CW00517990

"Duncan Smith is a firebrand for Jesus. The heat emanating I recognize as coming from the fire of the Holy Spirit. He is also a man of faith – reckless faith that is. This book is a vivid illustration of the same. Duncan's teachings and testimonies are very refreshing and edifying. We are friends and colleagues and I love him and his family dearly in the Lord."

Reinhard Bonnke, Evangelist

"Incendiary! Each page of *Consumed with Holy Fire* is tinged with the fiery Love of God. Duncan Smith's new book makes the beautiful paradigm of Trinitarian Love readily accessible to his readers through precise teaching and moving personal testimonies. His penetrating look at the Oneness purchased for us through the Love of Christ on the Cross is priceless. His concept of fully experiencing our Oneness within the Community of Burning Love and then extending that love through Kingdom ministry is a cutting-edge message for today. A must read for all!"

Ed Piorek, Pastor, Author of *The Father Loves You*

"It is such an honor to write an endorsement for a new book written by one of your spiritual sons. I am very proud of Duncan, his fiery, bubbly, happy personality and his amazing insights into Scripture. He has been part of our leadership team in Toronto for many years and we have travelled to the nations of the world together with many a challenge and many a victory. We preachers often have the ability to speak on a vast number of topics, but generally we have only a few that we might call life messages. I have mine, and Duncan has his. One of his main life messages is about the oneness that we have in Christ as believers in Jesus. This is is a fantastic and glorious revelation, not new, but freshly presented. It has helped and strengthened our leadership team in Toronto. It has helped me personally to continue to move out of my spiritual orphan tendencies and into my place as a son of my Heavenly Father, where I belong. Duncan has managed to get this down into a wonderful new book that will challenge and change your life. As you realize that you are one with Christ, and one with our awesome Trinitarian God, you will be propelled to new heights in relationship with Him and then into fruitful ministry for Him.

This book is a fun and exciting read. Through the stories you will get to know Duncan, but more importantly you will get to know the God of love as Jesus reveals the Father to you in a wonderful new revelation of your oneness with Him."

John Arnott, Catch The Fire, Toronto

"Once you read Duncan Smith's book, *Consumed with Holy Fire* I am confident you will have a new hunger for the fire of the Holy Spirit and the knowledge of your oneness in Christ. Duncan's hope is that we can walk into the wilderness of this world, confident that we too can demonstrate the gospel with burning love, accompanied by signs and wonders. His book is rich with scripture and stories of his own life that calls us to stay in the hidden place, consumed with great passion for God."

Heidi Baker Ph.D. Founding Director of Iris Global

"My close friend Duncan Smith is one fiery, passionate, vocal, electrified preacher of the Good News. The power and favor of God follow him wherever he goes, and he is utterly unashamed of all the extraordinary manifestations of love that the Holy Spirit pours out on the hungriest of the hungry. Duncan's understanding and appreciation of the entire Trinity excites him to no end, and that excitement is contagious among all who know him. God's love is all-consuming, and reading Duncan's book will help bring you all the closer to that perfect, blazing union with our God and Savior that is our ultimate destiny. The world desperately needs all that Duncan has expressed and described. May your appetite be whetted without measure!"

Rolland Baker, Founding Director of Iris Global

"Duncan Smith does an outstanding job in *Consumed with Holy Fire* of taking you into what it means to be one with Christ and in that oneness is found your identity and kingdom inheritance. The pages are filled with truth and transparency that causes a stirring and a hunger to rise up. Be prepared to receive revelation that will change you and your life forever and release you into the supernatural life God intended you to walk in to display His love to the world. I highly recommend this book."

Dr. Ché Ahn, Senior Pastor, HRock Church, Pasadena, CA
President, Harvest International Ministry & International Chancellor, Wagner Leadership Institute

"Duncan Smith is undoubtedly an inspirational man, both a passionate and articulate expounder of God's truth. In writing this book he without doubt both encourages and invites us to truly appreciate the truths of the gospel and the fiery union that produces new creation.

His exposition of the consuming love of God and the challenge of letting go of our rights to comfort propel us to the cause of Christ and our ultimate destiny. Duncan is a Holy Spirit Revolutionary; this book will inspire you to join him in his quest for more of the Father whom he passionately loves. I highly recommend it to you."

Ken Gott, Senior Leader of Bethshan Apostolic Community & Founder of House of Prayer Europe

"My friend Duncan Smith is a man who embodies his message. He humbly lays out his own life as an example of one consumed with passionate zeal, entirely fueled by a living relationship with the Trinity into which all Christians are invited. This book is a powerful combination of deep theological insight and personal experience which will inspire you closer into your oneness relationship with the God of Love Himself."

Rev. Nick Allan, Minister, St Thomas' Church Philadelphia, Sheffield, UK

"Duncan Smith's book fairly surges with the power of a loving relationship with the Trinity. Urgent, personal and at times poignant, Duncan's journey reflects the beauty of a life laid down and lived for his heavenly Dad. This book will set you ablaze as you understand that you are one with Jesus. Lord, may you make us all burning ones!"

Aled Griffith, Senior Leader, Community Church Derby, UK

CONSUMED WITH
HOLY FIRE

HEAVEN'S BLUEPRINT FOR A MIRACULOUS LIFESTYLE

DUNCAN SMITH

DESTINY IMAGE® PUBLISHERS, INC.
P.O. Box 310, Shippensburg, PA 17257-0310
"Promoting Inspired Lives."

This book and all other Destiny Image and Destiny Image Fiction books are available at Christian bookstores and distributors worldwide.

For more information on foreign distributors, call 717-532-3040.
Or reach us on the Internet: www.destinyimage.com

ISBN 13: TP 978-0-7684-5585-4
ISBN 13 EBook: 978-0-7684-5586-1
HC ISBN: 978-0-7684-5588-5
LP ISBN: 978-0-7684-5587-8

For Worldwide Distribution, Printed in the U.S.A.

1 2 3 4 5 6 7 8 9 10 11 / 24 23 22 21 20

To all who are longing for the world to rediscover that even our shadows can heal.

CONTENTS

FOREWORD

I love this book, just as I love this author. Duncan Smith is a gem, with a message that must be heard. Actually, this message must be felt, explored, and embraced thoroughly—and then nothing will ever be the same for the one embarking on this journey of journeys: being one with Christ. That union with Christ is at the heart of *Consumed with Holy Fire*.

Every chance I get to be with Duncan is sheer delight. His humble heart, combined with great love and joy, make him a pleasure to be with. I'm honored to call him friend.

Three vital expressions are woven throughout this book, each intricately designed to reveal another part of God's heart. The first is Duncan's story of his walk with Jesus, which is quite provoking, to say the least. His honest approach to God's dealings is refreshing and should give great hope to all who read it. He has invited us into his life with God by writing vulnerably about his life in a very endearing way. I pray that his encounter with God as a Father will leave its mark on your thinking as it has mine.

This is a place from which both Duncan and his lovely wife, Kate, live from day by day. It's tangible, appealing, practical, and so very compelling. I wept while reading of His encounter with Reinhard Bonnke. I was moved by the loving favor of our heavenly Father, who arranged for such an encounter to honor His hungry son. God is good at that. He is drawn to the hungry in unusual ways. He is really drawn to Duncan Smith.

The second part that adds such depth and perspective is Duncan's teaching. His insights into Scripture and life are a necessary part of the equation, and once again are woven beautifully throughout. Tragically, people's theology doesn't always have an effect on how they live. That can't be said of the Smiths. Their radical lifestyle of love results from personal encounters with Jesus along with the corresponding insights into His Word that unveils His purposes for our lives. Obvious to all who read this is that their instruction is not classroom theory, but practical and practiced—daily.

And finally comes the last part of this beautiful tapestry: power. Miracles abound in their lives as a great complement to this message of God's love. I'm so thankful to be able to say that there are now miracles that are commonplace in this present day. We see them almost daily. But this book goes beyond the common into the extreme heart of God for people, demonstrated through extraordinary miracles. The WOW factor is quite large as the wonder of Jesus comes dynamically to the forefront. He really is the same yesterday, today, and forever. And what a joy it is to discover He is delighted to reveal Himself through His surrendered sons and daughters.

Perhaps my favorite part of the book wasn't actually written directly. It's the intangible part that stirs the heart of the reader to say, "If they can live this way, so can I!" These pages contain an impartation of great courage that is rightly suited for everyone. I can't imagine anyone reading this book and remaining the same.

Something on these pages speaks to the deeply embedded divine design that lies in the heart of every person. *Consumed with Holy Fire* should draw it out beautifully. And for this, I give thanks.

Bill Johnson
SENIOR LEADER OF BETHEL CHURCH, REDDING, CA
AUTHOR OF *when heaven invades earth* AND *hosting the presence*

DEDICATION

This book is dedicated to our three beautiful daughters, Jessica Faith, Abigail Grace and Nathania Joy. You are so beautiful and I'm honored to be your dad. I have written this book that you might know the glorious hope of your eternal calling in Christ Jesus from before time began, that as the Father's beloved children, you are holy and blameless in love forever. You are each more precious to me than life itself. You were born for greatness and it will be my joy to spend all of eternity with you when our faces will shine like the sun and our eyes will blaze with Jesus' fiery love. I have written this that each of you may be filled to the full measure of all the fullness of God, embracing the way of the Cross and resurrection and living to see the one thing that counts on this earth: that Jesus receives the reward of His suffering, the nations as His inheritance. I love each of you with our Heavenly Daddy's great love. May you climb on my shoulders just like you did when you were little and go so much higher and further in this world than your mom and I ever will. You are the generation that will do the greatest miracles with Jesus the world has ever seen. I love you girls with all my heart.

ACKNOWLEDGMENTS

Without a doubt, if there is a platform that I speak from, it is the well-trodden path of the great men and women in Christ Jesus that have walked the way of the Cross long before me. I owe a debt of love to all my heroes in the faith who have blazed a trail of Oneness in Christ Jesus: the Apostle Paul, Irenaeus, Augustine, Athanasius, Anselm, Smith Wigglesworth, Watchman Nee, E Stanley Jones, DeVern Fromke, and Colin Urquhart. Through the revelation that these men have carried I have discovered who I am in Christ. Thank You Holy Spirit for leading me to the teachings of these mighty men. Thank You Father for the indescribable gift of Your Son to all humanity. Thank You Jesus for the extreme mercy, grace and love with which You have loved us through the Cross so that we could be raised in Oneness with You for all eternity.

Kate Smith, my beautiful bride, with all my heart I love you. You are an incredible woman of God and you constantly astound me with your beauty and wisdom. The Lord has truly fulfilled His promise and blessed me with a most amazing wife. Thank you for believing in me always and for spurring me on to greatness in Christ. Thank you for showing me the revelation of maturing in Oneness. Thank you for the price you've paid on this road of love. I could never have written this book without your sacrifice and love.

John and Carol Arnott, thank you for everything. Thank you for believing in us when you had nothing else to go by except the voice of the Lord. Thank you for showing us such godly, empowering leadership. Thank you for the giant bow wave that you've created for us all to succeed in. You are our greatest heroes. Thank you for the opportunity of a lifetime. It is the highest honor of our lives to be on your team and to walk in this revival with you both. You constantly show us the Father's love.

Bill Johnson, with all my heart, thank you for your love. You constantly inspire me to walk in the greatness of Christ. Thank you for writing the Foreword to this book and doing it with such love and affection as though you were doing it for Jesus. You have taught us all what true honor looks like. When I grow up, I'd like to be like you.

Rolland and Heidi, thank you for showing us what being consumed by love looks like among the "least of these." You are my heroes. Through you both we're learning to follow Jesus' example, not holding on to Oneness with God as something to be grasped, but emptying ourselves and giving our lives away for the sake of love as servants of all. Thank you for your love.

Evangelist Reinhard Bonnke, you have inspired me to preach the Gospel for over 25 years and given me a burning passion to win the nations for Jesus. Your friendship and love is one of the greatest privileges of my life. May the 747 jumbo jet take off at the greatest speed all the way to the end of the runway! Millions of souls won right to the end! Hallelujah!

Ed Piorek, thank you for revealing the love of the Father, and that the love that finds us, is the love that sends us.

Carlos Rodriguez, thank you for being an incredible son in Christ Jesus. When I look at you and Catherine, I catch a glimpse of that glorious day when all of our faces shimmer with radiant light as the paralyzed are brought into our presence without a trace of doubt that they will leap out of their wheelchairs instantly from one touch of our hands. I love you both so much. Catch The Fire Raleigh will be famous on the earth.

Murray Smith, thank you for saying yes to our invitation to come and join us for this adventure in Raleigh. You and Ash constantly inspire me with your love and wisdom. You have shown me how far Jesus can heal our hearts and mature us in this Oneness and my heart burns with love for you. I'm proud to be your brother.

Russell Smith, Thank you for being such a great brother. You're always an inspiration. You and Jo are fantastic friends.

Dad and Mom, thank you for the wonderful life you have given me. I am eternally grateful to you for showing me the Gospel of Jesus Christ from before I can remember. Thank you for your example of faith and sacrifice and for never letting go of my calling in Christ. You tenaciously held onto me before the One who sits upon the throne in the Heavens, especially when I needed that the most. Thank you especially Mom, for your over-the-top hard work on the early editing and for giving me so many hugely helpful tips. You are truly amazing.

Nancy Smith, of Authority Press, thank you for your excellent editing skills and expert advice. I've so enjoyed working with you. Thank you for pushing me on to the end.

Abby Smith, thank you for designing the beautiful cover for this book. You are a creative genius and I'm proud to be your dad.

Thank you Larry Sparks and the Destiny Image team for being so passionate for the Holy Spirit and spreading revival fire through books and media and giving me the privilege of publishing this book to somehow contribute to that mission. May the Holy Spirit use *Consumed with Holy Fire* to light a mighty flame in the hearts of everyone who reads it.

Thank you to all my friends and family at Catch The Fire Raleigh and our School of Revival. It is my joy to discover what Oneness with Christ looks like in an extraordinary community of radical lovers of Jesus, full of the Father's love. We are riding the wave of the next great move of God together, drawing the gaze of God until He baptizes us with unprecedented, undiscovered levels of His fiery presence and power.

Thank you to the millions of people who have come to our Catch The Fire events and churches throughout the world for over 25 years, especially those who have journeyed to the "mother ship" in Toronto. Because you came, we've all seen a glimpse of the future glories of the Kingdom. The love of the Father has been poured out and our lives have been ruined for anything less than this revival that I believe will never end and will be the greatest the world has ever seen.

INTRODUCTION

The revelation of our Oneness with Christ changes absolutely everything. My great hope writing this book is that you will encounter the God of Love Himself as you read it and be transformed by His presence and power forever. If you have never met Jesus, the Son of God, my purpose is that you will meet Him in the pages of this book. If you have already given your life to Jesus, no matter how long ago, my hope is that you will encounter Him in a way you never have before. May you be fully consumed by Love Himself. May the eternal God of all grace crash into you with the giant waves of the endless, infinite ocean of His love as you discover Jesus as the Person, the Place, the Price and the Power of Oneness.

Jesus came to show all humanity our Eternal Father who loves us with an everlasting love. He demonstrated the full extent of that love at the Cross. He came to lay down His life, so that by believing in Him and by receiving Him, every one of us would become sons of God just like Him. Jesus became one with you at the Cross and died, so that by believing in Him, you could be one with Him for eternity in His resurrection. He came into our lowliness, so that by faith we could live in His highness forever.

Jesus came into this world to show us God so that we could see ourselves; who we are created to be as humans. Because God is invisible it's easy to live so far below the full potential of who we really are. Jesus came to change that forever for each of us. He demonstrated fully what Love Himself looks like when He paid the consequences of all our selfishness and everything that has violated every human relationship throughout history. Jesus came and lived the perfect life we were all meant to live, so that the eternal debt of that life, which every human being owed God, could be paid on our behalf. Love Himself laid down His perfect life in death, so we could each live in His perfect resurrected life for all Eternity.

Our Oneness with Christ came at a price so beyond our comprehension that no book could ever do justice in attempting to describe the horrors of the Cross as He who knew no sin was made sin for us so that we could all be the perfection of God in Him. As you read glimpses of the sufferings of the Son of God for the whole world, including you and me, my prayer is that the knowledge of His incomprehensible suffering, the price He paid for our Oneness with Him, would anchor your faith in the eternal reality of that Oneness. My prayer for each of you is that you literally feel and experience the indestructible, eternal power that raised Jesus from the dead on the third day, when the Father by the Holy Spirit, raised the Son of God together with all who believe in His Son Jesus.

Of all the Apostles, it was Paul who writes the most about our Oneness with Christ.

Before his conversion, when he was first called Saul, he encountered the resurrected, glorified Christ on the road to Damascus when He appeared in brilliant, blinding light and asked, "Saul, Saul, why are you persecuting Me?" He didn't ask why he was persecuting His disciples and I believe that Paul could never forget that first encounter. As a deeply theological scholar he would have wrestled with Jesus' profound words. Since when did Jesus become His disciples and more the point, when did His disciples become Jesus? This theological mystery is at the very heart of the full Gospel of Jesus Christ. This book is about rediscovering the glorious Oneness with Christ that Paul walked in, turning his world upside down, preaching the Gospel to the entire known world of his day and winning multitudes to Jesus by doing astonishing miracles, miracles that the world is desperate for today.

God is a consuming fire, the very fire of Love Himself. As you read this book may your heart burn within you, set ablaze with the love of Jesus. Discovering the price of love that Jesus paid to separate us all from the power of sin and death and join us to Himself in Oneness, will destroy all doubt about your life, your future or what will happen to you after you die. My prayer is that you will catch fire as the God of the Universe, who created you, fills you with His fiery presence and power as you put your faith in Christ alone and willingly surrender to His invitation to die to all things in this world, fully consumed by love. You will learn how you too can live a life of Oneness with Christ, full of the most extraordinary, supernatural adventures and miracles with constant, direct access to His infinite treasures, walking in love and transforming your world by giving that love away. The riches of God are your inheritance and He's waiting for you to share them with the world. This book is for the hungry and thirsty, for all those who are longing for more of God. May you all be consumed with Holy Fire!

PART ONE

THE PERSON AND PLACE OF ONENESS

CHAPTER 1

SET ON FIRE

For by grace you have been saved through faith.
And this is not your own doing; it is the gift of God,
not a result of works, so that no one may boast.
Ephesians 2:8

I stumbled up a mountain path in the Rocky Mountains just outside of Estes Park, Colorado, tears in my eyes and heart racing. I had just rushed out of a meeting in a large auditorium where I had been listening to a preacher give a powerful message about Jesus Christ, and I just couldn't stay in the room any longer. I felt I had to get out for fresh air. *There's no way on earth God could want me,* I thought. *I've made a such a great mess of my life.*

Despite having wonderful missionary parents who introduced me to Jesus Christ at a very young age in Africa, I had totally gone "off the rails" as a teenager. I was a thoroughly self-centered 20-year-old hedonistic adrenaline junkie. I had no desire whatsoever to walk in the ways in which my parents had brought me up. My whole purpose in life was to have as much "fun" as I could, no matter how it affected anyone else. I was deeply insecure on the inside, yet I projected a confident, rebellious, adventurer persona on the outside, unafraid of anyone or anything. At that very moment, I was in America cheating on my English girlfriend. It's how I rolled.

The only time I ever gave God a thought was at the end of a runway when the plane I was on was about to take off and I needed "fire insurance" in case the plane went down. I'd learned how to "give my life to Jesus" to "save" me, especially if I thought there was any likelihood of death! I went to church services when I was with my parents just to please them, but my heart was far from the Lord. I absolutely hated church. It was unbelievably boring, and every church I had ever been in seemed to smell musty; sometimes the churchgoers smelled equally musty!

As I walked up the rocky path that day thinking about the message I had just heard, I began to realize just how horrible my heart had become. I was so full of deceit, pride and rebellion. I smoked a pack of cigarettes a day by the time I left high school. I smoked marijuana, used filthy language every sentence, was often drunk and had lost my virginity in Thailand while traveling around the world for nine months after leaving school.

Trudging along that mountain path, I felt totally ashamed. My whole life was messed up. For the first time in many years, I was acutely aware of how awful my heart was.

Just then I remembered a vivid dream I had had some months earlier; it had shaken me tremendously. It was one of those dreams that was so real, it was as if the dream was actually reality. In the dream, I was taking off in an airplane with my family from an airport I'd flown out of countless times, flying backwards and forwards from England and Nigeria, West Africa, between boarding school semesters and vacations.

But in the dream, the plane went down a few seconds after takeoff. As it hit the endless acacia trees of Africa, the airplane burst into flames. Everything went brilliant white, incinerated in the white-hot fire. I screamed in agony as my body burned in the flames. I felt the searing pain all over my body, and yet I couldn't see my body or touch it. I screamed for my parents but there was no answer, just white light all around.

I cannot describe the agony I experienced in that dream. Suddenly I could hear others screaming just like me. I couldn't see anyone, but I could hear their agonizing cries. I could hear millions of voices screaming. Sheer dread tore through my soul as I realized I was in Hell. For what seemed like an eternity I was stuck in the dream as though it had become my reality.

Finally, I woke up in my bed drenched in sweat with every hair on my body standing up. I rushed outside to have a cigarette to calm myself down. I was a wreck for days.

Now, on that mountain in Colorado, the memory of it came flooding back to me. A deep fear began to grip me as I looked around at the vast expanse of the Rocky Mountains all around me. I suddenly felt very, very small and very, very finite. I realized I absolutely deserved to spend eternity in that horrendous fire in my dream.

I thought that if there was a God, He sure must have been very angry with me. I was acutely aware that I had squandered everything that was good in my life and had pursued everything that was wrong and hurtful. I knew the Bible was clear about the consequences of sin: God hates sin and the result of sin is death, eternal death in the fires of Hell. But I also remembered that Jesus Christ came to save us from our sin so we don't have to die, but we can live with God forever, if we believe in His Son Jesus.

When I was very young, I had loved Jesus and invited Him into my heart. At 17, I had also gone forward at a Billy Graham Crusade. Yet despite these times when clearly God had met with me, I had been so unfaithful and turned away from Him.

I felt totally hopeless and condemned. I hated myself and felt so dirty. I had no desire to be a Christian anyway. I thought to myself, *There's no way I want to be like the people I grew up around in church.*

I reminded myself of how much I hated church. It was so boring, and all my parents' missionary friends were so uncool and untrendy. They were all nice enough, but as a 20-year-old about to go off to university, I simply did not want a boring life.

The only forms of Christianity I knew then were very formal. Church, as I knew it, was incredibly dull and had little meaning for me. I didn't like singing along to an organ and I hated listening to endless sermons. The last thing I wanted was to become a Christian, yet I was so shaken up and overcome with condemnation. I felt so awful and sinful.

Suddenly as I was walking up the path, I collided with an invisible wall of power the likes of which I had never encountered in my entire 20 years of life. I couldn't see anyone in front of me but I was stopped right there, dead in my tracks. I couldn't take another step forward.

I knew there was someone very powerful standing right in front of me.

My legs buckled under me and I crumpled to my knees. My heart was pounding in my chest, my breathing rapid and difficult. I had known about God, but I had never realized it was possible to encounter Him personally. I had never experienced His manifest presence. I'd prayed many times, but I never expected Him to answer.

Stunned by His power, I thought He was going to end my life right there. I was also convinced He would be completely justified if He did. But instead of putting me to death, I felt wave after wave of the most incredible, indescribable love. God poured His love over me and spoke to me tenderly in my heart. I cried out to the Lord Jesus, asking Him to forgive me for all my sin and save me.

He replied, *"I love you and I forgive you. I forgive you for all of your sins. All of them. I am setting before you life and death. Choose life and you will live. I have amazing plans for you, but you must choose life and you must choose to walk in obedience to My voice today. You can no longer go your own way. No more sitting on the fence, with one foot in the world and one foot in Me."*

Right there, I surrendered my whole life and gave my heart to Christ. I invited Him to be the Lord of my life and come in to all of me. I felt this tremendous surge of love and power and I was filled with joy beyond anything I had ever experienced in my life. My heart felt like it was burning on fire with love for God, like it would explode any moment with excitement and passion for Jesus. My body was trembling with it! Spontaneous gratitude welled up in me. All the terrible weight of condemnation for all my sin was gone.

I knew that Jesus had forgiven me forever. He gave me His faith to believe in the all sufficiency of Christ. I instantly knew that Jesus loved me, had chosen me, had saved me and had given His life for me. All the things I had vaguely understood about who Jesus was and what He had done for all of us, I suddenly understood with crystal clarity. He had done it all for despicable me, not just "nice" people.

I said to the Lord, "I will follow You for the rest of my life. I can't deny I haven't had fun over the past few years being a rebel, so I would like to ask You to please give me a very exciting life in You. Please, please, don't let me have a boring life like the church people I've known!"

He answered me. *"Done! You will have a very exciting life in Me!"*

I knew that He meant it. It was a done deal. My heart burned for God, set on fire from that moment for the rest of my life.

That night, I joined a late night prayer meeting under the gorgeous starry sky around a fire and sang songs with all the other church folk, all of whom I felt this incredible love for, something I would not have done in a million years before I'd met with the Lord that afternoon. The excitement in my heart was irrepressible.

I had been so radically saved and born again that I was unrecognizable to everyone who had ever known me before. When I got back to England a week or so later, my parents were thrilled for me, but I just didn't fit in at the church now. The Evangelical church had wanted me to get saved, but not that saved! My old school friends were saying, "Duncan's found God and gone weird."

From the moment I was born again on the mountainside that epic day, my heart has burned with love for Jesus. I knew instantly this love was not my own. The faith to believe wasn't even my own. It was way too strong and unrecognizable from any of my feeble efforts to believe in God in the past. I was in the glorious Kingdom of God.

I knew deep down in the very core of my being that God in His great mercy and love had saved me. This was not my doing; it was all His doing. I was His creation, and His alone. Christ did everything necessary for us to be saved and all that is required from us is our surrender to His great love, mercy and grace. My God had saved me; if He saved me, there is no one He cannot save! His love is unconditional and all encompassing.

Paul says it this way: *"For by grace you have been saved through faith. And this is not your own doing; it is the gift of God, not a result of works, so that no one may boast"* (Ephesians 2:8).

One touch from Jesus, one moment in His manifest presence had undone me and changed me forever. In the great kindness of God, He saved me just before I went to university. If I had gone to university before Jesus saved me that summer, I dread to think where I would be today. My journey into the everlasting riches of God's grace in Christ Jesus had begun. My heart was hungry for Jesus. I was so thirsty for His presence and my whole being craved to know the Living God, the creator of all things. It was my joy to lose my life and gain Christ.

I discovered that the secret place with God is the greatest place we can ever be. The Holy Spirit spoke to my heart, *"If you will hang out with Me in the secret place, I will hang out with you in the public place."*

I was hooked. Addicted. I spent hours and hours alone with the Lord Jesus, the One who really counts.

At the university Christian Union, I met Christians who were really cool, trendy, fun loving and inspiring people. Their eyes seemed to be full of 'fire' and their hearts brimmed with passion. They really loved Jesus and talked excitedly about Him and how awesome the Christian Union was as a community of radical, "on fire" Christians. I had never met Christians like that before. I quickly realized these people were experiencing Jesus in the same way I was now. They weren't shocked by my enthusiastic talk about Jesus. They were full of love.

As I walked toward a Christian Union meeting for my very first time, a few minutes late, my heart leapt in my chest. Long before I reached the auditorium I could hear music that sounded like U2, one of my favorite bands of all time, with electric guitar riffs and bass guitar rhythms, drums and synthesized keyboards. I had never associated this kind of contemporary music with Christianity before. All I'd ever known in church was organs, traditional pianos and boy choirs. The vocals were sensational, with soaring anthems and heart-rending melodies that made my spirit burn.

As I reached the doorway, to my complete astonishment, the place was packed with several hundred young people my age, dancing, jumping, swaying, clapping and singing with all their might. Almost everyone had both their arms stretched up, hands held high above their heads, just like I'd only ever seen at a football game with my grandfather. The congregation was a huge, heaving mass of radical young people who were all absolutely, fanatically in love with Jesus. It was incredible! I had never seen anything like it in my life.

Standing in the doorway, feet frozen, I took it all in for a few minutes. I started seeing other things happening I'd never seen before in church either. Some of the students were shaking violently, some still on their feet and others lying prostrate on the floor. I noticed some people laughing uncontrollably, and others were even crying. I wasn't sure whether it was the weirdest thing I'd ever seen or the coolest thing I'd ever seen.

My first thought was, *"Run, Duncan, run! Get out of here, these people are total freaks!"* Yet I was so irresistibly drawn to join in. I knew somehow this was what I'd been looking for all my life, a place where I could freely worship Jesus the way my spirit had always wanted to. I walked the few yards to the back row guys and jumped right into the middle of them. I've never looked back.

After worship, the president of the Christian Union got up to speak. Just like everyone else, this student was absolutely in love with Jesus. Even from the very back of the room I could see her face was radiant, shining with the glory and love of God. Her words were full of power, and there was so much authority exuding from her, it was as though Jesus Himself was literally standing in front of us all speaking, except in and through this petite, fiery young student. I listened intently to every word she spoke. Not only was she talking excitedly about Jesus, she was also talking about the Holy Spirit. The Holy Spirit! She was talking about the Holy Spirit as though He was a person just like I knew Jesus was a person.

This was a brand-new concept for me. I had always known the Holy Spirit was the Spirit of God, but I'd never given any further thought about Him other than He was like a dove that had descended on Jesus at His baptism. I understood enough to know God was One God, revealed in three Persons, but that was merely a theological statement. All I knew was that you gave your life to Jesus, and He came and lived in you so you could go to Heaven. I never imagined you could know the Holy Spirit like you can know Jesus.

My new friends told me about the "Baptism of the Holy Spirit" and that I too could be baptized in the Holy Spirit if I asked God. They reassured me I had the Holy Spirit "in" me already because I was born again, but God wanted me to have the Holy Spirit "on" me, so I could begin to be a powerful witness of Jesus Christ and start operating in what they referred to as the supernatural gifts of the Holy Spirit.

This was awesome. I couldn't get enough of their teaching. My eyes were being opened to the realities of the Kingdom of God in ways I had never known before. I regularly watched my friends lay their hands on people who were sick or had injuries, healing them in the name of Jesus— just like I read in the New Testament that Jesus and the Apostles did. I had no idea any of that was possible for me, but my eyes were seeing it and my heart instantly believed. In my inner being I somehow knew it was absolutely what God wanted for all of His children. My spirit was on fire with the love of God being demonstrated in power in front of my eyes whenever I witnessed Jesus doing miracles through my friends. I became very hungry for the presence of the Holy Spirit, not just in me, but on me.

Growing up as a missionary kid in Nigeria, I had always gone to church, yet I had never experienced the presence or power of God in my life. My experience was so far from this fullness I saw in my university friends. I was desperate for the Father to give me the Holy Spirit like Jesus promised (Luke 11:13). My friends had made it very clear that it was the Holy Spirit doing the miracles through them and not they themselves. I wanted to be baptized in the Holy Spirit more than anything in the world. I pleaded with God. I read the books my friends recommended and went forward at every invitation for prayer and ministry. I wanted the Holy Spirit on me so that I could be a powerful witness too. I yearned for so much more!

In that glorious moment in the Rocky Mountains when I walked into the invisible presence of Jesus, He changed me forever, making me a brand-new person inside and out. I thought I was going to die because of my sin. What I've discovered is that He died because of my sin. He became my sin and death so that I could become His perfection and life.

Having died with Him at the event of the Cross, the invitation of Jesus is that we take up our cross and follow Him on the way of the Cross. His invitation to us all is to die to ourselves, our destinies and our love of this world, sharing in His death and resurrection, so that our life is truly His life in us. Jesus, the Person, the Place, the Price and the Power of Oneness, made Himself one with us at the Cross 2000 years ago. Becoming one with us by His death, He experienced the greatest suffering so that we could be one with Him forever by His resurrection.

Now, it is our privilege to learn to live a supernatural life here on earth as we grow in the knowledge of who we are in Him, living fully in the benefits of our resurrection life in Jesus. The world is waiting for the sons of God to bring Heaven to the nations through our churches, our homes, our workplaces, our supermarkets, our gyms, the bars and all the darkest places of the world. In this way, we will manifest Jesus wherever we go as we live our lives from a place of Oneness with Him in the Father's love.

It is His joy that we have the infinite power and the infinite treasures of His Kingdom. His invitation to each of us is that we learn how to access that power and treasure through our Oneness with Christ, so that we can serve the world with the endless miracles, delights and riches of our Father. The Holy Spirit wants to "blow your socks off" and bless you beyond your wildest imagination so that you can win the world with the mind-blowing power and love of God.

I wanted the fullness of sonship. I wanted everything I stood to inherit as a glorious son in Christ Jesus. I wanted the Holy Spirit, I wanted to do miracles, I wanted Him to prosper me, but I had no idea that Oneness with Christ was my inheritance. God is our inheritance now! One with Him, His love is ours, His power is ours, His miracles are ours, His presence is ours and best of all He Himself is ours. We can share in all that is His, even the invitation to share in His suffering. Nothing is impossible for those who know they are one with Christ.

My journey into this Oneness with Christ began when I was 20 years old, in the Rocky Mountains of Colorado. I didn't know it at the time, but there, in those wild mountains when I walked right into the fiery presence of Jesus Himself, I wasn't just saved so I could go to Heaven, I became one with Him forever.

Since that day, He's opened my eyes to my Oneness with Christ and it has changed absolutely everything in my life. It's my joy to take you on a journey into the revelation of your Oneness with Christ, plunging you into the depths of the magnificence of the Cross of Christ, the place where the unimaginable price of this Oneness was paid in full, so that you might believe fully in Jesus and live the rest of your life in the power of His indestructible life, consumed by His love and full of His grace and glory.

Knowing that you too are one with Christ will change absolutely everything in your life. From this revelation of Oneness, you can set the whole world on fire with the love of your Eternal Father, because you are consumed by love.

My prayer for you as you read each chapter is that you will encounter the One whose eyes and heart burn with fierce love for you and the world: Jesus Christ the Savior of all humanity. Every moment of encounter with Him will change you forever and set your heart burning with His love.

CHAPTER 2

YOUNG FIREBRANDS

From this day on I will bless you.
Haggai 2:19

Sometimes the greatest things are worth waiting for. They are worth pressing in hard for. As I waited on the Lord for the things I'd asked Him, the Holy Spirit drew me deeply into Jesus' great heart of love. I was smitten. I realized that Jesus is overwhelmingly lovely and beautiful, truly the "*fairest of ten thousand.*" I was wrecked by His love for me, and His lovely presence.

It took nine months of earnest prayer before I was gloriously baptized in the Holy Spirit. One particular Sunday an awesome pastor from Uganda preached on the Holy Spirit, and after the message, I rushed down to the front asking him to pray for me to receive the Baptism of the Holy Spirit. He told me to hold my hands out in front of me, and then he simply asked God to come and baptize me.

Suddenly I felt a surge of joy and excitement. As I tried to verbalize my thanks to Jesus for who He is and all He'd done for me, I started speaking in another language I'd never spoken before. Words just poured out of my mouth as I spontaneously tried to express my worship to Jesus. I was filled with so much joy—and I let it rip! I went home, feeling as if I were walking in the clouds.

I was so excited for the Wednesday night meeting in the Christian Union that next week. Even though I had just experienced the first downpour of the Holy Spirit on me that previous Sunday, I wanted more. A guest speaker again preached on the Holy Spirit and invited us all to stand. The excitement in the room was tangible as hundreds of us stood expectantly, hungry and thirsty for the living God. The speaker told us to ask the Holy Spirit to come upon us. People started being touched all over the room. As I stood at the very back in the highest bleachers in one of those amphitheater rooms, I suddenly felt a very slight, very faint buzzing in my fingertips, a little bit like "pins and needles." As soon as I became aware of it, it intensified and went down my fingers into the palms of my hands. My hands started really buzzing.

I opened my eyes to see if anyone else immediately next to me could feel what I was feeling. No one else seemed to be particularly touched. By this time the buzzing was all over my arms and started coming up from my feet too. It intensified into what I can only think a million volts of electricity must feel like, with the likeness of extreme "pins and needles" raging throughout my body. It was surging so powerfully in my torso, especially my abdomen and chest areas. My whole body felt like I was dressed in a very heavy, thick blanket or chain mail coat of armor. It was so strange because I felt extremely hot and yet my hands felt cold all at once. It was utterly supernatural and outside of anything I had ever experienced before. The feeling that started in my fingers faintly at first, gathered such momentum and strength and eventually was sweeping through my entire body like a rushing fire.

At first it felt amazing and I started saying, "More Lord, please come with even more!"

Then, I'd feel the power go up a notch each time. As I continued to ask Him for more it began to get increasingly intense so that my breathing became rapid, my heart rate fast. I fell to the floor, eventually feeling so consumed with the manifest presence of the Holy Spirit I knew if He came with one more wave, I would instantly die and be with Him in His glory. My entire life rushed before me. I just wasn't ready to die right there. I wanted to get married and have children.

My cries instantly turned from, "More Lord, come more!" to, "*Stop Lord, please stop!*"

I had been asking the Lord to make me like Enoch, who walked with God and was not, but suddenly I wasn't ready to be "was not!" Just then the level of power went down just a little and I stayed this side of glory.

My earthly body literally could not contain that level of manifest power. I could not see the form of the Holy Spirit. I could not see any physical "fire" nor could I see what was coursing through my body, but I could feel it. I knew it was His presence. That moment marked my life forever. I have been a God-chaser of great passion ever since.

The sensation of His beautiful presence remained with me for hours. I was buzzing, fizzing with the presence of the Holy Spirit. I felt one with God, immersed in burning Love. I knew that He loved me and was in me and with me in a way that made John 14 so real to me, when Jesus said the Father would give us,

Another Helper, to be with you forever, even the Spirit of truth,
whom the world cannot receive, because it neither sees him nor
knows him. You know him, for he dwells with you and will be in you.
John 14:16-17

My heart burned within me. I literally felt supercharged with love. I loved God so much I thought I was going to burst. I was saturated in every fiber of my very being with His great love for me and I was exploding with the Father's great love for Jesus. I loved Jesus in a way that was beyond anything I had ever experienced.

Sometime just before midnight, I was walking from the meeting with my friend, telling him the whole way home about my experience. We were both hungry, as I have found is often the case for me after I've had a dramatic experience with the Lord! As we walked to our favorite local kebab shop, two men bristling with aggression confronted us. They deliberately walked right at us, knocking us both sideways on the sidewalk, spinning us around. They yelled foul language at us and were clearly ready to physically hurt us very badly. My friend, who happened to be about six foot six, took off running down the road yelling at me, "Duncan get out of there! Run, Duncan, run!"

For some reason I just stood there. I could still feel the tangible presence of the Holy Spirit but I couldn't move.

I put my hand out and said, "In the name of Jesus..." and was about to say, "I rebuke you"—but they both went into a karate stance. Without warning, one of them spun around in a 360-degree turn and kicked me, right in my stomach.

As if the whole thing was in slow motion, I saw myself being hit and falling to the ground, being kicked and beaten until left half-dead on the sidewalk. But an amazing thing happened. His foot hit my stomach, but it was as though my stomach was made of iron. It seemed that an invisible person took hold of his outstretched foot and jammed the entire man several feet backwards into the sidewalk, like he was body slammed. Bam! The man and his friend went deathly white as though they had seen a ghost. The man scrambled to pick himself off the sidewalk, and they both took off running as fast as their legs could carry them.

My friend had seen the whole thing from several yards away, and said he'd never seen anything like it before. He said the man was crushed onto the ground when he tried to kick me. I was shaking with shock, but we both felt so much love in the midst of our bewilderment. I knew it was the presence of the Holy Spirit that the aggressive man encountered. I truly was clothed in a mighty coat of the Holy Spirit. When I went to bed that night I was shaking all over, overwhelmed by God's power and goodness.

The Holy Spirit has fascinated me so much since that unforgettable night. Of course I have wanted to experience Him like that again and again. I have had many moments since then, where I have felt the tangible feeling of His presence and power. I have regretted asking God to stop ever since. I've realized I was given a foretaste of the glory awaiting us; what we were truly born for. Most of the time I don't feel Him at all, but I know He is living in me and is with me, on me, just like Jesus said. I think we'd barely be able to function if we felt the presence and power of God all the time like I felt Him that night. I love what my pastor John Arnott says: "The miracle is not that God touches you, but that when He does, you get to live through it!"

From that night on, I have burned with an unquenchable boldness and passion for Jesus. Everything the Lord did for me that night is what He wants to do for everyone and so much more. We can all be gloriously immersed in an ever-increasing measure of His Spirit on us. We just have to ask for more.

Since then, my heart has been filled with love and compassion for all of humanity. I couldn't bear the thought of billions of people spending eternity in that dreadful place I had experienced, burned alive, in my dream. The good news of Jesus Christ was literally like a fire in my bones just like the prophet Jeremiah said:

> *Is not my word like fire, declares the LORD,*
> *and like a hammer that breaks the rock in pieces?*
> *Jeremiah 23:29*

I had to preach the word of God. I just had to. I became an unstoppable force of fiery, burning love in my university. The Student Union Bar was always a scary place before, filled with a sea of heaving, drunk, ultra-cool students. The Student Union was a liberal, antiestablishment, anti-religion, atheistic, humanistic, pro-abortion, dark society—whose bar was packed every day at lunchtime. It was suddenly irresistible to me. I had to go in and do whatever I could to save as many students as would listen. I would regularly go into the Student Union Bar with friends, jump on one of the tables and shout at the top of my voice that I had good news. The crowd would go quiet, listening to me preach for about 30 seconds before someone threw a beer bottle at me, then others followed with many shouts of "Boo!" "Get him off!" and so on.

To my amazement, people came over, some to argue, but others because they were interested. We were able to invite them to the Christian Union meetings. It was so fantastic. I knew then, I want to spend the rest of my life making Jesus Christ famous throughout the earth. John's statement in John 1 became my life's mission:

He came to His own, and His own people did not receive Him. But to all who did receive Him, who believed in His name, He gave the right to become children of God, who were born, not of blood nor of the will of the flesh nor of the will of man, but of God.
John 1:11-13

We were very successful, with so many salvations and healings. We experienced ongoing revival and the presence of God was so intense with us. We saw the Holy Spirit do so many spectacular miracles. One of my best friends had suffered her whole life from epilepsy and could not drive as a result. During one of our meetings, she was totally and instantly healed from severe epilepsy and has never had to take the medication again. She gained her driving license a year later because she was cleared to drive by the medical profession. Today, well over twenty years later, she is happily married as a vicar's wife and has three strapping sons.

For my friend's sake, and so many others like her, I'm so thankful that we didn't have a theology that Jesus couldn't heal her because healing is not for today. Sadly, so many churches in the world believe this way.

That's My Wife!

It wasn't long after my conversion both my two brothers also experienced powerful encounters with the Lord. Our parents witnessed such a transformation in our lives that they wanted more than they were experiencing in their evangelical church and found a new church. They had recently returned to England after working for 20 years in Nigeria with an evangelical missionary organization. They were hungry for more of God themselves. I'm so ever so grateful for my heritage and godly parents who have pursued God their entire adult lives.

The first Sunday we walked into that church I noticed this gorgeous blonde sitting across from me. My heart skipped a beat as I thought to myself, *That's my wife! Oh my goodness, I'm looking at the girl I'm going to spend the rest of my life with!*

I just knew it. I knew I was going to marry Kate Daniels from that moment. As it happened, my parents had chosen Kate's mother and father's church, and it was her first Sunday home too. She had just flown home from Los Angeles, where she'd completed a Youth With A Mission (YWAM) Discipleship Training School. She was on fire for the Lord and there was a burning flame for missions in her heart.

I fell head over heels in love with her. She was, and is, such a mighty woman of God and loves Jesus passionately with all her heart. She gave me a good run for my money, though, making sure that I worked really hard to catch her!

The first night I kissed her I read from the book of the prophet Haggai. The whole book was about ancient Israel's restoration through God's forgiveness and promise to prosper them even though in the past they had been devastated through their sin and rebellion. The words leapt out at me through tear-filled eyes,

From this day on I will bless you.
Haggai 2:19

I've held on to that promise through thick and thin, throughout our relationship, in every circumstance and fiery trial we have been through together. Our God promised to bless us from that day on and He has been true to His word!

We were both extremely hungry for God before we began our relationship. Now as we fell in love, our hunger for Jesus skyrocketed. We became fully committed to making ourselves available to Jesus to use us for miracles and healing.

During a one-day seminar we attended together, the preacher emphasized the importance of being a pure vessel so that the power of the Lord could flow through us without any hindrance. The more he preached, the more I became aware of my need to pray through with someone about the sins I had committed before I came to Christ. I had already confessed and repented on a general level, but had never received specific ministry for some of the really defiling sins I had committed; particularly sexual sins, alcohol abuse, smoking nicotine and even marijuana on occasions.

I was so in love with Kate, and she was the purest girl I'd ever met. I wanted to marry her so badly! The Holy Spirit had whispered into my heart earlier that week, "*I want you to tell Kate about your past as a teenager and that you lost your virginity in Thailand.*"

My heart almost stopped beating.

"You have to be kidding, Jesus! I can't tell her about all that stuff, especially my sexual sin. I'll lose her forever! There is no way she will want to marry me. She'll be so disappointed in me and think I'm dirty."

I'd gone into a tailspin that whole week, feeling so inadequate and dirty. For the first time since my radical conversion, I felt the weight of guilt and shame trying to come all over me again. I've come to realize that we can confess things to the Lord in private, but it is when we confess our sins to someone as well as to the Lord that the power of that sin is truly broken. It is the power of walking in the light.

After the session ended I shared my situation with the speaker. He was very tied up so he handed me over to one of the pastors I knew well from the church. I shared everything with the pastor. He prayed some very deep and powerful cleansing prayers, ministering healing from all the effects of my sins.

As he ministered I felt the Holy Spirit falling on me so powerfully. It was like He was pouring liquid fire all over me, especially over my chest and in my lungs and onto my lap and over my legs. I felt the sensation of fire all over me to the point that it verged on being painful. The Holy Spirit was thoroughly cleansing me from all the effects of my sin in my body and healing me from all the abuse of my body's organs.

The speaker began to invite different people publicly to practice different types of healing methods. Suddenly, I felt the strangest sensation in my hands. They went cold, really cold, inside and out. I whispered to Kate to feel my hands and she was shocked that they were so cold. I realized that maybe the Lord was showing me what someone else was suffering.

Being the young firebrand I was, I couldn't help myself from jumping up and blurting out that I was experiencing something "cold" in my hands. The preacher looked at me and recognized me as the young man who had come to him confessing some serious sin. He looked reluctant to allow this to go any further, but then asked if there was anyone with cold hands. For what felt like an eternity, no one moved a muscle in the room. I stood there feeling increasingly self-conscious.

Suddenly a 17-year-old youth jumped to his feet on the far side of the room. He was sitting next to one of my aunts who was at the meeting as well. He yelled out very loudly that he had Raynaud's Syndrome, a blood condition that constricts the flow of blood to the extremities. He said he always had cold hands and feet and it was so severe, he could no longer play the sports he enjoyed so much. I could see in his face the earnest desperation to be healed.

The preacher told me to "send" the anointing across the room. I had never heard of anything like that before, but I simply obeyed. I said, "In the mighty name of Jesus I command Raynaud's Syndrome to leave your body now! And I command the blood to flow normally as God always intended it to. In Jesus' name be healed right where you are!"

To my complete joy he started yelling immediately, "Wow! Wow! Wow! My hands are on fire. My hands are on fire. I can feel heat burning in my hands!" He was so excited, because he was totally healed. I saw him later that day, and for the first time in his life, his hands and feet felt perfectly warm.

Kate and I went out that lunchtime and my heart was filled with courage to tell her everything. I knew I was healed and cleansed. I shared with her the devastating news that the man she was in love with was not a virgin and as a teenager had blown everything that was precious, but that the Lord Jesus had gloriously forgiven me and restored to me my innocence. She was stunned, and of course was very upset and saddened by what I told her.

She looked at me through her tears and with the kindest voice said to me, "I forgive you Duncan. I'm really sad of course, but you're not the same man who did all that sin. You're a brand-new creation and I love you with all my heart."

I burst into tears and we embraced each other in the longest hug. As I held her I whispered into her ear, "You've made me realize that I really am a brand-new man. A new creation. I am a virgin. When I marry you, you'll be marrying a virgin!"

Two months later, I asked Kate to marry me and she said, "Yes!"

Called to the Nations

A year later, while at a Christian summer camp, I heard Colin Urquhart say, "This afternoon as I was praying, asking God what He wanted to do tonight in this meeting, I heard Him say He wanted to commission the next generation of radical, passionate men and women of God that He wanted to use in extraordinary ways to bring His Kingdom on the earth. You know who you are, because there is a tangible sensation of God's presence all over you. If that's you, young person, come down here to the front right now. We're not going to start the worship until we have done this."

The sensation of electricity was pouring all over me again, just like I had felt two years earlier at university that epic night. I ran down to the front of the converted sheep shed, jumping over the chairs. I joined hundreds of young firebrands who loved Jesus passionately. I don't remember much of what Colin prayed, but he told us all to hold out our hands and receive a powerful impartation of the Holy Spirit as he commissioned us to carry the glory of God.

My whole body was filled with that beautiful, supernatural, pulsating, surging fiery power of the Holy Spirit. I stood there, barely able to hold myself up, shaking and trembling as the power of God overcame me again, wave after wave of burning love. Eventually Colin finished and told us all to go back to our seats.

As we all settled back in our seats he addressed the crowd again. "All of you young people who were just up here, we're going to wait on the Lord for a moment before go any further. The Holy Spirit is going to show you what He wants for each of you in your lives."

As I stood there with my hands out in front of me, the Holy Spirit coursing all over my body, I heard the voice of the Lord speak directly to my heart: "*Duncan, I have appointed you and today I have anointed you to be a light and a herald of the Gospel and to preach the Gospel to the ends of the earth!*"

Those words are forever burned and etched into my heart. My calling was engraved onto the fibers of my heart and every cell in my body. I knew who I was as a son in the Kingdom of my God and now I knew what He wanted me to do for the rest of my life. Those words have been the compass of my life ever since.

I married my beloved Kate a month later, still in the afterglow of that fiery moment. She was my beautiful bride and together we were going to change this world forever. Two radical firebrands, ready to go to the ends of the earth with the powerful message of salvation in our hearts. But what I didn't realize was that the Lord wants to take each of us on a long journey of discovering what the Gospel of the Kingdom really is. Before we give our lives to Christ, we must be willing to give up everything, dying to all things in this world. However, once we've given our lives to Christ and lost everything, we realize that what we had previously thought was everything, is nothing. Contrary to becoming nothing, by losing everything, we've gained all things. Resurrection is only for the dead!

CHAPTER 3

LIGHT IN THE DARKNESS

The light shines in the darkness, and the darkness has not overcome it.
John 1:5

"Duncan and Kate, stay here for at least three years. Duncan, get a job and at the end of three years we'll send you out to the nations." I was jerked back to earth by my pastors' response. I had just announced that we were off to be missionaries in Cameroon, one month after our wedding. They looked at each other, smiled graciously at me and then shared some wise words with us.

Utterly stunned, I sat there in a daze. I knew he was right. My desire for Cameroon was not based on any word from the Lord. It was just a whim, springing from a wrong mindset that the only way to please God was to be a missionary somewhere in the darkest regions of the world, preferably Africa.

I had been to the local job center that day and found out that my bachelor's degree in environmental biology didn't really help me much for anything other than being an environmental officer. The salaries were terrible, and I really didn't want to spend the rest of my life counting "indicator species" of grasses in a quadrangle in a field.

I'd walked out of the job center just as a police car rolled by with two smug-looking officers sitting in the front and I suddenly thought, *Wow! I should look into becoming a police officer.* I spun around and walked straight back into the same job center. The woman showed me all I needed to know to join the police.

As I sat there listening that night in our little kitchen, I knew our pastor was right. I would apply to become a police officer. Kate was already an occupational therapist, and she loved her job and our new lives together. That night as we went to bed, we agreed I should apply and see what would happen. We both felt peace about the shift in our plans. We knew God had our best in mind.

Our Mission Field

Being a police officer was tailor-made training for leadership in the church and Kingdom. I walked with the Holy Spirit as an officer, bringing glory to Jesus in every area of my working life. I was made fun of at first for being a Christian. My colleagues were stunned that I refused to participate in my shift's weekly corporate entry to the national lottery. My sergeant would ask me in front of everyone each week at briefing,

"Duncan, are you doing the lottery with us this week?"

"No, Sarge," I'd reply. "You know I don't need to win the lottery to gain a great life. I've already won everything I could ever want when Jesus found me!" I was already a multimillionaire in the spirit.

Everyone would groan and the sarge would say, "Oh well, don't come running to us when we're all multimillionaires!"

Then he'd smile. I knew he respected me.

I loved asking the Holy Spirit to tell me where the crime was going on. I'd follow His lead and sure enough, He'd lead me to where I needed to be to do my job. I shared about the Love of God in Christ Jesus with almost everyone I met. It didn't matter whether it was my colleagues in our cafeteria, in the patrol cars, or with the criminals in custody. I loved Jesus and I shared His love with everyone.

Work is our mission field, and I was a happy missionary. It wasn't Cameroon, but there were many pagans needing Jesus. I was burning with the love of God in my uniform! I've since realized that the developed nations of this world are in as great if not greater need of the Gospel than the developing nations. We can burn with God's love no matter what our jobs are.

I was a police officer for three years before heading off to Kingdom Faith Bible College in the south of England, with Kate and our 10-month-old eldest daughter, Jessica Faith. We left everything, our jobs, our home, our friends and our families. The Lord blessed us tremendously and our faith muscles grew as we learned to trust entirely on the Lord Jesus to provide everything. We learned so much and we are so grateful to Kingdom Faith Ministries for teaching us who we are in Christ.

One night while we were at Kingdom Faith Bible College, we were in the home of the academic dean, John Mackay, at Small Group. John asked us all to prophesy over each other. He called Kate and me into the middle of the group and began to speak prophetically over us. He told us that he felt that the Lord was calling us to the nations and then said these powerful words that we've never forgotten.

"Duncan and Kate, you and the people that you will raise up will be a raging bush fire. I see you and a company of people blazing a trail all over the world, starting Heavenly bush fires everywhere you go in the nations." We were both knocked off our feet as the power of God came all over us. Looking back, John Mackay's words have dramatically come to pass.

A few months after leaving for Bible college, while we were on vacation at home, our pastor shared a stunning story with me about two officers who'd come to Christ through my witness. Having been an atheist, my former custody sergeant was now a member of the church. He told the church that a young officer, PC Smith, had treated the people who were in his custody with such dignity and honor, despite them being criminals that he could no longer deny that Jesus existed. He saw Jesus in me in uniform! He asked Jesus into his life and became a Christian.

I was ecstatic. Then my pastor shared the second story. Apparently, I had been in a deep conversation with another colleague, also a devout atheist.

I had said to him, "You're a police officer and you're trained not to discount anything until you've considered the evidence, yet you discount Jesus without ever considering the evidence?"

I remembered the conversation. I had so many of those kinds of discussions with my colleague. I ended it saying, "I double dare you to say, 'Jesus Christ, if you are real then show me some evidence!'"

My pastor shared with me that a detective inspector (DI) had been sitting at the table next to us that morning at breakfast, reading a newspaper. I vaguely remembered. The DI was like a god, though, so we didn't disturb him, not even to greet him. He was mean and a very tough detective. However, the DI had been listening intently to our conversation, and he never forgot my challenge about asking Jesus for evidence.

Some time later he was at his house on his cycle exercise machine, rigged up to a pulse monitor. His second marriage was on the rocks and his life had taken a very bad downward turn. He was desperate and cried out into the atmosphere of the room, "Jesus Christ, if you are real, then just like PC Smith said, show me some evidence!"

No sooner had those words come from his lips when suddenly the DI felt a great surge of invisible power hit him that sent his pulse rate racing and something knocked him clean off his cycle machine onto the floor and pinned him there for two hours. His whole life flashed before him, and he saw clearly how mean he was and how much he had hurt both of his wives. He saw how he had treated everyone around him so terribly and how badly he was conducting his life. He wept and wept on the floor for the entire two hours and asked Jesus' forgiveness, finally accepting Jesus into his life as his Lord and Savior.

I was blown away by both of these stories, hugely encouraged. I've realized what John meant when he said,

The light shines in the darkness, and the darkness has not overcome it.
John 1:5

Wonderfully, the DI went on to be so successful as a Detective, especially with drug dealers and addicts, that eventually he was given the job of running a center where people in the drug crime world can receive prayer and the Gospel from the Christian staff, including the DI. This center serves as a halfway house, before they are sent on to a rehabilitation center.

The mission field of our work places is there, just waiting for us all. I'm so thankful to Jesus for baptizing me with His fire and power. It really does make for an exciting life.

Jesus told the disciples they were "the light of the world." In ancient times they didn't have electricity so there were no light bulbs. To have light at night they had to rely on simple oil lamps. A vessel containing oil with a wick into the oil could be lit with fire and this fire would provide light in a room. When we become born again, we are filled with the Holy Spirit, who is the everlasting supply of oil from the Anointed One, Jesus who dwells within us. The baptism of the Holy Spirit is the fire that comes and lights the oil so we, the light of the world, can shine in the darkest places wherever we are. We are Jesus' missionaries whether we're at work in a career job, at home, at church, in the shopping malls or in the pubs or bars. I've learned that the light shines best in the darkest places!

"Walk in the Mighty Name of Jesus"

After Bible college, my first job was helping set up large-scale events for an evangelist. My first assignment was in northern Ghana, where the vast majority of the people were Muslims.

On the second night a woman, dragging her nine-year-old son by his armpits, eventually managed to get close to me at the edge of the large platform. She was shouting loudly to my interpreter that her son was healed. She told us her son had been paralyzed from the waist down since having been in a tragic accident when was a baby. He had never walked or moved his legs. She said that during the preaching, suddenly her son started to move his legs a tiny bit, something absolutely impossible before.

I realized there was something powerful happening with this boy. I had never seen God do anything on that magnitude before, but I asked her to hold him up on his feet as best as she could. I commanded him to walk in the mighty name of Jesus. The interpreter was all the time translating my instructions.

The boy clumsily moved one of his feet forward, then the other. His mother pulled back, as her son leaned and tottered for a second on his terribly thin legs. I raised my voice and commanded the boy,

"Walk, in the mighty name of Jesus!"

The boy took a couple of very unsteady, weak steps almost collapsing, then, as if hit by a bolt of power, his legs instantly seemed to strengthen. Immediately, he began to walk towards me. I walked backwards away from him and he chased me, walking faster and faster. I had to break into an awkward backwards run to keep him from catching me as he was almost running towards me.

By this time the crowd around the side of the platform was all screaming with excitement. I turned round and began to run away from him and he broke into a full on run, chasing me. I ran across an open area behind the platform where the team was working, down the full length of the platform, in front of a large crowd of several thousand that were several yards behind the platform. The boy chased me everywhere I went. The crowd exploded with joy.

I took the boy back to the side of the platform where his mother was standing in shock and tears and then took him onto the platform to the evangelist. He ran all around the platform, chasing the preacher. It was absolutely amazing, and I will likely never forget it. By the time he came down off the platform his thin legs were the size of a normal nine-year-old's. His legs had physically grown to a normal size. I worship you Jesus!

As I left the event field that night, I walked in the midst of the crowd as they made their way home; the atmosphere was electric. Everyone was so excited. Despite being Muslims, they had seen the reality of the glory and power of Jesus. The Kingdom of Heaven had been revealed to them for the very first time in their lives and they were hungrier for God than ever. A strong passion came in my heart to see people healed in Jesus' mighty name.

I realized during that time in Ghana that the Gospel of Jesus Christ is only truly preached when it is accompanied by demonstrations of the Spirit and power, through signs, miracles and wonders. An unknown person famously said, "Preach the Gospel on all occasions and if necessary use words!" (Saint Francis of Assisi is often wrongly credited for this quote; but still, this is a powerful reminder.)

The Gospel of Jesus Christ is not just a matter of words, but must be accompanied by miracles, signs and wonders. When the full Gospel is preached like this there is a powerful clash of two very distinct and radically opposed realms, the Kingdom of Light, ruled majestically by the King of kings and Lord of lords, Jesus Christ, and the dominion of darkness ruled by Satan and his wicked fallen angels.

The devil hates it when he and his minions are confronted by ordinary men and women like you and me, filled with the power of the resurrected Lord Jesus by the Holy Spirit. When we preach the full Gospel of Jesus Christ with signs and wonders and demonstrations of the Spirit's power, Satan and his demons have to flee. Even more than that, people's eyes are opened to the reality of the Kingdom of Heaven and the King of that Kingdom. They see firsthand the King of Love and His great power to save. They see that He is kind and compassionate and that He cares for their every need. Miracles are an essential element of the true Gospel of Jesus Christ.

God attested Jesus Himself through signs, wonders and miracles. Peter, full of the Holy Spirit on the day of Pentecost preached to the crowd saying,

Men of Israel, listen to these words: Jesus the Nazarene, a man attested to you by God with miracles and wonders and signs which God performed through Him in your midst, just as you yourselves know...
Acts 2:22

The Father sent Jesus to reveal the true nature of God, the true nature of Love Himself. He could not do that without doing great signs, wonders and miracles. Nothing has changed; God is determined to reveal Himself to all people throughout the world. Now that we are one with Christ, His mission is to reveal Himself to the world through us, His sons in His Son. He wants to do today, through Christ in you and me, all that He was able to do in and through Christ when He walked on the Earth 2000 years ago.

One of the greatest privileges of being a son of God in Christ Jesus is that the Holy Spirit wants to do the works of the Father in and through His Son, in us. Sadly, today most believers in Christ don't know that. They're stuck, still believing that being a Christian is merely about putting your faith in Christ so you can go to Heaven when you die. To many, it is all about trying to live a good life, going to church and being a good person; being the best you that you can be. Being nice and towing the theological and doctrinal party line of the denomination you belong to is not the fullness Christ died to give you.

Millions of Christians have little understanding that they are one with Christ and that the Father wants to do His supernatural works of miracles through them by His Spirit. God is greatly glorified when He does something through us that only He can do!

My experiences introduced me to the reality that nothing is impossible for God. He is passionately committed to doing miracles through those who make themselves available to Him. I discovered that God is not looking for those who are clever or smart. He is not at all reluctant to do extraordinary things through ordinary people in their ordinary lives, ones who simply believe in Him and trust Him to do what only He can do through them.

My own journey of walking in the supernatural was gathering momentum. I knew without a shadow of a doubt that the things Jesus did are the very things the Father wants to do through us by His Holy Spirit—the very same Holy Spirit He anointed Jesus with. I also knew I wanted to give the rest of my life to doing those things and to teaching others that they too could do all that Jesus did; and even greater things than He did, because He went to the Father.

55

CHAPTER 4

DIE TO YOUR CALLING

He considered that God was able even to raise him from the dead,
from which, figuratively speaking, he did receive him back.
Hebrews 11:19

Sitting on the airplane on the flight from Ghana to London's Heathrow airport, I was quietly congratulating myself on the success of my first major event in Africa. Surely the evangelist would let me be the preacher on one of the main nights at the next event. My mind started to drift and I could see myself in front of a crowd of at least 100,000 somewhere in Africa preaching the glorious Gospel better than anyone had ever preached it in the whole world and throughout all history.

Ok, wait a minute. That sounds a little prideful, I thought to myself and chuckled.

I was so full of excitement at what we had just experienced. I was in Heaven thinking I had the rest of my life as a preacher doing these kinds of events. I was really pleased with myself that I had got off to such an incredible start. I remembered fondly the moment that the young boy who had been paralyzed began to take his first steps as I commanded him to walk. What a moment that had been. I had struggled so hard not to let it go to my little head. I kept rebuking all pride. I was so blessed that it had been me that had ministered to him. The evangelist had looked so pleased with me when I presented the boy to him on the platform.

What a moment! I thought again.

Just then I had another thought, "You must be pretty proud of your son after this event," I said to the Lord, referring to myself.

In an instant, Jesus whispered, *"Actually, Duncan, I'd like you to die to your calling as a preacher and an evangelist to the nations and resign from your position right away."*

I was utterly shell shocked by what the Lord said to me. Surely I hadn't heard right, I thought to myself, trying hard to cheer myself up after such a devastating answer. I decided to push those thoughts to the back of my mind; I certainly wasn't going to mention anything to Kate. I just had this inkling that she might agree with the Lord. I was about to land in England and I'd had such an incredible time. I decided right there and then that I would keep that thought to myself and instead tell everyone what an awesome time I'd had. I would share how God had used me so powerfully to do such awesome miracles.

There were great celebrations when I met Kate at the airport. But despite all my best efforts to be happy I couldn't find any peace. I prayed for a month asking God to change His mind, but I knew it was futile.

Finally I surrendered and decided to tell Kate. Just as I had anticipated, she said she felt exactly the same way. We knew that the Lord was asking us if we would be willing to die to our calling to the nations. I was devastated.

Die to my calling? I didn't have a grid for that. I had no paradigm for doing something that was, in my mind, paramount to giving up. I wasn't a quitter. You don't become a university 1st VIII oarsman, as I had, if you are a quitter. Turning back was never an option for me. James 1 was indelibly etched in my heart,

Count it all joy, my brothers, when you meet trials of various kinds,
for you know that the testing of your faith produces steadfastness.
And let steadfastness have its full effect, that you may be perfect and
complete, lacking in nothing.
James 1:2-4

I sought the wisdom of our pastors. They too felt it was right for us to resign from the ministry we were in and come home. However, I knew how much they loved us and wasn't sure they were objective enough. I desperately wanted to stay where we were. I was really an African, having grown up in Nigeria until I was 18 years old. Being able to minister and preach the Gospel in Africa in fluent Hausa, the language I grew up speaking, as well as seeing Jesus do signs and wonders through me, was almost as good as being in Heaven.

The Lord spoke to me through two scriptures.

By faith Abraham, when He was tested, offered up Isaac, and he who
had received the promises was in the act of offering up his only son, of
whom it was said, "Through Isaac shall your offspring be named." He
considered that God was able even to raise him from the dead, from
which, figuratively speaking, he did receive him back.
Hebrews 11:17-19

No distrust made him waver concerning the promise of God, but
he grew strong in his faith as he gave glory to God, fully convinced
that God was able to do what he had promised. That is why his
faith was "counted to him as righteousness."
Romans 4:20-22

These scriptures burned into my spirit like a laser beam. In that moment, I began for the first time to see that the Cross of Christ is not just an event through which we gain salvation; it is an invitation to walk in the way of Christ. The Kingdom message is the way of the Cross, as well as the event of the Cross.

Only through sharing in Christ's death can we experience the power of His resurrection. We share in His death whenever we accept His invitation to lay down our lives, our desires, our callings, our destinies, our ideas, our agendas, our will, our relationships, our opportunities and our rights. However, the way of the Cross is the way of His resurrection.

He is able to raise everything we lay down before Him from the "dead," including our callings. Without death there can never be resurrection. This is what Jesus meant when He said we were to deny ourselves and take up our Cross and follow Him. He's inviting us to share in His resurrection power on a day-by-day basis as we die to ourselves and follow Him. In this way we live in His power to fulfill His promises in us and through us.

The Holy Spirit's invitation was more than I had seen at first. I thought He was inviting me to "die" but in reality, He was inviting me to "live." He is inviting us all to believe in His resurrection power so that we can truly live. The very same Spirit that raised Jesus from the dead is the very same Spirit that enabled Abraham and Sarah to conceive as He had promised, even though they were 100 and 90 years old respectively.

Shortly after resigning, Kate and I visited my family farm. It had been in our family for several generations, but we had not had much to do with it because my parents had been missionaries in Nigeria.
As we walked over the fields, I asked Kate, "How would you feel about being a farmer's wife?"

She looked at me for a moment and replied, "I could do that, I think."

We both laughed out loud. It seemed ridiculous but as I thought about it, I couldn't help thinking, *There's no better proof that I've died to my calling to the nations as a preacher than if I became a farmer!*

I said to the Lord, "Jesus, if it's right for me to move here and become a farmer, let one of my uncles invite me to do just that, without us saying anything."

The next day we called in on my eldest uncle to greet him before we left town. During our conversation, he turned to me and said, "Have you ever considered coming down here and farming with us? There's no one in your generation who's shown any interest in farming. You'd have to do a university postgraduate course in agriculture and perhaps a master's degree in business, but we'd sponsor you through it all."

I was stunned. I could barely believe my ears. It was such an incredible confirmation. It was as though my uncle had been walking along with us the day before in the fields. Kate and I were completely shocked by the clarity of God's direction in our lives at a time when we really needed to know what to do. Everything fell into place and for three years I "died" on the farm.

The Lord spoke to me one day while I was alone that summer, sweeping another giant barn floor, as seemed to always be the case working on our family farm. I felt His presence come all over me and He spoke into my heart, "Son, the reason I brought you to this farm was because I wanted you all to Myself. You have always been so busy thinking you're doing My work that you've had little time to hang out with Me. I want you to know I don't need you to get the job done of saving the world. I love you and I want your friendship. That's what really counts. I want you to know that you bring as much glory and pleasure to Me sweeping these barns with your sweet-hearted attitude as you did when you were leading thousands to Me on the platform in Ghana."

My eyes teared right up. I knew right there and then that if I spent the rest of my life on that farm, I was a delight to the Lord. I told Him that even if it took until I was 80 years old to resurrect my calling to be a preacher in the nations, I trusted Him that He would do it. I had been praying that summer, "Lord, if possible, take me from this farm and get me back into my calling as a preacher."

I no longer needed to pray that.

Later, I shook Prince Andrew's hand as I received my master's degree in business management at the graduation ceremony. By the time all my studies were completed I really was ready to be a farm manager for the rest of my life. I loved our farm; it is beautiful and I loved working with my family. I guess for a missionary kid who's spent most of his life in another country, there's something special about knowing that your ancestors have lived and worked the land for many generations. I felt like I belonged for the first time in my life.

At the end of my training, my uncles and my father invited me to a special board meeting. One of my uncles opened the dialogue saying, "Duncan, we have not had any peace about you remaining on the farm. You've done very well in every way, but after prayer, we've decided you are not called to be a farmer. You're a preacher. You could be a farmer and do very well, but we just know the Lord has called you to the nations and we would like to release you to do just that."

My heart felt like it had frozen solid. I pleaded with them. I was not called to be a preacher; the Lord had asked me to die to that, as they all knew. However I soon realized they had made up their minds, my father included. Deep inside I knew they were right but my heart was shredded. I began to weep uncontrollably right there in the boardroom. Something to do with the feeling of losing my inheritance of working the land rose up from deep within me and I just couldn't close the floodgates. I asked them if I could pray for them, and I forgave each of them for the huge disappointment of not being able to be part of the family farm business any longer. I had read an incredible book by John Arnott called *The Importance of Forgiveness*, and I knew what I needed to do. I walked out of the meeting a free man in the spirit.

"Dying" to the farm was even worse than "dying" to my calling as a preacher. Here I was, dying to my inheritance and all that I had studied and worked so hard for over the past three years of my life. It was extremely tough. I found a job as a shepherd's assistant working on a nearby farm which provided our family with much needed income and gave me the space and time I needed to heal. All my ambition was gone.

Baptised In Heavenly Daddy

Kate and I had heard of the revival that had been going on at the Toronto Airport Vineyard church in Toronto, Canada, which by then was called the Toronto Airport Christian Fellowship (TACF). We had visited one night, while we were on vacation in Canada. We had many friends who had been several times and always encouraged us to make more of an effort to go. So when we found out from some friends of ours who were volunteering at TACF, that there was a small, invitation only, conference on church planting that very May 2000, we jumped at the opportunity.

While I was standing in a long line to receive a prophetic word, I found myself talking with a couple of pastors. As usual, I was doing a superb job of talking all about myself with the pastors.

Suddenly one of the men said to his friend, "I don't think Duncan's ever met his Heavenly Daddy do you?"

What are you talking about? I thought to myself. *How dare you insinuate that I'm lacking somehow in my spirituality? What's more, how dare you call God Almighty "Heavenly Daddy"! You're being far too familiar and way too irreverent with the Living God and you two call yourselves pastors.*

I was ready to punch them to be honest. His voice sounded so gooey and "nice." I was flat-out mad.

To my astonishment, his friend replied smiling ridiculously at me, "Yeah, I don't think Duncan has ever met his Heavenly Daddy before, have you Duncan?"

Despite my defensiveness, I knew they were right. The truth was, I had never met God in that way. I couldn't call God, "Daddy." I hated the word "Daddy"; it sounded childish and stuck in my throat. I could call God "Father," but I could never call Him "Dad" or "Daddy." I realized that deep down inside I had always been very uncomfortable with love, feeling that I couldn't really love anyone.

As I stood there angry, insulted and upset with them both, yet knowing how horribly right they were, I decided for the first time in my life, to show weakness and vulnerability and surrender to love, fully admitting the reality of my deficiency of love.

"You guys are right," I said. "I've never met my Heavenly Daddy."

"Well, you can meet Him now," one of them said, smiling.

As I held out my hands in front of me at waist level, he placed his hands very gently in mine and simply said, "Heavenly Daddy, come and reveal yourself to your son, Duncan."

I felt the sensation of something like warm, liquid, golden honey begin pouring all over me from the top of my head. At the same time, a tremendous, irresistible force of weighty glory hit the top of my head, and I crumpled to the ground in a heap at their feet. I couldn't have resisted it if I tried. If a locomotive could express kindness and love, I had just been hit by one!

As I lay there in a puddle of liquid love I heard a beautifully kind voice say to me as I was bathed in light, "*Duncan, you are My lovely son and I'm really pleased with you. I have loved you with an everlasting love from before time began. You are My treasured possession. I have loved you long before you ever did anything right or anything wrong. There is nothing that you have done that I have not forgiven you for and there is nothing that you will do that I will not forgive you for. There is nothing you can do that will make Me love you more and there is nothing you can do that will make Me love you less. I love you and I will always love you. You are My son.*"

I was absolutely undone. I lay there wailing like a baby in a pool of my tears. When I eventually came around after the longest time, everything was different. The grass was greener, the sky bluer. I felt so much love spontaneously in my heart. I felt a massive love for my wife and my children well up inside me. I *felt* it. I could feel love! I could call God, "Daddy!" My heart was no longer frozen and numb towards people.

I had always loved Jesus; He was my perfect Savior. But people? They hurt. I realized I hadn't trusted anyone, not even those closest to me. Now my heart was burning for people. I loved people. I knew I could trust them because I knew my Heavenly Daddy loved me. He could more than make up for any way they might hurt me.

I was revolutionized in my Father's great love. Kate was overjoyed when I later shared what had happened. I'm so eternally thankful to those two men for introducing me to the love of the Father, my Heavenly Daddy.

The next day was the last day of the conference. During the coffee break, John Arnott, the Founding Pastor of TACF, came over to me and invited Kate and me to lunch. However, it didn't happen that day, because the speakers came and laid their hands on us all to receive a greater measure of the Holy Spirit on us for church planting. Carol Arnott kept praying "more" over us both. We didn't stand a chance! As I lay next to Kate among a pile of bodies strewn all over the floor, John came and stood over me and asked if I still wanted to have lunch. I declined his offer. I was just too overwhelmed by the Holy Spirit.

We heard the next day that John still wanted to meet. We were so glad of the opportunity. He is such a great leader of a history making revival that has touched millions of people the world over. I thought to myself, *Perhaps the Lord has spoken to him about my plans to go into business in England and he is going to lay hands on me and bless me. That would be awesome.*

Over coffee the next day, John asked us to tell him our story. When we finished, we were all in tears because of the tenderness of the story of our experiences in dying to our callings and the promises of God, yet being fully persuaded that God was able to raise us up again.

John turned to me and said, "Son, I can see that you are really limping."

I replied with my head hanging down, tears falling on my cheeks, "Yes sir, I am really limping."

John then did one of the kindest things anyone has ever done to me. He stretched out his enormous hand and placed it gently on my shoulder. Looking me straight in the eyes, he said, "Well, I look for a man who's limping. I'd like to ask you to come and work with me and join our ministry as a pastor and help us with our business side of things at the same time." We were stunned and promised to give him an answer quickly.

Later, as we sat on the airplane heading home, we knew that this was the Lord. This offer had come while we were totally helpless to place ourselves in any capacity or position where we could fulfill our callings to the nations. It was the Lord. He is the God of resurrection power.

After sharing with a number of key people in our lives among our pastors, family and friends, we decided to go with the peace that was in our hearts.

Three months later, we moved to Toronto, Canada. I began working at TACF, this incredible revival center and enormous church, and I set about doing my best to enhance and contribute to the ministry. Everything I had learned in farming I was now putting into practice in a way I could never have dreamt. Within two months John invited me into his office and asked if I would be the executive director.

I replied, "I cannot do that!"

To which he said, "Yes, you can."

I said, "No, I really can't."

He said, "You're right, you can't, but we can do it together!"

To my amazement, John told me that the Holy Spirit had spoken into his heart the moment he saw me walk into the church planting conference back in May.

"*That's the tall Englishman I said I would give you, to be your first executive director.*"

After praying it over with Kate, I accepted the post. We were both 33 years old. I was a dead man, now coming fully alive. Everything that had taken place in our lives up until that point had been preparation for that very moment. Truly God works everything together for our good (Romans 8:28).

Our Heavenly Daddy is so big and so awesome that He is able to do far more than we can ever conceive or even imagine. His invitation to share in Christ's death was an invitation to share in the power of Christ's resurrection. I began to realize that the whole journey I had been on since I "died to my calling" was a journey that allowed me to begin to learn what the Gospel that I had been called to preach really was.

In August 1991, I had heard the voice of the Lord saying, *"I have appointed you and now I have anointed you to be a light and a herald to the nations and to preach the Gospel to the ends of the earth."*

I had assumed I knew the Gospel. Now, ten years later, I realized I had so much more to learn about the incredible Gospel of Jesus Christ. Now I was beginning to understand that my calling was really an invitation from the Holy Spirit to allow Him to plunge me into the mysteries of this glorious Gospel, and the depths of God's great love that He has demonstrated to us in Christ. It was an invitation to truly know Him, the author and finisher of our salvation. To meet with Him, feast with Him and be transformed by Him, in union with Him. I was more desperate than ever to understand the mysteries of Christ.

CHAPTER 5

BLIND EYES OPENING

Never since the world began has it been heard that anyone opened
the eyes of a man born blind. If this man were not
from God, he could do nothing.
John 9:32-33

God is so fantastic. It was no coincidence that the Lord made sure my first missions trip from Toronto was carrying the Father's love to Ghana: the very country in which He had asked me to "die to my calling" seven years earlier. I couldn't have planned that, but the Lord always loves the finest details in our lives. They are our Heavenly Daddy's kisses.

When I returned to Canada I knew we needed to create a new name and ministry to be the international face of TACF. It was a little awkward telling the Ghanaians that our ministry was called the "Toronto Airport Christian Fellowship." They had not heard of the Revival at the "Airport Church." For those who knew about the revival, the words "Toronto Airport" were synonymous with a great move of God. But to those who'd never heard of the revival it was bewildering. They had asked me in Accra, "Is your ministry based in one of the terminal buildings at the airport?"

I shared with John Arnott my thoughts and we formed "Catch The

Fire Ministries" as the international ministry based out of TACF. "Catch The Fire" was already the name of our annual signature conference since revival had exploded in 1994, so it was perfectly natural for us to start a ministry to reach the world with our values called by the same name. Revealing the Father's love through the Gospel by the Holy Spirit in signs and wonders through ordinary people manifesting the grace of Christ is our passion at Catch The Fire.

In Romans, Paul powerfully summarizes how he authentically preached the Gospel.

Through mighty signs and wonders, by the power of the Spirit of God;
so that from Jerusalem and round about to Illyricum,
I have fully preached the Gospel of Christ.
Romans 15:19 (KJV)

There is a profound connection between the preaching of the Gospel and the supernatural miracles of the Kingdom. As far as Paul was concerned, signs and wonders done in the power of the Holy Spirit is the authentic preaching of the gospel of Christ.

The Gospel of Christ is never just words but action; supernatural action, accomplished by Christ through ordinary people like Paul, the early church in Rome, and people like you and me. We can't authentically preach the gospel unless we allow Christ, through the Holy Spirit in us, to perform miracles, signs and wonders. God confirms that the message a preacher is preaching is an authentic message, by enabling them to do what only God can do. This was true even for Jesus' ministry. He did not just speak powerful words that carried authority in themselves, but He demonstrated the word by extraordinary works of power.

This rocks our world as we know it. We've preached far too many sermons and done far too few miracles. I've set my heart on learning how to do miracles as well as learning the Gospel. Miracles are the authentication of the very Gospel we preach.

As a child on the mission field in Nigeria I was always perplexed by the fact that we never expected, witnessed or did miracles. I was aware that many Evangelicals believe miracles ended with the first apostles. It bothered me as a kid, that people taught us God doesn't do miracles any more through His people.

Why would Jesus stop doing miracles after the death of the last early apostle? Were they the last and only apostles? Surely the Gospel is eternal and never changes. Surely if miracles were the authenticity of the Gospel, first in Jesus, then in the early church, it must still be today!

I'm so thrilled that when I went to university the Holy Spirit introduced me to that bunch of fanatical lovers of Jesus. They introduced me to the authentic Gospel of Jesus Christ, demonstrated by powerful demonstrations of the Spirit's power. Watching God at work doing extraordinary miracles, we can't help but know that He really is the most wonderful person in the universe. The same Jesus I am so in love with in the Gospels is truly the very same Jesus who is alive in the Heavens, seated at the right hand of the Father. He is the same Jesus who dwells in us and on us, through the Holy Spirit here on earth.

Jesus Christ Himself is in you and me! We have known it theologically, but let that reality collide with you. If Christ is in us then the best way we can reveal Christ to the world, is by preaching the Gospel of Christ through extraordinary signs wonders and miracles.

One night, I was preaching at TACF on John 9, when Jesus heals the man born blind. As I read verse 32, the words just leapt from the pages,

Never since the world began has it been heard that anyone opened
the eyes of a man born blind. If this man were not
from God, he could do nothing.
John 9:32-33

Dynamite went off in my spirit. No one, throughout the entire history of the human race, had ever opened the eyes of the blind—until Jesus Christ. Throughout the Old Testament no one is ever recorded opening the eyes of one blind person. Elijah and Elisha had both raised the dead, Moses had done many outstanding miracles and many others had seen God do extraordinary things, but no one had ever seen the eyes of the blind opened.

The psalmist says:

> *The LORD opens the eyes of the blind.*
> *Psalm 146:8*

Isaiah, speaking of the Messiah's day, says:

> *Then the eyes of the blind will be opened and the ears of the deaf*
> *will be unstopped. Then the lame will leap like a deer*
> *and the tongue of the mute will shout for joy.*
> *Isaiah 35:5-6*

My heart raced. I knew instinctively as I thought about the blind being healed that it was one of *the* signs of the Messiah. It was as if the writers of the Old Testament were saying, "Israel, You will know your Messiah when He comes because He is the One who will open the eyes of the blind!"

Put another way, "Whoever you see among you opening the eyes of the blind, is the Messiah!"

Standing on the platform I heard my heart crying out to the Lord, "Oh, Jesus! The whole world throughout all ages is supposed to know You are the Messiah when they see You opening the eyes of the blind, but where are You today? If You were here right now, You would be opening the eyes of the blind. If You were present in your church as I believe You are, then why are we not experiencing blind eyes opening?"

Knowing the truth that Jesus is of course among us tells us that the problem is on our end. But we can ask the Messiah to reveal Himself in His church all over the world by opening the eyes of the blind through us, His people. I determined that night I needed the Holy Spirit to teach me how to open the eyes of the blind so the Messiah could be revealed in me as well as the church.

I resolved in my heart, "If Jesus Christ is the Messiah, which He is, and He lives in me, then He will open the eyes of the blind through me from this day forward! I will see the blind healed! We will all see the blind healed!"

May all the church go forth into the world in our spheres of influence that the Lord has given us and heal the multitudes, especially the blind. The joy of healing a blind or deaf person is beyond description and is quite possibly one of the most precious experiences we can ever have. It will be too late in Heaven to do it, as our friend Heidi Baker says!

I knew I needed to understand much more fully who Christ is in me and who I am in Christ. The Holy Spirit took me on a journey into the glorious riches of Christ and the Cross. He showed me that the key is understanding that we are one with Christ.

Without miracles, the church today has settled into a place so far short of where the Father desires us to live. They do not realize they are *one with Christ*. Miracles, signs and wonders done in the power of the Spirit through us are essential to us discovering the true power and authority of Christ and our identity in Him. We can't open the eyes of the blind until we realize that we are the flesh and blood manifestation of Jesus on the earth!

We don't take His place; instead, we are one with Him so completely that we are indistinguishable from Him. The miracles are the daily evidence of that truth, just as they were for Jesus when he walked the earth in the very same body as ours! (Acts 2:22) Oneness with Him is the key to doing miracles.

It has been 10 years since that night, and I am thrilled to say Jesus answered the cry of my heart. I have had the honor of seeing Jesus use me to heal many blind and partially blind people as well as deaf or partially deaf people, five of whom were born deaf and mute. We have been able to teach thousands of others to do the same and they too have seen Jesus heal the blind and deaf. If these kinds of miracles begin to take place regularly in the church throughout the world, we will have the greatest revival ever known. The key is knowing the power of the Cross and our union with Christ through it.

Imitate Me As I Imitate Christ

During our early days at TACF, I grappled with my insecurities, inadequacies and fears as a leader that had begun to surface. Kate and I went to a pastors and leaders retreat at a church in Bogota, Colombia.

As I sat listening to a pastor from that church challenging us, I was arrested in my tracks. He read,

> *Be imitators of me as I imitate Christ.*
> *1 Corinthians 4:16*

Paul's words to the Corinthian church were like dynamite in the very core of my being. I could not stop thinking about them.

Deeply challenged, I realized everything within me resisted ever saying those words to another person, especially our leaders—my followers. I was wired from head to toe to think, "Whatever you do, imitate Christ, not me!"

I was aware of my shortcomings; I wouldn't want anyone to imitate my life, my habits, my thoughts or my conduct. I would rather they learn from my mistakes, of which there have been many. How could I look one of our young leaders in the eye, back home in Toronto, and say to them with all sincerity, conviction and absolute confidence, "Be an imitator of me, as I imitate Christ"? No one with my track record and secret thoughts could ever be worthy of saying something like that to those around them. I would never dream of telling anyone to imitate me. Imitate Christ, sure, but not me!

I realized that the Apostle Paul must have known something fundamentally profound. His entire belief structure was on a completely different plane from much of the world's population today, including myself and the vast majority of Christians.

We can see that the church worldwide, on the whole, has lost much of the belief structure that Paul and the early apostles lived by. This structure is what made them such passionate men and women who lived every moment of their lives in the supernatural power of God, raising dead people to life, healing the blind, deaf and mute, and shaking entire cities with their preaching. Many Christians today have little idea of what Jesus Christ, the Messiah, actually accomplished for humanity. If we did, the church would be radically different; and as a result, so would the entire world.

I wonder if the words of Jesus to Saul of Tarsus on the Damascus road were the very words Saul, who later became the Apostle Paul, could never forget.

Saul, Saul, why are you persecuting me?
Acts 9:4

Those words are so profound. They led Paul to his conversion, ultimately leading him to understand Oneness with Christ through faith in Him. To persecute the believers was to persecute Jesus, because His believers are one with Him. Paul later discovered the place of that Oneness was none other than the Cross and resurrection.

Many have a church-centered experience rather than a Christ-centered experience, living in what I call "Churchianity" rather than experiencing who we are in Christ—true Christianity. Whatever our particular denominational persuasion, we often have a far better understanding of the ways of that denomination than we do of the ways of the Kingdom of Heaven.

Unfortunately these ways are often based on theologies, doctrines and church dogma, more rooted in unbelief than in faith. This "knowledge" quenches the fire of God birthed in the human heart the moment we are born from above. This very quickly leads to a loss of our first love, and any purpose in God's heart for us to experience His supernatural life and power is extinguished.

Our experience of the church becomes one of attendance at Sunday services and possibly attendance at another weekly meeting. If we are very keen and attend faithfully, we spend most of our time listening to others. We just warm up the pews or the seats. Rarely do we get to "do the stuff." We see very few miracles done by Jesus through others, let alone ourselves. The only time we might ever see miracles is by going to a conference or a healing crusade by a well-known healing evangelist; but again, we're simply observing, not doing.

So the result of all this is that our experience of Christianity is often routine and boring. Every time we seem to take one step forward we get knocked back at least two steps. We become more acquainted with our weakness and failure to live the Christian life than anything else. Our "righteousness" as Christians becomes based on our behavior, clothes, church attendance, tithing and offerings, prayer life, fasting and cleanliness of our speech and conduct in life—all of which the Bible calls "dirty rags."

Whatever Christian denomination or culture we are from forms the basis of how "holy" we feel at any given point in our lives. These cultures become law to us. Not the Law of the Old Testament, but our own cultural version, which is a good mixture, or "pseudo-Christo-Judaic" law. It is a Christian version of the Law, dressed in our culture. We are quick to claim we are not under Law, but instead are living under the grace and the freedom of the New Covenant in Christ. However the reality of our day-to-day experience is that we are living under church cultural rules and regulations that dominate our lives and are law to us, defining how we live and feel spiritually.

When we have read our Bibles and prayed in our quiet time, we spend much of the day feeling settled that God is pleased with us and we are holy, or almost! On the other hand if we haven't done either of these, then we might feel very anxious and discouraged that we have slipped in righteousness, although many of us are not too sure what that long word means anyway! Some even go so far as to think any "bad" things that might happen to them can be attributed to a lack of "quiet time"!

The specific spiritual actions we call "spirituality" vary from church to church and Christian to Christian. Some might think nothing of missing their quiet time. Others may not even believe in having one. Instead, they may have a strong doctrine on mercy missions and almsgiving to the poor. As long as they are serving the poor, they have a settled feeling that they are holy. However, if for any reason they have a period of neglecting this area of their lives they can quickly come under the very same anxiety, fearing a loss of holiness or righteousness.

I have found this belief system is prevalent as strongly in Renewal or Revival circles as it is elsewhere in mainstream churches. The "works" are different, but nonetheless still easily become the substance of a person's sense of well being before God.

Waiting on the Lord, often called "soaking," or "soaking prayer," is a wonderful spiritual activity, but can easily become the thing which people's sense of holiness is dependent upon. When they have a really good soaking session they feel at peace with God, that somehow He is now more pleased with them. We need to learn that when we soak, we do it to simply be with Jesus, for Jesus. It neither adds nor takes away from our righteousness in Christ. Soaking in His presence reminds us of our righteousness in Him and lifts our eyes off our own attempts at righteousness. It tunes us to the reality of His presence and glory in us and on us. If we believe in Jesus as our Savior, we are one with Christ whether we soak or not. However, if we soak, we are more likely to live in the knowledge and experience of our union with Him.

To be "holy" growing up was very much based on what I did, or did not do. I knew nothing of the tangible presence of God or the power of God. I was familiar with the "religion" of our particular strain of Christianity, but the presence and power of God was absolutely alien to me. I didn't know who the Holy Spirit was other than the third person of the Trinity. Holiness was defined by adherence to the rules and regulations of the household and the mission organization's acceptable theology, doctrine and code of behavior and conduct.

What this meant was that as long as I wore the right clothes on Sundays, didn't watch TV on Sundays, never went shopping on Sundays, but went to church at least once without fail, preferably twice or three times, then I was a "holy people set apart unto the Lord." My siblings and I even had a special toy each that we were only allowed to play with on Sunday afternoons to "make Sundays special!" We were never allowed to drink alcohol as that was deemed particularly sinful and in many church circles around the world to this day, to drink alcohol such as beer is paramount to losing one's salvation. I'm so glad that the Kingdom of Heaven is in the Holy Spirit and is not dependent on what we do or don't do! It is a matter of whether we believe in the King of the Kingdom. Paul says,

> *The kingdom of God is not a matter of eating and drinking but of*
> *righteousness and peace and joy in the Holy Spirit.*
> *Romans 14:17*

In today's church culture, holiness is defined so often by what you do or don't do. In some churches, people would laugh at this, thinking they are "free," but in reality each type of church has its own version, equally based in dos and don'ts. Do you speak in tongues or not? Are you an intercessor? Do you soak? Do you manifest? Do you minister to the poor? Which denomination do you belong to?

I believe with all conviction that this is not God's heart for His church. His heart for the church is that we would have the most exciting lives of all human beings. He sent His Son into this world on a mission that involved both the Father and the Son paying the highest price, the greatest overpayment that has ever been paid in the history of the entire universe. He did this so He could have many sons walking in the supernatural realm with Him every day of their lives on this earth and on into eternity. Sons, one with Him, consumed by Love Himself.

My parents have both since come to wonderfully experience the supernatural presence and power of the Holy Spirit and are still traveling in the nations as witnesses of Christ's resurrection life and power.

Spiritual disciplines, whether fasting, prayer, spending time reading the Bible, giving to the poor, caring for widows and orphans or soaking are all extremely important to our growth in fruitfulness and maturity in Christ. However they neither add nor take away from our righteousness or holiness before God. That is dependent upon what Christ alone has done for us.

In Christ we embrace spiritual disciplines because our Heavenly Daddy loves us and not to make Him love us. My pastor Carol Arnott tells the story all over the world of how the Lord spoke to her heart, "Carol I have many servants, but very few lovers."

There is nothing we can do that will make God love us any more or any less than He already does. We can love Him with the same love with which He has first loved us (1 John 4:10).

In Colombia, I asked the Holy Spirit to teach me the depths of Christ and the Gospel that Paul and the early apostles preached, which was confirmed and demonstrated by signs, wonders and miracles. They were able to see virtually the entire known world in their day turn to Christ. I realized I needed a total transformation of my core belief structure.

The Eternal "Well Done!"

The Holy Spirit led me to read the first few lines of Mark 1. The word "Gospel" stuck out to me and I realized I had always taken it for granted I knew what the word Gospel meant. I knew it to mean Good News, which it does.

Nevertheless, I looked up the Greek and quickly discovered the word in Greek translated "Gospel" is *euaggelion*. It is made from two Greek root words, *eu* and *aggelos*. Eu means "well done" and *aggelos* is most commonly translated angels or messenger.

Putting these two words together, we see the Gospel is literally the "Well Done!" announced by the angels. My heart started racing as I began to see revelation in these two Greek words used together. I began to think of the moment when Jesus re-entered Heaven after He rose from the dead and returned to the Father. As He returned to the Father He took us all with Him, leading many sons to glory (Hebrews 2:10).

I began to think of the story of the Prodigal Son, which I prefer to call, The Loving Father, that Jesus told in Luke 15. Let's see how Jesus, the Eternal Son of the Father is totally different from the eldest son in the parable. Adam can be compared to the youngest son and therefore we too can be compared to the youngest sons, because we were in Adam. In the parable the youngest son went to the foreign land and squandered all that was his inheritance on loose living and then enslaved himself to the "citizen of a foreign land," who I can't help thinking is such a type of Satan. The son found himself in the pigpen; a pen full of the most unclean animals, again for me, a type of the demonic realm. The world of sin and death was a totally "foreign land" to humanity. We were created for our Father's house not for the pig pen.

Jesus the Eternal Son, was willing to leave the Father's house on the most incredible rescue mission ever witnessed within the universe. He came into the "foreign land," stepped right into the pigpen of our sin and demonic affliction and rescued us forever. He gave His blameless life for our filthy lives.

He took off His robes and clothed us in them. He took off His sandals and put them on our feet, along with His ring on our finger. Then, having risen from the grave, He took us back to our Father. As I meditated on this moment, I imagined what that must have been like. That incredible moment, when all the angels of Heaven watched as the majestic, triumphant Eternal Son of God, returned into Heaven and came up to the Ancient of Days, His Father, with all of us clothed in His glorious garments of salvation and robes of His righteousness that He won for us at the Cross in the "pigpen" of our broken, sin-filled world.

I realized that the angels of Heaven witnessed the Eternal "Well Done!" It was spoken by the Father over the two sons in all eternity, heard by all the heavenly angels (messengers) when the Eternal Son came home with the youngest son that was lost. Well done to the eldest for rescuing us and all that it cost Him to do so and well done, to the youngest, us, for just believing in the Eternal Son and being willing to come home. Oh, the love and immense grace and kindness of the Lord.

The "Good News" for all humanity is that there is an eternal "Well Done!" spoken over us that the angels of Heaven witnessed and heard. They have been joyously announcing the "Good News" ever since!

The Father has already spoken an eternal "Well Done!" over your life if you believe in Jesus; which is why, despite all our sin, the word we shall hear on the Day of Judgment is "Well Done!" What a comfort to know there has already been spoken an eternal "Well Done!" over your life. No matter what, God says "Well Done!" over you. Now, that is good news for people like me who have spent most of our lives really making a mess of things.

If the Father has already spoken the eternal "Well Done!" over our lives then why did I, and so many Christians the world over, have such a problem with knowing we are truly holy? I decided once and for all to tackle the issue of holiness, and embarked on a study of what the word "holy" in the scriptures really meant.

Two verses leapt out at me,

Consecrate yourselves, therefore, and be holy,
for I am the LORD your God.
Leviticus 20:7

I am the LORD your God. Consecrate yourselves therefore,
and be holy, for I am holy.
Leviticus 11:44a

The Hebrew word translated to English as "consecrate" is the word, *qadash*. It means "set yourself apart," "sanctify yourself" or "consecrate yourself."

The Hebrew words translated into English as "holy" in these scriptures are the words *qodesh* and *qadosh*. Both words mean the same thing and are used interchangeably in the Hebrew text. They both mean "The place of apartness." In other words, holiness is not behavior, it is a position and that position is a person!

When the Bible says God is "Holy," it means He is "The Place of Apartness." He is not "Holy" because He is Perfect; He is "Holy" because of who He is and where He is. He is the Place and Person of Apartness.

I saw it right there. Of course God is "Holy!" He is the only uncreated Being inside and outside of the universe. Everything else is created. God is the Creator. He is apart from us. He is "Apartness" Himself.

Putting this all together, it is as though the Lord is saying, "*Set yourselves apart, and be in the Place of Apartness; and by the way, I am the Place of Apartness, for I am the Lord your God.*"

Looking at it backwards we can see the Lord is saying, "*I am the Lord your God, which means I am the Place of Apartness, therefore you too can be the Place of Apartness if you are willing to set yourselves apart.*"

Revelation flooded my mind. Now it was my "blind eyes" that were opening as I grappled with the enormity of what the Lord was showing me. Under the Old Covenant, this verse was impossible for anyone to fulfill, even the Israelites, God's chosen people included. You cannot come to a person who is Apartness Himself and join Him without ruining His apartness. Not only that, but He has also ruined your apartness. Two people cannot be together and be apart. To be truly apart, there can only be one of you!

To join God and be apart *with* Him you cannot be separate *from* Him. So under the Old Covenant there was no provision yet for true holiness, or apartness. The commandment in these verses as part of the Law was to point to a coming Kingdom reality that would not be fulfilled until Jesus their Messiah came. It was an invitation to realize that only God is truly "Holy," and therefore we can only be "Holy" *in* Him.

Under the Old Covenant, God would not compromise His nature as Holy. He has never intended for man to be Holy apart from Him. That's why God says to Moses and Isaiah,

> *You cannot see My face; for man shall not see Me and live.*
> *Exodus 33:20*

> *I am the Lord; that is my name; my glory I give to no other.*
> *Isaiah 42:8*

What they could not do for themselves, God did for us all in Christ Jesus. Christianity is the only religion (for want of a better word) in the world that does not teach you to try to get to God, or find God. Christianity is about God coming to rescue you. It's about Him finding you. All other religions are about man preparing sacrifices for God, but Christianity is about a God who prepared His eternal sacrifice for us, His own dear Son.

Paul tells us in Romans 8 that what we could not do for ourselves—come to God, because our flesh separated us from God—God did for us, by sending His Son in our likeness. We couldn't get to Him, but He came to us!

> *For God has done what the law, weakened by the flesh, could not do.*
> *By sending his own Son in the likeness of sinful flesh and for sin,*
> *he condemned sin in the flesh.*
> *Romans 8:3*

The Son of God became the Son of Man so that the sons of men could become the sons of God. What a Gospel! The Cross of Christ was His entire journey of being made in the likeness of our sinful flesh. His purpose was to give the Father the many sons He had always desired, just like His Son Jesus. Paul sums up Christ's mission so beautifully in Galatians:

> *When the fullness of time had come, God sent forth his Son, born*
> *of woman, born under the law, to redeem those who were under the*
> *law, so that we might receive adoption as sons. And because you are*
> *sons, God has sent the Spirit of his Son into our hearts, crying, 'Abba!*
> *Father!' So you are no longer a slave, but a son, and if a son,*
> *then an heir through God.*
> *Galatians 4:4-7*

The glorious reality of our sonship in Christ is anchored in the enormity of what it cost Him to become who we are in every way in our humanity, sin and depravity in time and space. He did this so that we could become all that He is in His deity, righteousness and holiness forever. May our eyes be fully opened as we look into the enormous price that was paid for our Oneness.

PART TWO

THE PRICE OF ONENESS

CHAPTER 6

THE SON OF ABBA

Abba, Father, all things are possible for you.
Remove this cup from me. Yet not what I will, but what you will.
Mark 14:36

And being in an agony he prayed more earnestly; and his sweat
became like great drops of blood falling down to the ground.
Luke 22:44

I was in Moscow with John Arnott, speaking at a conference at one of the leading non-denominational churches. John asked me if I would do one of the sessions. As I was preparing to speak, the Holy Spirit began to open my eyes to the suffering of Christ. I was drawn to the Baptism of Jesus.

In Christianity, baptism has long symbolized our sharing in His death, burial and resurrection, but I had never thought that it was just as symbolic for Jesus. As He came to the water's edge in front of thousands of people, He knew the icy cold muddy floodwaters symbolized the waters of our death. In becoming like us in every way so that we could become like Him in every way, He would have to be willing not only to share in our life, our flesh and blood, but also share in our sin and death.

Jesus illustrates His absolute resolve to be fully associated and identified with us as He got into the water and presented Himself to John the Baptist to be baptized. He had never sinned, yet He made no attempt to make that known to any of the onlookers.

Jesus knew going into the river risked His reputation. Everyone was getting into the water for one reason: to repent and have their sins washed away. Getting in Himself, He risked the crowd thinking that He too was a "sinner," but Jesus was never worried about His reputation, or what everyone thought about Him. He came for one thing alone: to do the will of the One who sent Him, His Father. He was willing for His reputation to be ruined in order to rescue us.

He got into the icy waters of the Jordan because of His great love for you and me, as well as His great love for His Father, unashamedly throwing His reputation away. It was precisely because Jesus had come to identify with us as sinners and take all our sin, guilt, shame and even the punishment we deserve, that He was willing to get into our waters of death. John tried to stop Him, saying Jesus should be baptizing him (John was right about that), yet Jesus says John must baptize Him to fulfill all righteousness. This was necessary so righteousness could come to all.

Jesus had a dramatic foretaste of the suffering He would go through three and a half years later as His head and body were plunged into the Jordan. I don't imagine for a moment that John lowered Jesus gently into the River Jordan. John the Baptist has always struck me as being a real tough guy with his clothing of camel's hair and leather belt.

I don't know if you have ever had the experience of being plunged into an ice pool, or icy river. It is an experience I shall never forget, and I don't wish to experience it ever again! It was awful. My entire body exploded with searing pain. Every nerve ending screamed to my central nervous system, "Get out now!" The strangest thing is that even though it's freezing, it feels like fire on your skin, as though you are being burned alive.

I remember our girls jumping out of our hot tub in their bathing suits and rolling around in three feet of snow when they were young and we lived in Toronto, Canada. Jessie, our eldest daughter would always be the first to jump in the snow. She would roll for a few seconds and then jump back into the tub screaming that she was on fire. Then her two sisters, Abby and Nathania, would pluck up the courage to follow suit. Once or twice I also tried it. I was shocked to find that sure enough, it felt like my entire body was burning on fire, even though it was bitterly cold.

One of the most notable memories for me of being plunged into an ice pool was that it literally felt like nails or sharp thorns were being driven into my scalp all over my head. Jesus would have felt a taste of the crown of thorns in that very moment as He was plunged into the Jordan.

As John the Baptist plunged Jesus under the water, searing pain would have burned along Jesus' body as His skin crawled with the fiery sensation of ice-cold water covering Him. It was His first foretaste of death, burial and resurrection.

Jesus the guiltless, immersed in our sin and therefore our death, so we could be forever immersed in His righteousness and His life, one with burning Love Himself. He was so secure as the Eternal Righteousness of God Himself that he didn't hesitate for a moment to get into the muddy waters of our sinful humanity. He knew His righteousness was so much more powerful than our sin. Hallelujah!

The Waters of Burial

We have taught the Body of Christ about sharing in Christ's death, but we don't often preach much on sharing in Christ's burial. Burial is so significant; it is the moment when we finally realize they are gone from this life into the next. When Kate's mother, Ann, died, it wasn't until her ashes were interred in the ground that we all realized she had truly gone. Until that moment there was always the hope of her resurrection, but once she was in the ground that was it. We knew it was over in this life. Of course, Ann is now more alive than she ever was on Earth!

We need to understand that not only have we died with Christ, we have been buried with Him. This means we are really, really dead! We no longer live. In the tomb, nothing of this world matters any longer, there is only one thing that really matters: "I must live again!"

What car you drive in this world, or what house or subdivision you live in is irrelevant. It doesn't matter how much money you made, or what college your kids went to. Nothing matters except one thing, "*I must live again!*"

Jesus experienced this burial after the Cross. He died and was buried in the tomb. He had to trust that His Father, by the power of His Spirit, would raise Him from the dead on the third day, just like He had promised. He had to trust His Father knew none of that sin was His own.

At His baptism, as He was thrust under the water, knocked off His feet and left at the total mercy of John to raise Him up, Jesus had a foretaste of His burial.

I have often wondered what went through Jesus' mind in that moment under the Jordan River. The battle of faith would have been enormous, perhaps with the question rampaging through His mind: Now that He was one with us, in our sin and death, would the Father be able to raise Him from the dead?

As Jesus is lifted up out of the watery grave, something so amazing and powerful happens. The Heavens are ripped open and the Spirit descends upon Him like a dove and remains upon Him. The voice speaks from the Heavens saying, "*You are my beloved Son, in whom I am well pleased.*"

In that perfect moment, when the Son of God comes out of the watery grave, figuratively "covered" in humanity, the Father speaks in the most dramatic way. He honors the Son and assures Him that He will raise Him from the dead. He does this not just by His words, but with a dramatic affirmation through the descent of the Spirit upon Him.

The very same Spirit of God that would fill His dead body on the third day three and a half years later, raising Him forever from the dead, descended upon the Son as He came up out of the water. Jesus knew that He knew, in that day, when He was one with humanity, the Father would still raise Him from the dead.

The extraordinary thing about this watery grave is that the Father opened the Heavens, the Spirit descended like a dove upon Jesus and the voice spoke when Jesus came up out of the water, not when He first got in. This moment was not just for Jesus' sake, but for ours. The Father's voice spoke over us too.

Jesus had to go through extreme suffering so we could live under an open Heaven and have the Spirit descend and remain upon us. He suffered so we can hear those words spoken over us for all eternity,

"You are my beloved Son, in whom I am well pleased."

The Crushing of the Son

This agonizing suffering, beyond anything we can ever imagine or conceive, began in a Garden called Gethsemane.

At the foot of the Mount of Olives there is an olive grove. Tradition states that this is the very garden called Gethsemane, the place Jesus went to pray the night before He was crucified, after He had finished the Last Supper. It was in this garden that the last and greatest crushing of the Son of God began, ending in His death on the Cross. But this time it wasn't just the waters of Baptism in the muddy Jordan River. I have no idea how to gauge the enormity of the crushing that took place when the unfettered Son of God who had created the entire universe by His spoken word, allowed Himself to become an invisible baby in a human mother's womb, let alone the Cross.

We have a powerful glimpse into the suffering of Christ in the Old Testament. The psalmist says that God gives,

Wine to gladden the heart of man, oil to make his face shine,
and bread to strengthen man's heart.
Psalm 104:15

All three of these are provisions of the Lord to humanity. Wine, oil and bread are provided by Jesus both in the natural for us and in the spirit, representing the terrible crushing at the Cross. None of them are produced without going through a pressing and crushing process. Wine can only be made from crushing grapes, bread comes by crushing grains and oil is from pressed olives.

The Holy Spirit is referred to as the Oil of Joy. When we receive the Holy Spirit, joy unspeakable is one of the glorious fruits that explode on the inside of us; our very faces shine with it. However, John tells us the Holy Spirit had not been given before Jesus had been crucified because He had not yet been glorified (John 7:38-39). The Holy Spirit had never been given on the inside of a human being before.

Now, through faith in Christ Jesus, because Jesus has been to the Cross, been resurrected and glorified, whoever believes in Him can now be born of the Spirit and be joined to Him, one spirit with Him forever. Our faces can shine with it!

In Jesus' day the only oil that was used regularly was olive oil from pressed, crushed olives. Oil could only be gained through the hard work of crushing by treading upon the whole olives and then pressing them, using a large stone that was worked downwards by a donkey or bull turning the stone on a large spindle, forcing the oil out of the olives as they are crushed by the stone.

Jesus the Messiah, which literally means the Anointed One, was the "Everlasting Supplier of Oil." It was in the heart of the Father to allow His

Son, filled with the "Oil" of God, to willingly offer Himself and be crushed so we could become His sons forever in His Son, filled with the very same Oil of the Holy Spirit, the Oil of Gladness. The Messiah had to be willing to be crushed with unimaginable agony in the olive press of God: the very Cross of Christ. No wonder Jesus cried out to the Father to take the cup from Him in the middle of an olive grove. There may have been an olive oil press nearby as a visual representation of that very agony He was about to suffer. The Father had anointed Him from all eternity with the Oil of Gladness, the Oil of Joy. As the writer of Hebrews says,

> *You have loved righteousness and hated iniquity, therefore God, even*
> *your God, has anointed you with the oil of*
> *gladness above your companions.*
> *Hebrews 1:9 (KJV)*

Jesus allowed Himself to be crushed so all we need from the Father could be ours. He gave us His flesh for our eternal strength and His blood for our forgiveness, for freedom from condemnation and setting our hearts ablaze with joy. And He gave us the oil of the Spirit to make our faces radiate with His glory for all Eternity.

The Bible tells us that God saw what He had created in humanity, and declared that it was *"very good"* (Genesis 1:31). He loves you and is very proud of you. He who created you says this about you,

> *For he who touches you touches the apple of my eye...*
> *Zechariah 2:8*

How happy do you think God is that people have hurt you your whole life? Have people lied to you, cheated you, abused you, insulted you, falsely accused you; hurt you physically, emotionally, maybe sexually and even spiritually, your entire life? Do you think the Lord is happy with what others have done to you? No, He is not at all happy!

The One who calls you the "apple of His eye" is very angry that His beautiful son or daughter has been so terribly mistreated, hurt and sinned against.

In Hebrew tradition, the "apple of the eye" is the pupil in the middle of the eye, the thing that we look through. It is the most delicate part of the eye, the part that must be protected at all costs so the eye can see. When it comes to God telling us how important we are to Him, He will not compare us to something else He has created.

There is nothing in all of creation God considers more lovely and precious to Him than us, so He compares us to something of Himself. He could have said we are as important as His pinky toe and it would have been an honor (although I must admit it wouldn't have the same ring to it).

No, the only part of God's anatomy He can compare us with are His burning, love filled eyes. The Lord says of you, "You are as important to me as my pupils!" He demands that those who have done these things to you must pay in full with their very lives, because He is a God of justice. The Law of God demands a life for a life and an eye for an eye (Exodus 21:23-24). If someone sins against you they are literally stabbing God in His eye!

Love Demands Justice

Imagine if love did not demand justice. When you get to Heaven, there in front of you are all the people who have hurt you, your whole life, every one of them. You hear the Lord saying, "Oh, by the way, not only was I happy for them to hurt you on earth during your lifetime, but I've decided they can carry on here in Heaven for all eternity. Let's try to pretend they didn't hurt you, nor are they hurting you now. Put on a brave face, it's forever this time!"

That would not be Heaven; that would be Hell! No, thankfully God is a God of justice and He demands that every individual who has ever hurt you, the apple of His eye, will absolutely pay the full penalty for his or her sin, by their death, followed by an eternity burning in fire.

At this point the dilemma of sin, justice and love is revealed. In order for God to deal justly with those who have sinned against you, who He loves, justice demands He would have to do the same with you for your lifetime of sinning against all the other "apples of God's eye" around you, that He also loves! He would have to wipe us all out. Heaven would be empty and Hell full.

Justice demands that because the one sinned against is also a sinner in the same measure, both the sinner and the sinned against must suffer the same punishment, eternal death. When we realize this we begin to see the depth of God's love for us in sending His Son Jesus to become who we are in every way as both victims of sin and sinners ourselves.

To be a human being means to experience both sides of Adam's sin. To be fully human is to experience a lifetime of being sinned against as a victim; it also means to experience a lifetime of sinning against others. For Jesus to be made in the likeness of men and in the likeness of sinful flesh, He had to be made just like us (Philippians 2:7, Romans 8:3-4).

The writer of Hebrews says a body was prepared for Jesus,

Consequently, when Christ came into the world, He said, "Sacrifice and offering you have not desired, but a body you have prepared for me" ... then I said, "Behold I have come to do your will, O God."
Hebrews 10:5-7

Paul says He became the last Adam (1 Corinthians 15:45). He had to experience what it meant to be Adam, the victim of a lifetime of being sinned against, culminating at the Cross where He was unjustly tortured for sins that He, the innocent One Himself, never committed.

However, He also had to experience the other aspect of what it means to be a human being in the likeness of the first Adam, the perpetrator of a lifetime of sin. It is so hard for us to imagine how Jesus could have experienced this aspect. To save us, it was absolutely necessary that He never sinned, which we know He accomplished. This is one of the greatest mysteries of the Cross of Christ, one of the greatest demonstrations of burning love in its purest, most extreme form.

On the Cross, Jesus Christ, God Himself in the flesh, who knew no sin, was made sin for us by the will of the Father and the Son. In that moment, He fully experienced the weight of sin.

> *For our sake He made Him to be sin, who knew no sin,*
> *so that in him we might become the righteousness of God.*
> *2 Corinthians 5:21*

Love beyond measure reveals the full extent of that love. *For our sakes*, the Father makes the Son, who knew no sin, to be sin for us. We as created beings owed the Creator the perfect life He created us to live. Having sinned, we no longer have the means to pay what we owe; yet justice demands we pay it.

God on the other hand, the Creator, is the only One that has the perfect life to give, yet justice demands He shouldn't have to give it. Jesus Christ, fully God who could pay, became fully Man who should pay. He fully obeyed the Father and laid down His perfect life. He went to the Cross and gave His life for the world. He allowed the Father to put all the sin of the whole world on Him so completely that He made Him to *be sin*. He literally *became* our sin.

He simultaneously had to trust that the glorious Father had recorded that though He was tempted in every way just as we are, yet He was without sin.

For we do not have a high priest who is unable to sympathize with
our weaknesses, but one who in every respect has been tempted
as we are, yet without sin.
Hebrews 4:15

At the Cross, Jesus fully satisfied the wrath of God that rightfully stood against the sin of the entire human race. He fully satisfied the justice of God. The sin of those who have sinned against us, the Apple of God's Eye, was fully paid for as justice demanded; *and* the sin we have committed against all the other apples of God's eye around us was also fully paid for.

By this act of love Jesus fully settled the dilemma of the sinned against and the sinner. The eternal justice of God was fully satisfied by one immeasurable act of Grace. Now when we arrive in Heaven, we will see all those who sinned against us throughout our lives and we will know they are there because the same blood of Jesus that paid for us paid the price for them as well. He paid for their sin done to us and our sin done to them. We will all join the entire host of Heaven,

And they sang a new song, saying, "Worthy are you to take the scroll
and to open its seals, for you were slain,
and by your blood you ransomed people for God
from every tribe and language and people and nation."
Revelation 5:9

The consequence for making Him who knew no sin to be sin for us was more terrible and devastating than we can ever imagine.

As Jesus hung before the Father, as our sin and for our sin, the Father gave Him the cup of wrath to drink. This cup, full, foaming and dreadful beyond all our imaginations, Jesus drank until it was empty. He had to empty it forever and He did it!

When He cried, "It is finished," He may well have been referring to the cup among other dynamics. In Luke we read,

> *And being in an agony he prayed more earnestly; and his sweat*
> *became like great drops of blood falling down to the ground.*
> *Luke 22:44*

Medical professionals know that this phenomenon of blood mingled with sweat occurs when a human being experiences extreme emotional pressure and stress. It is known as *hematidrosis*. The blood capillaries in the skin layers can burst, thereby releasing blood onto the skin.[1]

Facing this impossible cup of the wrath of God against the entire sin of every human being throughout all history, Jesus faced the justice against sin and the judgment of all sinners. As He looked at the foaming, bubbling cup of the fierce wrath of God (Isaiah 51:17, 21), the mercy contained in His blood began to spontaneously spill out onto the dust of the earth. The scriptures refer to us being made of dust and we can easily see the symbolism of the blood and sweat falling onto the dust, onto us. In that moment, as He looked as a Man into the gigantic cup of wrath in the supernatural realm of the spirit, mercy triumphed over justice (James 2:13).

Jesus began to plead with His Father, as recorded in Mark,

> *Abba, Father, all things are possible for you.*
> *Remove this cup from me. Yet not what I will, but what you will.*
> *Mark 14:36*

The cup of wrath and suffering was so immense that Jesus pleaded with the Father that it might be taken from Him. He says all things are possible. Matthew says He said, "*If it is possible let this cup pass from me.*"

---

1   Elvira Mora and Javier Lucas, "Hematidrosis: blood sweat." The journal of the American Society of Hematology, Vol. 121, February 2013, http://bloodjournal.hematologylibrary.org, doi:10.1182/blood-2012-09-450031

In other words He was pleading, "If there can be another way, Father, please take this cup from Me."

Yet He knew there was no other way for all humanity.

The only way He and the Father could spend eternity with us was for Him as a Man to pay the price in full for the sin, transgression and iniquity of us all and drink the entire cup of bubbling, foaming wrath of God. One drop was enough for him to have cried out to the Father to find another way and take the cup from Him, because just one drop represented the fires of eternal punishment. Each drop in the cup was the drop you and I deserved, yet Jesus drank the entire cup filled with billions of drops, one for each human that has ever lived, and will ever, live.

Justice demanded that a human drink the full cup of wrath. But love demanded that God the Son drink it, because only He could do it without dying eternally, because He was without sin. It was the only way that the perfect blood could be squeezed out of the "Grape" and presented eternally before the Father (Hebrews 9:14). It was the only way the "Olive" could be crushed so the oil of the Holy Spirit could be forever given to us. It was the only way the strength in His body, the "Bread of Heaven," could be given for us so we would have His Eternal Life. It was His joy to be crushed for us in time and space, so we could be whole in Him for all Eternity.

Jesus, the beautiful champion Savior of all humanity, willingly faced that terrible cup on the Cross. As He became our sin, He willingly took the cup in our place, and drank it down until He declared, "*It is finished!*"

The cup has been emptied forever. The wrath of God is removed from those who believe in Jesus. Wrath only remains on those who refuse to believe in the Son. Justice was fully satisfied, and love was perfectly revealed forever.

Whoever believes in the Son has eternal life; whoever does not obey the Son shall not see life, but the wrath of God remains on him.
John 3:36

"Lord Jesus for all eternity we will gaze upon Your beauty and marvel at Your immense gift of love in giving Yourself for us and to us. You alone are truly worthy of our lives and all our worship forever. It will be our joy to give You our praise and our love, to give You whatever it was You and the Father saw in us that You desired forever. Whatever that was, we give it to You with all our hearts. We are Yours forever. Your treasured possession and Your eternal reward, Your inheritance. Amen!"

CHAPTER 7

ROASTED LAMB

So Pilate, wishing to satisfy the crowd, released for them Barabbas,
and having scourged Jesus, he delivered him to be crucified.
Mark 15:15

Do not eat any of it raw or boiled in water, but roasted, its head with
its legs and its inner parts.
Exodus 12:9

The gaze of Rome must have been on Palestine, and especially on Pilate.
I imagine powerful political pressure was on Pilate to ensure that there
was peace in Palestine and to keep the all too frequent uprisings at bay.
It may well have been for this reason Pilate was so reluctant to hand Jesus
over to death.

Pilate's escape route from this predicament was to release one of
the prisoners at the time, something that had become a tradition. All four
Gospel writers tell us that a man in Roman custody by the name of Barabbas
was chosen, to bring before the chief priests and elders of ancient Israel.
Mark records,

The man named Barabbas had been imprisoned with the
insurrectionists who had committed murder in the insurrection.
Mark 15:7

Barabbas had been convicted of murder during the insurrection. He was a criminal who fully deserved to be punished according to the law of the Roman Empire by crucifixion, the usual torturous means of executing the enemies of the Empire.

One day as I was reading the events of the Cross, I decided to look up the meaning of the name "Barabbas." I was astonished to discover what his name meant. *"Bar"* was used by the Jewish people to denote the "son of so and so." For example, *Bartimaeus* means "son of Timeaus," *Barjonah* means "son of Jonah," *Bartholomew* means "son of Tholomew" and so on.

Barabbas literally means "son of Abbas!" *Abba* was the intimate Aramaic word for "Daddy." Barabbas' father and mother loved him so much they wanted him to be known his whole life as "son of Daddy."

How could a man seemingly so loved by his parents at birth, now be in the prison of Pilate, guilty of murder? Whatever his beginnings were, here he was in the Roman prison as a murderer. Of all the criminals and murderers in Jerusalem, it was the one called Barabbas who the soldiers brought out before Pilate. This was no accident or coincidence. This was the Father's eternal good purpose being fulfilled down to the very last detail.

Jesus Christ, the Son of God, the true "Son of Daddy," was now face to face with a murderer and criminal who had been named "son of Daddy" at the beginning of his life, but was now a murderous criminal. A man who utterly deserved to die, according to Roman law.

I cannot begin to imagine what it must have been like for Jesus to look at Barabbas, who was no doubt grinning gleefully at Him. I have no idea how He must have felt as every fiber of His humanity was screaming out the injustice and humiliation, yet in His heart, He knew it was for this very reason that He had come into the world. He came to seek and save the lost just like Barabbas, ones born as "sons of Daddy"; yet because of sin, every one of them murderers.

If we are guilty of breaking one aspect of the Law, for example lying or stealing, we are guilty of breaking the whole Law (James 2:10), making us guilty of murder. Jesus says that if a person is angry with their brother in their heart they are guilty of committing murder (Matthew 5:21-22).

It is clear according to the perfect Law of God that we are each guilty of breaking the whole Law, and therefore we are *all* guilty of murder before God. As Barabbas stood before Pilate, Jesus and the Father, he represented the entire human race. He represented you and me, murderers named "sons of Daddy." We were created to be sons of our Heavenly Father, but through our sin turned away from Him, broke His entire Law and became guilty of murder, deserving not just death in this world, but death for all eternity.

What must that have been like for Jesus who was fluent in Aramaic and knew instantly what Barabbas' name meant? Having already been beaten earlier so that His vision was bloodied, He looked up at the murderer Barabbas, called "son of Daddy," and saw you and me.

He saw all of us and knew that the only way we could spend eternity with Him was for Him to take our place and go to the Cross. He would have to take the Cross set for Barabbas, set for you and me. He the true "Barabbas," *the* "Son of the Father" was willing to go to the Cross so the impostor Barabbas, the "son of Daddy," representing you and me, could go free.

Under the Mosaic Law we read that once a year the High Priest was to present two goats before the Lord, one slaughtered and the other set free (Leviticus 16:7-10). What a moment that must have been as Jesus looked at Barabbas and saw you and me! God is love and this was perfectly revealed at the Cross. Barabbas, representing us all, was set free because Jesus was willing to be the atonement offering for all sin upon the "altar" of the Cross in Barabbas' place.

It is highly likely the very Cross Jesus died upon was the Cross Barabbas would have been crucified on with the other two criminals. The Innocent, Jesus, willing to die in the very place of the guilty, us, so that the guilty can live, forever innocent. No wonder nothing can ever separate us from His love (Romans 8:39).

"Lord Jesus, I worship You and thank You with all my heart that You, the true Son of Daddy were willing to take the place of a murderer and criminal like Barabbas, whose very name meant son of Daddy, even though You knew You had never sinned. You took our place as You took Barabbas' because You knew it was the only way we, the lost sons of Daddy, could ever be set free from the power of sin, death and the devil. When You took Barabbas' Cross, You took our Cross that we equally deserve. I'm eternally grateful for Your immense love and sacrifice for us all. Amen!"

The Passover Lamb of All Time

When the Lord gave Moses specific instructions as to how the Israelites were to prepare the Passover Lamb, He told them they were to roast the Lamb. They were not to prepare it any other way,

> *Do not eat any of it raw or boiled in water, but roasted,*
> *its head with its legs and its inner parts.*
> *Exodus 12:9*

The rule was that the Lamb had to be roasted as a prophetic sign to the world of what would be necessary for the true Passover Lamb to go through for Him to save the world from its sin. Jesus Christ willingly offered Himself for us all as the Lamb of God, who takes away the sin of the world (John 1:29). He became the ultimate sacrifice of all time: He became the Passover Lamb of all time and went to the Cross intended for Barabbas; and not only him, but intended rightfully for all of us, the lost sons of Abba.

Christ took upon Himself something so terrible that I don't think you or I could ever experience in a million years of suffering every imaginable torture. As He became the sin of the world, He experienced the full punishment justice demands the guilty must take. By instructing the Israelites to roast the Passover Lamb in the fire, God gives us a tiny glimpse of what Jesus Christ the Eternal Son of God, the true Passover Lamb experienced as He was roasted alive in His body. As He hung on the Cross, He was burned alive in the fire of God's wrath. He was roasted alive as us, for us, so we would never face the wrath of God for all eternity.

It is little wonder that as Jesus was hanging naked, burning alive in the fire of God, He cried out the first line of Psalm 22,

> *My God, my God, why hast thou forsaken me?*
> *Why art thou so far from helping me,*
> *and from the words of my roaring?*
> *Psalm 22:1 (KJV)*

In most modern translations the last word is translated "groaning." However, the King James Version more accurately translates it as "roaring." The Hebrew word here at the end of this verse is *shagah*, meaning *roaring*. This word is derived from the root Hebrew word, *sha'ag*, which means *to roar mightily*.

When a wild animal is suffering and about to be slaughtered it can roar with a terrible bloodcurdling roar. I discovered this firsthand when I was 18 as I was helping cull some of the rabbits on our family farm. It was awful. I had no idea a rabbit could make such sounds; I will never forget it.

I cannot imagine what it was like on that terrible day of Calvary when the Eternal Savior of the world let out the most bloodcurdling scream—the roar of death, like a wild animal—as He experienced that terrible fire as He, the Passover Lamb, was roasted alive.

The blood He shed as He hung there, roasting, was the very blood He was able to offer to the Father, once and for all atoning for the sin of you, me, and all humanity, purging our consciences (Hebrews 9:14). Because He allowed His blood to be spread on the "lintel" and "posts" on the "doorway" of our lives, as He gave His life, we can put our faith in the same God. The God who caused the Angel of Death to pass over the houses of the Israelites when he saw the blood will cause him to pass over us, and we will live forever with the Lord.

In the second book of Chronicles, King Josiah held one of the greatest Passovers in the entire history of the Ancient Israelites (2 Chronicles 35:18). As I read the account of Josiah's Passover I noticed an interesting verse,

> *And they killed the Passover,*
> *and the priests sprinkled the blood from their hands,*
> *and the Levites flayed them.*
> *2 Chronicles 35:11 (KJV)*

What caught my attention were the words, "*... and the Levites* flayed *them.*"

The Hebrew word *pashat*, translated "flayed" here, is fascinating, because it means to skin, to spread out, or to strip off. This opens our eyes to some amazing things. The Passover Lambs, flayed in Josiah's great Passover, gave prophetic insight into what would happen to Jesus at the Passover of all Passovers, when the Son of Man, the Lamb of God, would be flayed of His very skin.

The flaying of the Passover Lamb of God began when the Roman legionnaires stripped Jesus of His clothing and scourged Him with the Flagellum (Matthew 27:26-28). This was a dreadful short leather whip with pieces of bone and metal tied into the ends of the leather thongs, used by the Romans to severely punish convicted criminals for serious crimes that may not necessarily warrant death. The Jews' ancient law prohibited more than forty lashes (Deuteronomy 25:3), but these were Romans and it is likely that these soldiers whipped Jesus until he was unrecognizable. Isaiah testifies this prophetically when he says,

> *His appearance was marred more than any man*
> *and His form more than the sons of men.*
> *Isaiah 52:14 (NASB)*

As the Romans scourged Jesus, they literally would have stripped Him of his very skin all over His body, flayed just like the animals of King Josiah's Passover. The psalmist says that God will punish His people's transgressions with the rod and will punish their iniquity with stripes (Psalm 89:32). Isaiah says that the punishment that brought us peace was laid upon Him. He says the Messiah would be pierced for our transgressions and crushed for our iniquities and that by His scourging we would be healed (Isaiah 53:5). Jesus was willing to take the punishment that Justice demanded must be paid for all our transgressions and iniquities, and that punishment had to be borne in His flesh. He had to be flayed, stripped of His very skin.

In the Garden of Eden, the immediate effect of sin and rebellion was a deep sense of shame, causing Adam and Eve to feel naked and afraid and therefore the need to hide from God. Jesus was stripped of His skin so He truly hung "naked" before God, fully taking that very shame.

Another consequence of their sin caused the ground to be cursed so that only with great toil would it produce food.

> *Cursed is the ground because of you; in pain you shall eat of it all the*
> *days of your life; thorns and thistles it shall bring forth for you;*
> *and you shall eat the plants of the field.*
> *By the sweat of your face you shall eat bread,*

till you return to the ground, for out of it you were taken;
for you are dust, and to dust you shall return.
Genesis 3:17b-19

As Jesus the Son of God became fully identified with humanity, He was willing to be stripped naked of His skin and take upon Himself our nakedness and our shame so that we could be forever clothed with Him. Made just like us, He took the punishment of the curse of sin. In the garden as He contemplated His suffering, blood mingled with sweat, His Life contained in His precious blood, mingled with the very sweat of His humanity and kissed the "dust," the very dust of humanity.

By the sweat of your face you shall eat bread, till you return to the
ground, for out of it you were taken; for you are dust,
and to dust you shall return.
Genesis 3:19

We've already seen how He suffered in His skin. With the crown of thorns, He suffered in His face, taking the curse (Mark 15:17).

Ultimately, He bore the curse of the dust for us in His body that was dust just like ours. When He was buried He took the ultimate punishment that the Fall brought on humanity. His body of dust, made one with us carrying all our sin, was laid in the dust in the rock when He was buried. Jesus took the entire curse for us.

Into the Thorns

While I was on a mission trip to The Republic of Niger, I experienced an unforgettable, tiny glimpse of Christ's sufferings through sweat, thorns and the dust. We were ministering with Terje Liverød, who leads World Outreach Missions in Niger, in the far bush on the very edge of the Sahara Desert. Something extraordinary happened that opened my eyes to the power of sharing in Christ's sufferings and death.

One night after ministering to some of the most unreached people in the world, the Fulani and the Tuareg, we were all exhausted. Terje and I looked for a place to sleep that night, under the stars. We drove and drove in the bush for hours unable to find a suitable, safe place to sleep. All of us were at the end of ourselves.

Finally at almost midnight we found the perfect spot. We jumped out of the Land Cruisers and were about to get all our mats and sleeping bags out when Carlos Rodriguez, who absolutely loves extreme missions in Niger, pointed out a loud hissing sound, coming from a punctured rear tire of one of the Land Cruisers.

As I went to change the rear tire, we discovered that the standard jack that had come with the Land Cruiser was not tall enough for the aftermarket suspension. It was just comical. There we were in the Sahara Desert at midnight with a flat tire, an exhausted team and a jack that couldn't work with the vehicle it had come with. It was a big opportunity for frustration, to say the least. I asked everyone to go hunting for rocks to gain some height with the jack and we managed to raise the car.

As I was changing the tire, sweat pouring off me, I suddenly felt the presence of the Holy Spirit. I realized the whole night was a set up for an encounter with God! I told everyone and at once, the Spirit fell on us all. Suddenly one of the Norwegian girls from Terje's team fell onto the desert sand with a squeal.

As I saw her falling, I thought, *Don't fall down into the sand. It's covered with terrible thorns called burrs.* She lay there, shaking violently as the power of God came on her. She began to laugh uncontrollably.

I know from growing up on the edge of the Sahara in Nigeria that no one ever falls into the sand without being covered in thorns. They are about a quarter of an inch round, clusters of extremely sharp needle-like spikes, very painful to touch and they stick fast to any clothing or hair. Often there can be small twigs from the Acacia thorn trees, covered in two or three inch thorns of the kind that were likely threaded together and thrust on Jesus' head as a crown.

She has to be covered with those tiny, deadly thorns, shaking in the sand. She has to be in a huge amount of pain. They're for sure matted in her clothes and her long hair. It will literally take hours to remove them all from her body, hair and clothes. There's no way I would do that! I thought to myself.

Just then, I felt a surge of power from the Holy Spirit come on me and I too was almost knocked backwards into the sand. But there was no way I was going into the thorns, and I stopped myself from falling, resisting the weighty glory.

In that moment, I knew the Lord was giving me a choice. Would I yield and surrender to the invitation from the Holy Spirit to go lower with Him, into the dirt and the thorns? Or would I resist and stay as I was? I knew instantly that falling into the thorns was somehow, for me at least, an invitation to embrace the sufferings of Christ. I knew I was being invited into the joy of sharing in His suffering. You see, I would have gladly allowed myself to be knocked to the floor on a lovely church carpet, but into the sand filled with thorns? I knew there and then the Holy Spirit was more precious to me than anything in the world.

I yielded in my heart and determined that yes; I was willing to fall down into the sand and thorns. Just then Terje, who was full of joy in the Holy Spirit, came right up to me laughing and laid his hand on my chest. I felt the power of God hit me and I flew back into the sand at the edge of the road, near the Norwegian girl.

As I hit the sand, fiery, searing pain exploded all down my back and legs as I was instantly covered in the tiny Saharan thorns, confirming all I knew about falling into the sand. It didn't matter one bit to me. Being in the dirt with the Holy Spirit, sharing in a tiny, tiny part of the sufferings of Christ was more precious to me than anything else in all the world. I lay there laughing, overwhelmed by the love of God and His pleasure in me as His son. It was a Heavenly kiss from the Father.

When we eventually got the new tire on and found another spot to sleep the night, it took a long time, with the help of our respective friends, to get all the thorns out of our skin, hair and clothes. We got to bed very late that night, several hours beyond midnight. Early in the morning, when we all got up and headed back into the village to meet our Fulani friends, I noticed something dramatically different about my thoughts.

Usually whenever I experienced personal discomfort, such as being away from home in a foreign country, ministering to people when I'm tired, or hungry and experiencing extremes of temperature, I would have to force myself to overcome a deep reluctance to do what I am supposed to do. My thoughts would center on, *"How many days are left before I'll be back home with Kate and our girls, where I can relax, take a hot shower and sleep in a decent bed?"* Honestly, deep inside, all I could think was, *"I can't wait to go home."* I'd preach to the unreached, because I knew it was my calling, but I always had to push myself.

But that morning, everything was different. I jumped out of my sleeping bag and couldn't wait to be with our Fulani friends. My heart was filled with such love for them, and instead of longing to go home, my heart longed to be with them and help meet their needs. I was full of joy unspeakable. I suddenly had this fiery passion in me to be with my beloved African friends. I could hardly wait to preach that night at the next outreach to the unreached villagers. I was burning with Love Himself.

That night after we showed the Jesus Film, I preached and we all began ministering to the sick and needy. Some of my Fulani friends brought one of their unsaved cousins to me. He was 27 years old and had been born deaf and mute. He had never heard or spoken anything in his life. I laid my hands on his ears and mouth in the power of the Spirit, in Jesus' mighty name. Immediately, he could hear perfectly and the Lord Jesus loosed his tongue and gave him full speech. Right away he gave his life to Jesus Christ.

His brothers were overjoyed.

When we drove the two-hour journey from that village back to the main missions base in Zinder, everyone was so excited because the Lord had done extraordinary things through us all. The young Norwegian girl who had been the first to fall into the thorns the night before was bursting with so much joy and so were her Norwegian friends. They had witnessed her lay hands on someone that night that was blind with two "milky" eyes. The normal irises of the person's eyes were covered completely in thick white tissue, so that they were completely blind. As my Norwegian friend had laid her hands on the person, suddenly, right in front of them, the person's irises went from opaque white to clear brown. She was totally healed and could see perfectly. It was a fantastic miracle by the Lord Jesus.

Later that night as I reflected on the previous 24 hours, I could hardly recognize my own thoughts. Instead of wanting to go home, I was filled with love and tenacity to preach, minister, heal and pour out love and affection on everyone, especially the unreached poor. I asked the Holy Spirit, "What happened to me last night Lord?"

I heard Him whisper, "*Last night, Duncan, you gave Me permission to take away your right to comfort. I can do anything through someone who has let go of their right to comfort.*"

Jesus perfectly surrendered His right to comfort as the Son of God, and surrendered His perfect life, saying to the Father,

Not My will be done but yours.
Mark 14:36

Satan, referring to Job, says to God,

Then Satan answered the LORD and said, "Skin for skin!
All that a man has he will give for his life."
Job 2:4

Satan accused humanity before God, saying humans will always give away all that is theirs just to hold onto their life, just to save their skin. Jesus vindicated humanity as a Champion on behalf of us all and for all time. He came as a Man and gave His life, gave away His skin, to hold on to all that were His from the Father: His redeemed people.

Jesus, being intimately acquainted with the scriptures, as the Eternal Word of God made flesh, may well have been anchoring His faith on the words Job had cried out centuries before,

> *After my skin has been thus destroyed,*
> *yet in my flesh I shall see God.*
> *Job 19:26*

What a Savior Jesus is! He was willing to be shredded of all His skin, so that one with Christ we too shall see God in our flesh.

A deeply mysterious verse concerning the nature of Adam and his wife before and after they sinned for the first time is recorded in Genesis.

> *The LORD God made for Adam and for his wife*
> *garments of skins and clothed them.*
> *Genesis 3:21*

I have often wondered whether before the Fall, the Lord God originally created Adam and Eve in such a way that they were not limited by human skin as we know it. Their life was God's "breath of life" in their breath.

> *Then the LORD God formed the man of dust from the ground and*
> *breathed into his nostrils the breath of life,*
> *and the man became a living being.*
> *Genesis 2:7*

In other words, their spirit was the dominating faculty of their souls rather than their physical bodies. Could it be that being limited almost entirely to their physical bodies, encased in skin, was one of the consequences of the Fall, and that after the Fall, their life was in the blood and no longer in the breath? What if sin caused us to lose our life in the Spirit and instead our life was confined in the blood? Moses writes in Leviticus,

> *For the life of the flesh is in the blood, and I have given it for you on*
> *the altar to make atonement for your souls,*
> *for it is the blood that makes atonement by the life.*
> *Leviticus 17:11*

This is a mystery, and my purpose in sharing it is to provoke deeper thought and excitement at the possibility of what Christ has regained for us by His death on the Cross.

I have always thought that the Lord God slaughtered some animals, and the very first sacrifice in history was made, as animals gave their lives to give their skins to provide clothes for Adam and Eve, to cover their nakedness. That could be what is meant, although it doesn't say that precisely. It simply says that the Lord God made garments of skin for Adam and His wife and clothed them.

The Hebrew word used for "*made skins*" in this verse is neither the word used for when the Lord God *formed* man in Genesis 2, nor is it the same word used when the Lord God *made* woman from Adam's rib.

In Genesis 2:7 of Adam, Moses uses the Hebrew word *yatsar*, which means he roughly molded him like a potter forms clay. In Genesis 2:22, when describing the Lord God making the woman, Moses uses the Hebrew word *banah*, which means He built her together piece by piece, meticulously. The word *banah* is used throughout the Old Testament whenever something such as a house is built.

In Genesis 3:21 the word is neither *yatsar* nor *banah* but is *mad* from the root word *madad* which means *to stretch out by careful measurement a measured vesture*. Maybe this refers to the Lord God giving them their very own clothing of skin, perfectly measured from head to toe. It may well have been in that moment they lost their capacity to relate freely and easily with the realm of the spirit with their senses. This is deeply mysterious and exciting in its possibilities.

However, we must leave it at that. Genesis 2 says the Lord God made man of the dust of the earth and most of our household dust is our skin! That clearly contradicts any notion that Adam and his wife were not given earthly skin right from the moment they were created.

However, it may be that although they were still made of dust, their actual skin was somehow different from what it was after the Lord God clothed them in skin. Perhaps before the Fall, their bodies were not limited, confined, or trapped by skin, like an earth suit, as ours are now. Perhaps it's even deeper as a powerful glimpse of what Christ would do for all humanity for those who believed; that He would give His very skin for us, something Satan thought no man would ever do. In so doing Christ has liberated us from our confinement to our finite bodies. We are now no longer simply clothed in skin, bound to time and space. Instead, we are clothed with Christ, His eternal garments of salvation and robes of righteousness. Already seated with Him now in the Spirit in the Heavens, one day we'll also be given our new bodies. It is a mystery, and one day we will have full understanding.

What we do know is that when Jesus had risen from the dead and He appeared to the Apostles in Luke 24, He said these amazing words,

See my hands and my feet, that it is I myself. Touch me, and see.
For a spirit does not have flesh and bones as you see that I have.
Luke 24:39

These words show us that unlike a ghost that has no physical body, Jesus was resurrected fully in a Heavenly body that could be touched and could eat, enjoying food just like our earthly bodies. Yet His body was not of the substance of our temporary physical earthly bodies. Nevertheless He had a "physical" body, a brand-new glorious body that was not confined to anything of the natural earthly realm, because it was of the Eternal realm of the Spirit. He could enter a locked room without opening any doors, appear anywhere He wanted on earth at any time He wanted, and He could fly! He could fly in this atmosphere and slip out of this realm and into Heaven, as He did when He ascended in front of the Apostles on the Mount of Olives forty days after His resurrection and the cloud hid Him from their view as He went through the Heavens.

Jesus triumphed over another of Satan's great accusations before God against humanity. On behalf of us all, as a human, He allowed the Father to stretch out His hand and touch His bone and His flesh, allowing Him to die on the Cross. Jesus triumphed over even death and was raised flesh and bone.

But stretch out your hand and touch his bone and his flesh,
and he will curse you to your face.
Job 2:5

Jesus' words are remarkable. He refers to His body as being flesh and bones. He doesn't say flesh and blood, but says flesh and bones. I know from my studies in biology that blood is created in the bones. I know when we refer to ourselves, we say that we have flesh and blood. The natural life is in the blood, which is created in the bones. We talk about our offspring as our "flesh and blood." We never say our "flesh and bones." Could it be that there is significance in this statement and mystery is wrapped up in these words "flesh and bones"?

When God made woman from a rib from Adam's side and meticulously fit her together piece by piece, He presented the woman He had made to Adam and the man said,

This is now bone of my bones and flesh of my flesh. She shall be called Ishshah, because she was taken out of Ish.
Genesis 2:23

It was a fantastic picture of Oneness, providing a picture of what Christ would do thousands of years later when He, the Last Adam, would be willing to be "put to sleep." From His pierced side, a new glorious "woman," the one church, Jew and Gentile together, would be "made," meticulously fitted together piece by piece, living stone by living stone. He would build His church into a glorious Bride for all Eternity, bone of Jesus' bones and flesh of Jesus' flesh.

Jesus took upon Himself our flesh and blood. He made a way, as the sacrificial, roasted Lamb of God, for His Eternal life to be given to us. His Eternal life filled His blood and His flesh. The blood that He shed on the Cross and offered up by the Eternal Spirit to God, giving His life in the blood as an everlasting atonement for our souls. His life is one with His Father, through the Spirit. He gave His flesh to us so that by eating His flesh and drinking His blood by faith as we eat and drink the symbolic elements of the bread and wine, we now have that very Eternal Life of Christ in us. We will have bodies just like His, flesh and bone, with the resurrection life of the Spirit in us now. The life no longer confined to our blood, but the Spirit in our bones, and in every sense fully alive, burning with Love Himself.

CHAPTER 8

THE TWO TREES

The LORD God commanded the man, saying, "From any tree
of the garden you may eat freely; but from the tree of the knowledge
of good and evil you shall not eat, for in the day that you eat
from it you will surely die."
Genesis 2:16-17

In the beginning, God created Adam to be a son of God forever, just like the Son Himself. We were made in Love's image. We were created to receive and give love from God, to God, and to one another, just like the Trinity. God created us in the sheer delight and unfettered joy of glorious, unadulterated, selfless, perfect Love. Love by nature is only true Love if it is absolutely free to choose.

For us to enter into Eternal Love, Love needed to know we truly love Him. Knowing we cannot love Him with the love He deserves, God knew He needed to fill us with His life and His love so we could love Him with *His* love. The Gospel is about Love, giving us His life, so we could be one with Him forever, filled with Himself, immersed in burning Love. The very love of God in us so we could love Him with the love with which He first loved us.

We love, because He first loved us.
1 John 4:19

God created a beautiful garden, the Garden of Eden, to be an incredible realm in which He could pour out His love upon Adam. Adam could return that love to Him, demonstrating his desire to enter into the Eternal Love: the very Godhead Themselves. God placed two essential trees in the Garden of Eden in order for His purpose in love to be worked out.

The first tree is the Tree of Life, in the middle of the garden. It was the greatest tree in the garden, not necessarily in its stature or beauty, but in its identity and therefore in its significance. To eat the fruit of this tree would mean the eater would gain Eternal Life.

Then the LORD God said, "Behold, the man has become like one of
us in knowing good and evil. Now, lest he reach out his hand
and take also of the tree of life and eat, and live forever."
Genesis 3:22 (emphasis added)

This tree is symbolic of Jesus Christ, Eternal Life Himself. He is the Tree of Life, and His presence in the Garden of Eden was God's provision of grace for all humanity. God's hope was that, in Love, Adam would reach out and eat from the Tree of Life.

When we eat food we chew it and then swallow it, where it enters our digestive system. Once there, it is assimilated into us so it is not just in us, *but becomes us.* We are what we eat. Whatever we eat we become that. Each part of our food does its work in us and becomes us.

As we eat, the proteins, carbohydrates, fats, minerals and fiber, they each do their thing and are turned literally into us, becoming one with us. This dynamic is extremely helpful in understanding our salvation in Christ Jesus.

God's purpose and design was that Adam and Eve would reach

out and take the fruit of the Tree of Life and eat it. The fruit would become one with them. It would be assimilated into them, and they would become that fruit and do what that fruit does: become a tree of life themselves, just like the Son. They would exist for the benefit of others in perfect love, just like Him. They would be eternal beings, just like Him, and eternally produce the fruit of Life and Love Himself. What an awesome plan God had for humanity!

God planted a second tree in the garden, right next to the Tree of Life. The Tree of the Knowledge of Good and Evil provided the proving ground of Adam's love. Jesus said that if we love Him, we would obey Him (John 14:15). This tree existed to prove obedience and thereby reveal love through the demonstration of free choice: to obey, or not to obey. The Lord is looking for lovers for eternity, not reluctant servants who feel they have no choice.

The Lord God spoke first to Adam, before his wife was created, and gave him explicit instructions.

And the LORD God commanded the man, saying, "You may surely eat of every tree of the garden, but of the tree of the knowledge of good and evil you shall not eat, for in the day that you eat of it you shall surely die."
Genesis 2:16-17

The Lord God had already declared all things "good." If Adam had obeyed the Lord, Adam could have reached out and eaten the fruit of the Tree of Life and gained Eternal Life, without ever tasting evil, which was God's very best intention for Adam.

I believe that the Lord, knowing the snake—Satan—was in the garden, hoped Adam would so love Him that when confronted by the snake, or any evil for that matter, he would not take on the snake on his own. He would wait for his Daddy God to come and deal with it. The Lord gave Adam the commandment to test his obedience and therefore love, as well as his capacity to share those instructions accurately with his wife and all future offspring. It was Adam's job to tell his wife very clearly the Lord's command.

I have often thought about the moment Adam was confronted by the snake. Rather than answering the snake first, he allowed his wife to be the first to answer the snake's dreadful, cunning questions. Adam stood by and lamely watched the whole tragedy, despite being the one the Lord God had given the instructions to.

Adam had already done a poor job of communicating to Eve the most important instructions. To the snake's question, "Did God really say you shall not eat the fruit of any tree of the garden?" she replied inaccurately enough to give away her uncertainty concerning the Lord's original command.

And the woman said to the serpent, "We may eat of the fruit of the
trees in the garden, but God said, 'You shall not eat of the
fruit of the tree that is in the midst of the garden,
neither shall you touch it, lest you die.'"
Genesis 3:2-3

Comparing Eve's answer with the Lord's original command to Adam, it is amazing how much inaccuracy and doubt there is already.

The Lord did not refer to the "middle of the garden" when He gave Adam the commandment and warning. Genesis 2:9 tells us that *both* the Tree of Life and the Tree of the Knowledge of Good and Evil were in the middle of the garden. However when the Lord God gave the command and warning to Adam in verses 16 and 17, He was very careful not to refer to the Tree of the Knowledge of Good and Evil being in the middle of the garden. This would have been very confusing to Adam because there were *two* trees in the middle of the garden. One was the Tree of the Knowledge of Good and Evil, which they were not to eat from, and the other was the Tree of Life, the one the Lord absolutely wanted them to eat from. Yet Eve adds to His words saying, "You shall not eat of the fruit of the tree *that is in the middle of the garden*." The Lord never said that exactly.

Adam and Eve had not eaten from the Tree of Life at this point. We know this because they would have already become eternal beings. So why had they not eaten the fruit of the Tree of Life, which was in the middle of the garden? What was it about that tree which caused them to hesitate to eat its fruit?

Maybe it was opposite in its external nature to the Tree of the Knowledge of Good and Evil, which the Bible tells us was good for food, looked like it tasted good, was delightful to the eyes and good for gaining wisdom (Genesis 3:6). The fruit of the Tree of Life could have looked very different. Perhaps it revealed something of the nature of the Cross, strangely unpleasant to the eyes and seeming very unlikely to give the eater Eternal Life. Perhaps it was the only thing in the entire garden that spoke of death; after all, there can only be resurrection if there has been death. Maybe it looked so much like death the onlooker would be persuaded that if they were to eat of it, they would die, somehow portraying the Lamb slain from the foundation of the world (Revelation 13:8, KJV).

Faith pleases God; without faith it is impossible to please Him (Hebrews 11:6). The fruit of the Tree of Life may well have looked like it would kill its eater, but that was the mystery. The eater would "die" on a natural level, only to be raised from the dead by the fruit and live forever. Faith was required to believe that. Faith was required to eat the fruit of the Tree of Life! In the very same way, faith is expressed as we eat His flesh and drink His blood, sharing in His death so we live forever, one with Him.

Adam and his wife had not eaten the fruit of the Tree of Life. Instead they chose to believe the lies of the enemy and ate the fruit of the forbidden tree that looked good, yet brought permanent death to the eater.

The Two Trees were side by side in the middle of the garden. The Tree that looked like death brought Life to the eater. The Tree that looked like life brought death to the eater. It seems upside down, like everything in the Kingdom of God.

The second inaccuracy in the woman's reply to the snake was that they were "*not to touch it*." There is no record of the Lord saying to Adam that they could not touch it. God made man before any of the trees had come forth from the ground and man's job was to tend to the garden and guard it (Genesis 2:5-15). That would be difficult to do without touching it.

Adam's work was to be the vinedresser for all the trees. He was responsible for the growth and development of all the trees. This meant at any point he could have destroyed the Tree of the Knowledge of Good and Evil. He had been given dominion over everything on the earth, which included all the trees and so he could have cut down the Tree of the Knowledge of Good and Evil while it was a sapling, before it produced its terrible fruit. That's always the best way to deal with sin and its fruit. Cut it down, out of your heart, while it is a small sapling, long before it grows into a full-grown tree bearing fruit.

Imagine what it could have looked like. There Satan is, appearing as a snake, languishing in the branches of the forbidden tree, perhaps casually munching on one of the fruit, juggling it up and down from hand to hand, between mouthfuls. (Evidently snakes had limbs then!)

From the moment the snake asked the first question, Adam could have stepped forward as the champion God created him to be and said, "Snake—yes that's right, I'm calling you by the name I gave you! I don't like what you're saying, the sound of your voice, or the doubt you are sowing about my Heavenly Daddy. In the mighty name of our God and with the authority He has given me over everything that flies in the air, swims in the oceans and creeps along the ground—yes, that would be you—I command you to stay right there in this tree until my Father gets back!"

Then, turning to his wife, "Come on darling, let's go and rest while we wait for our Daddy to come back. He'll know what to do with that strange creature, Snake!"

The snake and all the evil represented by him and contained within him would have been overcome right there and then. He would have been glued to the branches of the Tree of the Knowledge of Good and Evil. And when the Lord God came walking in the cool of the day, the couple could have run up to their Father and excitedly reported to Him all they had done concerning the snake and the forbidden tree.

With great pride and love in His eyes the Lord would have looked at Adam and his wife and said something like, "Come on you two, hop on my back. Let's go deal with that terrible snake. I have an eternal lake of burning sulfur prepared for just this moment!"

Sadly, we know it didn't end that way. Instead of using his authority and trusting his Heavenly Father, Adam allowed his wife to reply to the snake each time; and then after she reached out and took the forbidden fruit and handed it to him, Adam also ate.

The consequences were devastating. They were instantly made one with sin and therefore death. For the first time in their lives they were ashamed of themselves. Shame, fear and control came rushing in like a flood. Adam told God that they were naked and were afraid, and hid themselves (Genesis 3:10).

The fruit entered into their bodies and like the way of all food, it became them. They became one with that food. Sin went into every cell in their bodies. It went right into their very DNA. They were the father and mother of all who were ever going to live on the earth. All humanity was within them both, and therefore sin became one with all humanity. All of us. To rid the world of sin, the Lord would have to rid the world of us.

Adam and Eve, right there and then, became one with that forbidden fruit, and fruit multiplies its own kind. They became Trees of the Knowledge of Good and Evil, bearing fruit in keeping with themselves. Instead of becoming Trees of Life, full of love, able to give their lives away in selfless acts of love just like the Son of God Himself, they were now Trees of the Knowledge of Good and Evil, behaving like self-appointed judges of both good and evil, determined at all cost to hold on to their lives in acts of endless selfishness. And ever since then, humanity looks at everything and declares judgment: "That's good, but that's not good. They're good, but they're not good. I like them. I don't like them. I'll do this, but I won't do that."

We have all been living, breathing, walking, talking Trees of the Knowledge of Good and Evil ever since the Fall.

The very children God created to experience Him and His love, dwelling with Him for all eternity, were now one with sin and death, condemned and judged as Lawbreakers. They had become the very curse of the Law. They were lost forever, unless they could be saved, something only the Lord Himself could do. Adam and His wife could never save themselves. It was too late. Only a sinless life could save them by dying, paying the price for us all.

I have always imagined that God was very angry, and in a rage removed Adam and his wife from the garden, so they were cut off from ever gaining access to the fruit of the Tree of Life. I have found most people I've spoken with about this imagine, like me, that the Lord God was so angry He almost smoked them there and then. I imagined Him kicking them out in a fit of angry rage. This view, of course, came from my wrong image of God as an angry, hard to please judge, rather than a beautiful, patient, kind, loving Father.

My pastor, John Arnott, helped me see an entirely different picture. He showed me it was an act of immense love when the Lord God removed Adam from the garden. I realized I had been wrong for years about that moment. Having eaten of the fruit of the Tree of the Knowledge of Good and Evil and becoming one with that fruit, Adam and his wife were now one with sin and death. If in that condition they had reached out and eaten from the Tree of Life, they would have made themselves *eternally irredeemable*. They would have been eternal beings, but irredeemable beings, just like Satan himself and all the fallen angels.

I imagine the scene so differently now: the Father, Son and Holy Spirit all firmly yet tenderly, walked Adam and Eve over to the gates of the Garden of Eden and said goodbye to them as they put them out of the Garden with much tears all round. As they walked off into the distance, the Son of God, waved at them with His hands, perhaps even scarred hands, because He was the Lamb slain since the foundation of the world (Revelation 13:8 KJV). He could easily have said under His breath, "We have a plan, little children. You cannot come to me any longer, but I will come and rescue you one day; that glorious day, when I will demonstrate my love and my Father's love for you and the world." The love story that began in a Garden with two trees, at the very beginning of the creation of the world, ended with two trees, on the edge of another Garden, at Golgotha, just outside the Garden of Gethsemane, in the greatest demonstration of love the universe has ever witnessed.

The wooden cross represented a tree, made from the wood of a tree and standing upright above the earth just like the tree it was made from. The upright piece of the Roman cross was typically fixed at the site of execution. It remained there constantly, in the place of death. From the moment the Son of God said, "Let there be light" and there was light, He was fixed by His own will and obedience to the Father in the place of execution. Jesus knew that to create us would cost Him his very life. He was willing to pay that price. By His will, He was fixed in our site of execution from the foundation of the world.

He was forced to carry the heavy crosspiece from Pilate's court to Golgotha. What a powerful representation of His willingness to carry all of our sin and each of us, to the site of execution prepared for Him. He carried our sorrows and our infirmities (Isaiah 53:4). He carried us, represented by the crosspiece, to the upright piece, representing Him and was willing to be nailed to us through death and into eternity.

The first Adam was a living being. He depended totally on the Life of God. Adam had no life in himself. To become a giver of life he had to reach out and eat the fruit of the Tree of Life and become one with that Tree.

Instead he cut himself off from that Life, by disobeying the Lord. Rather than becoming a Tree of Life, just like the Tree of Life, Jesus Himself, Adam chose instead to become a Tree of the Knowledge of Good and Evil and died. He became a Tree of Death.

The Lord of Glory was willing to become the Last Adam. He became a Life-giving Spirit (1 Corinthians 15:45). He was the Tree of Life Himself in flesh and blood. At the Cross, the Tree of Life was willing to be nailed to the Trees of the Knowledge of Good and Evil, namely all of humanity. It is profound. The Son of God was willing to be nailed to the sons of men. The Tree of Life Himself was willing to be nailed to the Trees of the Knowledge of Good and Evil, forever! The Fire of God's wrath fell on the sacrifice. The One Tree, the Tree of Life, Jesus, was burning in blazing fire and yet was not consumed by that fire. The other, the Tree of the Knowledge of Good and Evil, us and all of humanity, was utterly consumed and burned up forever by the fire.

Moses and Elijah both saw glimpses of that moment at the Cross. It is so significant that of all the prophets in the Old Testament it was Moses and Elijah who appeared with Jesus on the mountain when Jesus was transfigured in front of Peter, James and John. Luke tells us,

> *And behold, two men were talking with him, Moses and Elijah, who*
> *appeared in glory and spoke of his departure, which he was*
> *about to accomplish at Jerusalem.*
> *Luke 9:30-31*

Moses represented the Law and Elijah represented the Prophets. I love the Father's words when He spoke from the bright cloud of His presence. The cloud enveloped them and the voice spoke, "*This is my beloved Son, whom I love. Listen to Him.*" He was saying to Jesus' disciples, "Listen to my Son. Moses and Elijah are the Law and the Prophets, of whom the Law and the Prophets testify. It is all about Jesus my Son."

We need to hear the Father's voice today. The church around the world is so divided over whether they are more Bible-based or more law-based, or whether they are more Spirit-based or prophetic-based. Both are necessary so we have a revelation of the Glorious Son, and it is the Son who counts. He has come to reveal the Father to us. Jesus Christ, the Son of God is the Word made flesh. He is the One who has the Spirit without measure.

Moses, representing the Law and Elijah, representing the Prophets, spoke with Jesus about the cross, His soon coming departure and exodus from this world. Moses saw the bush on fire, yet the fire did not consume it (Exodus 3:2). In the spirit, prophetically, he saw the Tree of Life, Jesus the Son of God, nailed to the Cross, burning in the fire of God's wrath, yet He was not burned.

> *He looked, and behold, the bush was burning,*
> *yet it was not consumed.*
> *Exodus 3:2*

Elijah saw the other side of the Cross, when the fire fell from Heaven on Mount Carmel and burned up the entire sacrifice. He saw the fire burn up everything: the wood, the sacrificed bull, the stones and even the water.

> *Then the fire of the LORD fell and consumed the burnt offering and*
> *the wood and the stones and the dust, and licked up*
> *the water that was in the trench.*
> *1 Kings 18:38*

Prophetically, he saw the Tree of the Knowledge of Good and Evil—you, me and all of humanity—burned up and consumed. No longer our own, but now fully His, consumed by the fire of His burning love. The Tree of the Knowledge of Good and Evil burned up forever, with absolutely nothing left.

What a glorious Savior Jesus Christ the Son of God is. It truly is all about Jesus! He has delivered us forever from our union with the Tree of the Knowledge of Good and Evil and with sin, death and Satan himself since our ancestors ate its fruit. Now we are forever in union with the Lord of Glory, Christ Jesus Himself. Jesus said,

> *Whoever feeds on my flesh and drinks my blood has eternal life, and*
> *I will raise him up on the last day. For my flesh is true food, and*
> *my blood is true drink. Whoever feeds on my flesh and*
> *drinks my blood abides in me, and I in him.*
> *John 6:54*

We have direct access once again, through faith, to the Tree of Life. We can eat His flesh and drink His blood and by feasting on the Son of God, we have eternal life. Jesus said those words as He took the Passover with His disciples at their very last meal together before He went to the Cross, during Passover. The very Lamb of God Himself was about to become the ultimate Passover Lamb for all humanity for all time to make an exodus from the dominion of darkness—the realm where Satan had been reigning over humanity since the Fall.

He gave His disciples bread and told them that it was His flesh, His very body, given for them. He gave them the cup of wine and told them that it was His blood of the new covenant and that they were to drink it as often as they could in remembrance of Him.

By doing so, Jesus set the new Passover for every believer. The invitation and commandment was given. We are to come and eat from the Tree of Life. We are to feast on His flesh and drink His blood. The promise is there for every human being. Whoever eats of Jesus by faith, shall receive eternal life. In eating the bread and drinking the wine, we are literally eating from the Tree of Life. By eating of that fruit we become one with the Tree of Life and become Trees of Life ourselves for the world, re-presenting Jesus

CHAPTER 9

THE TWO THIEVES

And he said, "Jesus, remember me when you come into your kingdom."
And he said to him, "Truly, I say to you, today
you will be with me in Paradise."
Luke 23:42-43

There were two criminals who were sentenced to death with Jesus of Nazareth. Pontius Pilate must have considered their crimes so terrible they deserved the death penalty by crucifixion, one of the cruelest forms of death known in history. They were crucified with Christ, one on His right and the other on His left. Jesus was placed in the middle of them both, separating them.

And with him they crucified two robbers,
one on his right and one on his left.
Mark 15:27

There they crucified him, and with him two others, one on either side,
and Jesus between them.
John 19:18

Christ, the Tree of Life, these two criminals represented the entire human race being crucified with Christ. Their very different responses to Jesus and being crucified with Him encapsulates the two opposite responses of every human being to Christ, His death and resurrection. All of humanity, regardless of belief, was crucified with Christ, but only those who believe in Him will be with Him in Paradise. Although Jesus gave His life for every human on the Cross, only those who believe in Him will spend eternity with Him. According to Jesus Himself, those who refuse to believe in Him will spend eternity in the fire prepared for them.

These are some of Jesus' last words to His disciples, in the parable of the Sheep and Goats, just before He went to the Cross.

> But when the Son of Man comes in His glory, and all the angels with Him, then He will sit on His glorious throne. All the nations will be gathered before Him; and He will separate them from one another, as the shepherd separates the sheep from the goats; and He will put the sheep on His right, and the goats on the left. Then the King will say to those on His right, "Come, you who are blessed of My Father, inherit the kingdom prepared for you from the foundation of the world" ...
> Then he will say to those on his left, "Depart from me, you cursed, into the eternal fire prepared for the devil and his angels"... and these will go away into eternal punishment, but the righteous into eternal life.
> Matthew 25: 31-34, 41 and 46

The thieves were physically separated by Jesus in their death. They were separated by their belief in who He was when they died, a profound separation that went beyond their death and into resurrection. Only one thief inherited the Kingdom on the other side of death in the everlasting "Today" that Jesus called "Paradise."

Mark and Matthew call the men robbers, although crucifixion was the ultimate punishment for the most heinous crimes so they were far more than petty thieves. They may have been the equivalent of armed robbers today, who would not hesitate to murder those who stood up to them. We don't know their crimes, but we know they were bad enough to warrant a punishment reserved for things like murder. Luke uses the Greek word *kakourgos*, which literally translated means *a worker of sheer evil*. They were criminals of the worst kind, sentenced to death by crucifixion.

> *One of the criminals who were hanged railed at him, saying, "Are*
> *you not the Christ? Save yourself and us!" But the other rebuked him,*
> *saying, "Do you not fear God, since you are under the same sentence*
> *of condemnation? And we indeed justly, for we are receiving the due*
> *reward of our deeds; but this man has done nothing wrong." And he*
> *said, "Jesus, remember me when you come into your kingdom."*
> *And He said to him, "Truly, I say to you,*
> *today you will be with me in Paradise."*
> Luke 23:39-43

Let's take a look at the first thief. He was hurling abuse at Jesus (v 39). Even in the face of death there was no fear of God in him. The first thief is absolutely unrepentant, full of hatred and scorn even towards Jesus. He had no revelation that Jesus really was the Messiah. He may have felt justified in believing Jesus could not be the Messiah, the Son of God, after all, Jesus was dying on a cross with them. He was looking at Jesus according to the natural.

The First Thief

The first thief was focused on this natural realm, on saving his own life for himself. He wanted Jesus to prove He was the Son of God, but only for his own self-centered motives. He wanted to save his own skin! Even in the possibility of being in the presence of God, his reaction was, "God, do this, or do that for me." He wanted to be rescued from the cross so he could continue living his life here on earth as he had always done.

This is so often the motive in the hearts of humanity before God. *"God, if You love me, then do this or do that."* When we're faced with things that haven't gone well for us, we can think, *"God if you are real, or if you really loved me, why didn't you rescue me?"* In this, we betray our self-centered motivation. Our orientation is always earthly, concerned about the cares of this world and our own selfish desires.

The first thief could only see Jesus according to the natural, according to the flesh. He did not have faith and had no desire for the eternal realm. He did not have a desire for God or Heaven. He had faith for one thing only: being saved from the death he was dying in this life. He was steeped in selfishness, living for the moment with no care about the next life, even as he faced imminent death.

He personified hedonistic, self-preservationist, self-serving humanity that only looks out for "number one," that has no sense of eternity, care for others, or fear of God. One can imagine he might have been thinking, *"All I want is to get off this cross. I know I deserve to be here, but all I care about is saving my skin and going back to my life. I was just unlucky that I got caught and now here's my chance to get off, but it turns out this so-called Messiah can't save me."*

He was only interested in using Jesus for his own ambition to not die in that moment. He had no honor for Jesus and who He truly was as the glorious Son of God.

Before we judge him, though, recognize that this is the essence of sinful humanity's heart, in every one of us that has ever lived. Yet Christ came to our place of execution to die with us and for us while we were yet sinners (Romans 5:8).

The Second Thief

Matthew tells us the second thief started out the same way, hurling insults at Jesus.

> *The robbers who had been crucified with Him were also*
> *insulting Him with the same words.*
> *Matthew 27:44*

However at some point on the cross, the second thief had a revelation of Jesus Christ, the glorious Messiah, as his personal Lord and Savior. The resulting very short dialogue between him and Jesus perfectly reveals all that is necessary for a human being to be saved by grace alone through faith. It is the gift of God (Ephesians 2:8).

The dialogue is so deeply profound and shows us the purest essence of the Gospel of Jesus Christ. It is what makes the "Good News" of Jesus Christ such incredible good news to every human heart.

Having lived a life of crime as a worker of sheer evil, the society that prided itself on being the most civilized and just society, found him guilty and condemned him to death. This man was deserving of death and then Hell. He was absolutely undeserving of life or Heaven. On top of this, a short while earlier, he had been hurling insults at the Son of God—the only One who had the power to save him. His place in the everlasting lake of burning sulfur, described by John in Revelation, was surely inevitable.

Suddenly, just when he was truly *"without God and without hope in this world"* (Ephesians 2:12), doomed to destruction, the mercy of God flowed into his heart. He was forced to look at Jesus every time he tried to look at his friend because Jesus was crucified between them. Something about watching Jesus on the Cross caused him to realize He truly was the Savior of the world. The second thief suddenly saw something every human being is required to see to be eternally saved: He saw his absolute need of a Savior.

Somehow, he recognized there was something so different about this Man, Jesus, even in the face of death. This Man was the Savior of the whole world. The thief got revelation that salvation has nothing to do with what any human being, himself included, had done or not done throughout their lives. He realized it was a matter of who he put his faith in. Something in Jesus of Nazareth, in the way He hung on the Cross, enabled the second thief to know without doubt, "Jesus is my Savior and He is able to save me out of death."

He instinctively knew that death is the one thing we all deserve. Because of our sin, we cannot save ourselves from its eternal grip. We need a sinless person to die in our place for us, as us. The thief knew he was dying a death he deserved, but he could see that Jesus had the power to save him beyond their imminent death and give him the right to be with Him forever in paradise.

The second thief turned to the other criminal and rebuked him, "Do you not even fear God, since you are under the same sentence of condemnation?"

He demonstrated full understanding that their sentence of condemnation has devastating consequences for them because they would inevitably face God for their lives of sin. He understood that there is One person who is more to be "feared" than any other fear, including the fear of death. He illustrated by his words that he knew on the other side of death he would meet God. It is as though he had been there when Jesus had said,

I tell you, my friends, do not fear those who kill the body, and after that have nothing more that they can do. But I will warn you whom to fear: fear him who, after he has killed, has authority to cast into hell. Yes, I tell you, fear him!

Luke 12:4-5

There is no evidence that this man was there when Jesus had spoken these words, but his response now is exactly what Jesus was talking about. Suddenly, the second thief was no longer concerned about getting off the cross and being saved from those who were killing his body. It dawned on him that there was someone who he needed to be much more afraid of: *the One who, after he has killed, has the authority to cast into hell.*

In his first declaration of faith in Christ he turns to his friend, and says, "Do you not even fear God?"

Where the fear of the Lord fits into the New Covenant can get confusing. There are verses that could make us think that in the New Covenant, there is no fear of the Lord. For example, John wrote,

> *There is no fear in love, for perfect love casts out all fear.*
> 1 John 4:18

Of course, John is speaking the truth when he says there is no fear in love; however the words *in love* are very important here. There is no fear *in love.* Once we are in love there is no fear, but the fear of the Lord is an essential element in leading us to love Him. Once we believe in Christ we are hidden in Him, placed in Love Himself because God is love. In Christ, in love, there is no fear (1 John 4:8,16).

John is not saying this to negate the reality of the fear of the Lord, an essential component of our salvation. The word of God is very clear on the importance of the fear of the Lord in leading us to love and keeping us in love.

Many Christians misunderstand this, thinking that the fear of the Lord is an Old Testament dynamic and therefore not important today. However, the fear of the Lord is essential in leading us *to* Christ and is the constraining force of the Holy Spirit, Love Himself, that leads us *in* Christ to obedience of the Father's will.

The second criminal sees the importance of the fear of the Lord. So much so, he felt it necessary to rebuke the other criminal with the words, "Do you not even fear God?" He is clearly beginning to fear the Lord.

There are some amazing words in the book of Proverbs that help us to see why the second thief's words illustrate how he himself had suddenly been filled with the fear of the Lord. It was the reason he was now able to see Jesus differently, and it led to his salvation. The verses follow the wonderful progression of revelation that leads every human to salvation through faith in Christ.

The fear of the LORD is the beginning of knowledge.
Proverbs 1:7

There is little evidence that when he was first crucified, he had any knowledge of God. However, the fear of the Lord is the beginning of knowledge. Knowledge began to enter his heart and mind.

Then you will understand the fear of the LORD and
find the knowledge of God.
Proverbs 2:5

As he discerned the fear of the Lord, perhaps realizing, "This is it. I'm dying. I'm not going to make it this time. *I'm going to die!*"

He may have begun to consider the reality of his peril, not in this life alone now, but more importantly in the life to come, a split second after he died. The fear of the Lord led him instantly to the knowledge of God.

The fear of the LORD is hatred of evil.
Proverbs 8:13

The fear of the Lord caused a hatred of evil to rise in his heart. Perhaps for the first time in a long time, maybe for the first time ever, he became acutely aware of the dreadfulness of his sin. He began to hate evil, aware of the sin in his life and his great need to be separated from what he now violently hated.

The fear of the LORD is the beginning of wisdom.
Proverbs 9:10

The fear of the Lord filled him with wisdom, such that he may have realized it was his own sin that would keep him in death for eternity—and justly so.

The fear of the LORD prolongs life.
Proverbs 10:27

The fear of the Lord was the key to his life being preserved through death, prolonged for eternity beyond death.

In the fear of the LORD one has strong confidence
and his children will have a refuge.
Proverbs 14:26

The fear of the Lord gave him the strong confidence to believe in Jesus' power to preserve him and be his eternal refuge as a child of God.

The fear of the LORD is a fountain of life,
that one may turn away from the snares of death.
Proverbs 14:27

The fear of the Lord triggered in his heart a gushing revelation of the eternal life that would course through him, bubbling up in him as pure life forever and ever, preserving him from being ensnared or trapped by death. That eternal life would set him free from being a captive to death for eternity.

The fear of the LORD leads to life, so that one may sleep satisfied,
untouched by evil.
Proverbs 19:23 (NASB)

The fear of the Lord led him to Jesus of Nazareth, being crucified next to him, yet who was Eternal Life Himself. The King of Glory, whom death could not and would not hold because He was the perfect One who had never sinned. The Savior of the World, who was good enough and powerful enough to rescue him beyond the grave and keep Him forever untouched by evil, the evil he now hated so much. Jesus was able to remove from him his sin, by becoming his sin for him and preserving Him forever from sin defiling him again.

The reward for humility and the fear of the LORD
is riches and honor and life.
Proverbs 22:4

The fear of the Lord caused humility to spring up instantly in the second thief's heart. He was able to truly admit his sin and desperate need of a Savior and that the One being crucified next to him was indeed that very Savior. This man from Nazareth, nailed to a cross just like his, had emptied Himself and become a servant of all. He was laying His life down for His friends in the greatest demonstration of love ever witnessed by the universe.

The fear of the Lord enabled the second thief to walk in the same kind of humility that the Son of God walked in. He was able to believe that simply by believing in Him, Jesus would raise him from the dead, leading to an eternity spent with riches, honor and life.

He was willing to confront the other criminal, knowing he may well turn on him too. His appeal to his fellow criminal demonstrates that mercy was already at work in his heart. He wanted the other man to be saved too!

The beauty of the fear of the Lord is that the Holy Spirit was working all this instantly into the heart and mind of the second thief, even though he very likely had no knowledge of the scriptures concerning the fear of the Lord whatsoever. It was a work of pure grace, grace that was available to both thieves, but only one received.

Next he said, *"We indeed are suffering justly, for we are receiving what we deserve for our deeds"* (Luke 23:41).

He demonstrated here his absolute recognition of his sin and his willingness to confess his sin before Jesus, which he did right there as he spoke to the other thief. He was no longer in denial and deception. He brought his evil deeds into the light, confessing them aloud and fully acknowledging that justice demands the punishment he was receiving. He acknowledged that he deserved to die for his sin and that justice would be satisfied if he did.

Then he began to make the most amazing statements of faith in Jesus' power to save. He said of Jesus, *"This man has done nothing wrong"* (Luke 23:41b).

This is astonishing. He recognized that Jesus had never sinned. He understood that Jesus is dying as a "sinner," yet now he knew that Jesus himself had never sinned. Had Jesus sinned, He would not be able to rescue him from death on the other side of them dying. He realized that Jesus had done *nothing wrong.*

It is likely that as a Jewish man, this criminal would have been familiar enough with the story of Adam to know death came to humanity because of sin. He likely knew that no human had ever lived a life and done nothing wrong. If there ever had been such a man, he would not have had to die. Death is the result of sin.

Now here he was on the cross he deserved to die upon, watching the Man Jesus of Nazareth, accused of some terrible crime, such that He was being crucified. He is dying a death the thief recognized he himself deserves to die: yet he could distinguish somehow Jesus did not deserve to die this death.

There was something so radically different about Jesus and the manner in which He was dying on a similar cross that made this thief realize, *"This man does not deserve to die this death! We do, but He doesn't."*

We do not know what suddenly caused this thief to realize Jesus was dying a death He didn't deserve and that Jesus was the sinless Savior of the World. We know he could not look at the other thief without seeing Jesus. Maybe every time he looked across at the other thief or looked directly at Jesus, he could see Jesus looking at him with eyes of pure love and grace. Maybe even while he was insulting Jesus, looking with eyes of pure malice, despising Jesus, he could see Jesus looking back at him through His terribly swollen and smashed face with no condemnation or accusation; just pure compassion and mercy.

Maybe it was the "look" Jesus carried in His love-filled eyes that captivated the heart of the second thief, or maybe it was Jesus' words,

Father, forgive them for they know not what they do.
Luke 23:34

Maybe the thief was deeply touched by the forgiveness Jesus conveyed in His request to the Father for all those who had put Him on the

Cross. Maybe the thief even realized Jesus' reference to "them" might have been the entire human race, which included him, his insults of Jesus and his *entire lifetime of sin.*

We don't know, but something the thief saw or heard led him to place his absolute faith in the saving power of the grace of Jesus of Nazareth, because this man was truly God in the flesh.

He then directed his words straight at Jesus with a profound statement that again illustrates the Gospel in its purest form. He does not ask, "Jesus, *will* you remember me when you come into your Kingdom?" Instead, He makes a clear declaration of bold faith,

"Jesus, remember me when you come into your Kingdom" (Luke 23:42).

What incredible words from a man who recognizes he is absolutely deserving of death for his deeds, and that those deeds are more than enough to cause him to spend eternity in the fires of Hell. Yet he places all of his faith in Christ Jesus, whom he somehow knew could save him.

The thief called upon the name of the Lord using his first name, Jesus, which means "The Lord Who Saves." It is a gigantic statement of his faith in the capacity of the Man next to him to save him.

Then he says, *"Remember me when you come into your Kingdom."* These are most extraordinary words, under the circumstances. They reveal such faith and revelation into the nature of who the thief believed Jesus was. Jesus was dying next to him, nailed to a cross just like the one he was nailed to, yet he showed he realized Jesus is a King after all, of a Kingdom that is not of this world, but is on the other side of death.

The thief knows Jesus is the rightful King of that Kingdom, despite Him being on a Cross dying in this world. As the rightful King, He has the right to decide who does and who does not get to be in His Kingdom. His words show clearly that at this point he was now convinced Jesus is the sinless One. The One who has never sinned, therefore death cannot hold Him. Though He will die, yet He will live.

As the King of Life who has conquered death, He will have all authority over those who have died. In His goodness, He will remember each of them on the other side of death. He demonstrated that he realized Jesus is God, the all-knowing One, the omniscient One, who will remember everything that has happened in this life and therefore will remember him.

Jesus was all the thief could trust in. The thief's hands were nailed so he couldn't do anything. His feet were nailed so he couldn't go anywhere. He had nothing to give Jesus. He had nothing else. Nothing he had ever done qualified him for Heaven. Everything he had ever done disqualified him from Heaven. There was nothing he could give for his life. *He could only trust Jesus had everything to give Him.*

He put no faith in the other thief, or in the High Priest, or in the Pharisees, or in the Romans. He knew he deserved to die. No, it was this Man who did not deserve to die; He was the only one with the power to save him. No one else could die for him on a cross with him, except the perfect One who had never sinned. Jesus alone had the power to save him, and His payment of His perfect life upon the Cross was all sufficient to have paid in full the ransom for the thief's entire life of sin.

Jesus was his Messiah, and the Savior of the whole world. The thief surrendered to love. Surrendered to grace. He had nothing else but to simply believe in all Christ was for him. He put his trust in the perfect King, who was laying down His life for his friends: the ones like him, who knew they were sinners and desperately needed a Savior. The ones who knew they could never do anything to save themselves and in humility were surrendered to Love Himself. He knew by grace he was now one of those friends of Jesus forever.

Jesus turned and said to him, *"Truly I say to you, today you will be with me in paradise"* (Luke 23:43). Jesus spoke as the Eternal King He is. Knowing all He is about to accomplish by His death and resurrection, He gives the absolute verdict of mercy, grace and love. He replied, *"Today, you will be with me in Paradise."* Not *tomorrow*, but *today*. Not in three days, but *today*! Today is always today. There is never a day that today is not today.

The word represents the everlasting *now*! The realm where the I AM dwells in all eternity, where every day is Today.

It's fascinating that Jesus said, "Today, you will be *with me* in Paradise" rather than, "Today you will be in Paradise." The *"with Me"* reveals the essence of salvation: we will be with Jesus forever. Heaven is not our reward apart from Him. God is our exceedingly great reward forever (Genesis 15:1). To be with Him is to be in Paradise!

Tragically, there is no reference to the other thief, the first thief, ever having this kind of dialogue with Jesus. He died without surrendering to Love Himself. He refused to humble his heart. He refused the mercy that offered the fear of the Lord. He refused to put his faith in Jesus as His Messiah and Savior and there is no record of Jesus ever saying to Him those glorious words, *"Today, you will be with me in Paradise."*

Luke is clear Jesus only said it to the second thief.

Although two thieves were crucified with Christ and died with Christ, only one was saved by Christ's death. Only one died with the assurance of spending eternity with Christ. Both shared in His death, but only one shared in His resurrection. One died and burned for eternity with sin, death, the devil and his angels. The other was raised to life, one with burning Love Himself forever.

Their two different responses represent the two opposite responses to Christ of every human being, to His death and resurrection. They symbolize what was happening in the realm of the spirit. All of humanity, regardless of who they are, was crucified with Christ, but only those who believe in Him will die and go to be with Him today in Paradise.

I have at times met people who have said to me they cannot believe that being saved can truly be as simple as placing our faith in Christ and His death and resurrection. I have had people angrily say to me they cannot believe a person should be able to live a life of "sin"; and then on their death bed, put their faith in Christ, call upon His name, be saved and get to go to Heaven, even though they have done terrible things all their lives.

You see, that's the whole point! That's why the Gospel is such incredibly good news. That a person who has lived a terrible life as a sinner can place their faith in Jesus Christ as they die on their death bed is what makes Jesus and His work of salvation upon the Cross so indescribably good. There is no life any human can ever live that is good enough to qualify for eternity with Jesus in Heaven. The only qualification is a perfect life, lived perfectly.

A person who does their very best to please God through their own efforts is just as much in need of a Savior as the person dying on their death bed is, having lived a life of rebellion against God. The person who is dying, having lived a life that totally disqualifies them from Heaven, is more likely to trust purely in the saving grace and power of Jesus alone. They have nothing else.

Once, before you believed in Christ, you were one with sin. So much so that if you had died in that condition, in union with your sin, without Christ, then your sin's eternal destiny, burning forever in Hell, would have been your eternal destiny with your sin, even though God never made Hell for human beings. God made Hell to destroy sin forever and ever, together with the source of all sin, the devil himself and all the fallen angels. He did not make Hell for humanity. However, if anyone in humanity chooses to reject the Son of God, the One whose perfect sacrifice provided the means for our eternal separation from sin, then they remain in their sin, one with their sin. Their sin's eternal destiny becomes their eternal destiny, burning in Hell, separated from the Life of God.

I know there are some of you reading this book that may have realized you want to call out to Jesus today and tell Him how much you desperately need Him to save you. Not just to save you from all the troubles you might be in right now in this life, and not so you can selfishly carry on life the way you have always known it, like the first thief wanted Jesus to do for him. Rather, no matter who you are, or what you have done in your life, come to Him; and like the second thief, put your faith in Jesus Christ, for no other reason than you want to spend eternity with Him in Paradise. Not just for your sake to save your skin, but for Him, to give Him the eternal reward of His suffering: your heart of love and loyalty forever.

Like the second thief, put your faith in His perfection. Put your faith in Jesus' death as the sinless, perfect sacrifice, which paid for all your sin and mine. Put your faith in His power to conquer death because of His indestructible life, untainted by sin. Like the second thief, put your faith in Christ's resurrection. Confess with your mouth and believe in your heart that the Father raised Jesus from the dead.

> *If you confess with your mouth that Jesus is Lord*
> *and believe in your heart that God raised him from the dead,*
> *you will be saved.*
> Romans 10:9

Put your faith in Jesus as the King of the invisible, everlasting Kingdom of Heaven and accept Him as your Savior and the Savior of the world. Open your heart to Him and welcome Him into your heart. Even if you are on your deathbed, or you feel there is no hope for you. Even if you have done such terrible things in your life that you are convinced you have disqualified yourself from ever being saved. Tell Him all the ways you have messed up your life and the lives of those around you, sinning against yourself, others and Jesus Himself. Without Jesus, you, like us all, have been a "thief," who's tried to "steal" eternal life for yourself. There's no need to steal any longer; simply take the gift of Life Himself that He's freely offering you right now for all eternity.

Like the second thief, tell Jesus you realize you are guilty, and that you desperately need saving from your sin that clings to you. Sin you have always hated deep down in your heart, yet you've held onto it. You've never known how to get rid of it. As you do so, you will sense the power of Jesus' blood that He gave for us all at the Cross bringing complete forgiveness to all your sin and washing your guilty conscience clean.

Come to Him empty handed, with all your own efforts at being "good" left behind. Christ is your only, all sufficiency. His life is the only life worthy of the Father, the only life acceptable to the Father. There is nothing you or I have ever done or will ever do that will make us worthy of Eternal Life. All that is required is that we simply believe in the Lord Jesus Christ and that He died for us, though He Himself never sinned, as the only perfect sacrifice for our sin. Death could not hold on to Him, but the Father raised Him from the dead. Come to Him in humility, acknowledging your absolute need of Him and call upon Him to save you.

Like the thief, you will hear His words in your heart saying, *"Truly I say to you, today you will be with me in Paradise."* Paradise that will last for all eternity begins in Christ for you and me right now!

The life Jesus lived is the only life that qualifies for eternity in Heaven. By simply believing in Jesus, the Father has credited to your life the life Jesus lived on earth for 33 years, as if it was the life you lived. Perfect love has given you His perfect life forever.

CHAPTER 10

THE BRONZE SERPENT

As Moses lifted up the serpent in the wilderness, so must the Son of
Man be lifted up, that whoever believes in him may have eternal life.

John 3:14

Some years ago, I was about to preach at our TACF Sunday night healing service. I love healing services, especially in an ethnically diverse city such as Toronto, where people are from all over the world. This means there are often people from other religions, such as Islam, Sikhism or Buddhism, in the services. We have the privilege of seeing them healed and give their lives to Jesus Christ as they discover first hand for themselves He truly is God and their champion Savior!

On this occasion I was really getting concerned. I had been waiting on the Lord all afternoon, trying to prepare myself and the message. I still had no idea what He wanted me to preach on. I was getting really desperate as the last song was being sung. I had been studying the story of Moses and the Bronze Serpent in Numbers all afternoon, as it is a wonderful story to preach on at a healing service.

The LORD said to Moses, "Make a fiery serpent and set it on a pole,
and everyone who is bitten, when he sees it, shall live." So Moses
made a bronze serpent and set it on a pole. And if a serpent bit
anyone, he would look at the bronze serpent and live.
Numbers 21:8-9

Ancient Israel was grumbling in the desert. They had begun being bitten by snakes. They cried to Moses, Moses cried to God for mercy for the people. God instructed him to construct a fiery serpent, and hold it up on a pole for all to see. Moses constructs the serpent out of bronze, places it on a pole, and everyone who looks at it survives the snakebite. The powerful prophetic symbolism in the story points so clearly to Jesus dying on the Cross for all humanity who have been bitten by the "snake." All humanity, who have been poisoned by sin so they are dying, are instantly healed by looking to their Savior on the Cross.

The passage symbolically demonstrates the power of the Cross to heal all those who turn by faith and look to Jesus on the Cross. Sickness is death slowed down. He delivered up to death His own body, thereby saving us from all our sin, sickness and diseases.

As I joined in the worship, lying face down on the floor at the very front of the church, I began to focus on how much the Father and the Son love us. I took my eyes off my sermon and I began to worship God deeply from my heart. Suddenly I was struck by the fact that I had no idea what bronze was and most of all, I had no idea why God asked Moses to make a *snake*. Surely it would have been far more appropriate to ask Moses to make a figure of a *man* on a pole not a *snake* if it represented Jesus on the Cross! Figuring that no one else could hear me over the loud music all around us, I yelled out at the top of my lungs into the carpet, "What is bronze anyway?"

To my surprise I heard a man shout back very loudly behind me, *"Bronze is an alloy of two distinct metals, tin and copper, melted in fire they become one brand-new metal!"*

I was stunned as I lay there, revelation exploding in my mind. *Two distinct metals melted in the fire become one brand-new metal.* I later learned that he was right. Bronze is an alloy metal, not naturally found in nature. At a molecular level, tin and copper have extra electrons. One is slightly acidic, and the other is slightly basic. When the two are melted, they bond together and become bronze. It is a chemical process that cannot be reversed. Once tin and copper have become bronze, that bronze remains bronze forever. It is impossible ever to reverse that process and regain tin and copper! As bronze, it is fully tin and as bronze, it is fully copper! It has lost none of its tin-ness or copper-ness, yet it is something brand-new, bronze. Fully copper and fully tin, yet wholly bronze and therefore neither tin nor copper, as they previously existed.

I realized in that incredible moment, lying on the floor, that the Holy Spirit was giving us glimpses into the mystery of the Cross of Christ. In the furnace of the wrath of the Father, poured out upon the Son, Jesus allowed Himself to be forever melted into absolute union with all Humanity. We were literally and irreversibly melted together into Christ at the Cross. He in us, and us in Him.

I was invited recently by a famous sculptor in South Africa, well known for his beautiful bronze artistry, to join him at his workshop after he heard me preach this message. He had a professional kiln where he made his own bronze, creating his masterpieces. We arrived in the early afternoon. It had taken all morning to heat up the kiln close to the required 1085°C, or 1984°F, where tin and copper melt together to form bronze.

I dressed up in the required heat protection overalls and wore a large facemask with an extremely dark glass window where I could look through into the fiery furnace of the kiln. I saw that the tin had already melted into the mold and was liquid under the copper. Tin melts at 231.9°C, or 449.5°F. Everything looked shimmery with white light dancing about all over the tin and the copper glowed bright red in the fire. It was so beautiful. As I stood watching, fascinated, the thermometer registered 1085°C.

Instantly, the large block of copper collapsed into the pool of tin and the two were transformed into a brand-new metal, an alloy we call bronze. The two became one and were irreversibly, forever made one brand-new metal.

I saw with my own eyes the two metals become one. I caught a tiny glimpse of that moment when the Son of God became one with you and me forever, as I watched it all happening in the fiery kiln.

It was one of the most moving things I've ever had the privilege of seeing. The extreme melting points in the furnace required to achieve the melting for the union was overwhelming. Oh, how He suffered. His love for us is beyond our comprehension. Love so amazing, love so divine!

Jesus underscores this dynamic reality when He refers to the bronze serpent in his conversation with Nicodemus.

As Moses lifted up the serpent in the wilderness, so must the Son of
Man be lifted up, that whoever believes in him may have eternal life.
John 3:14

Tin and copper, melted in the fire become one brand-new metal, bronze. At the Cross, Jesus and sinful humanity were melted together in the Fire of God's wrath as Jesus Christ became the ultimate burnt offering, the ultimate sacrifice for sin. From that moment, the center point of all history, whoever would simply believe in Jesus and look to the Cross would be saved eternally from sin, death and the everlasting fires of Hell.

Why a Snake?

Now that I understood the amazing significance of bronze, a question I'd pondered many years flooded into my mind. I said to the Father, "I realize the significance of the bronze now, but why did Jesus have to look like a snake?"

Have you wondered, why a snake? Why couldn't God have asked Moses to make a man of bronze and fix it to a pole? Like a Catholic crucifix, for example. If it was a powerful prophetic type of Christ upon the Cross, why a snake on a pole?

The answer the Holy Spirit spoke into my heart in that moment as I lay on the floor completely undid me and I have never recovered! The Father spoke into my heart, *"Because that is what my Son Jesus looked like when He became fully you."*

I was utterly overcome. Jesus was made my sin at the Cross, so completely that He now looked like a snake! Again revelation exploded in my heart and mind as I realized that if all of my sin and the sin of all humanity came upon Jesus in that moment, Christ *was me and all of humanity hanging there.* Jesus was fully identified with humanity and all its sin and devastation. There was no distinction. He had become indistinguishable from you and me, truly the Last Adam. He became fully one with us all.

Only those ancient Israelites who looked at the snake on the pole in the desert were healed. In exactly the same way only those who believe in Jesus and look to the one pierced upon the Cross are made one with Him through faith.

To rescue us from the power of sin, death and Satan himself, Jesus had to be willing to go even further than becoming our sin. Our Savior, Jesus Christ was willing to be crucified on the Cross, to take upon Himself all of our sin and own it so completely that He Himself was the guilty One, me and you, before the just and righteous Father.

The pure, spotless, sinless Son of God laid down His life for His friends, thereby achieving and demonstrating the ultimate revelation of love.

Greater love has no man
than he lay down his life for his friends.
John 15:13

As his lifeblood drained away and the unthinkable happened, the perfect sinless one began to die. Death is the wages of sin. Without sin there is no death, yet here was Jesus dying. His sinless death created a dynamic which I cannot describe in any better way than to simply say it this way: His body, as He died, became a gigantic vacuum cleaner of all sin. Jesus' words, recorded by John, sum up this moment.

I, when I am lifted up from the earth, will draw all people to myself.
John 12:32

As a kid, I always used to imagine Jesus with a small group of Christians gathered around the Cross, huddling in a missionary prayer meeting. However, I don't think that was what Jesus was referring to at all. I think He meant that in the day He would die on the Cross, He would draw all men literally into Himself. To say it another way, He would make Himself one with all humanity.

Jesus' dying body literally sucked all the sin of humanity, from Adam to the last baby born before the end of the world, into Himself in those hours as He hung on the Cross dying. As His dying body sucked our sin into Him, so also He brought us into Himself, because you cannot separate the sin from the sinner.

He became our sin as He died our death, and in so doing *became us*. The fullness of what it means to be *"made in the likeness of sinful flesh"* took place. The ultimate state of being made in the likeness of you is for someone to become you. At the Cross Jesus became so one with us, He actually became us—you, me, and every human being in history.

Understanding this aspect of Christ's death has helped to settle for me a huge question that I have grappled with for years, being an ex-police officer. Anyone who understands the essential elements of justice knows there are two sides to justice. First, it is an injustice for a guilty person to

go free, unpunished. Second, it is a grave injustice for an innocent person
to be punished. The scriptures confirm this in Proverbs,

> *He who justifies the wicked and he who condemns the righteous are*
> *both alike an abomination to the LORD.*
> *Proverbs 17:15*

Knowing both these aspects of justice, I've always wondered how
the God of justice could have justified you and me, the wicked, guilty ones,
and do it by condemning to death His righteous innocent Son, without this
entire act of the Cross being a travesty of justice. Love is not love without
justice. How could the Cross be the greatest demonstration of love, if it was
the greatest injustice of all time? Justice must be justice for love to be love.

Justice Satisfied

> *Mercy and truth have met together, justice and peace have kissed.*
> *Psalm 85:10 (NKJV)*

Somehow in the great mystery of the Cross, Jesus became our sin and in
becoming our sin, He literally became us, each one of us. When He died,
He died our death as us, so that before the Father, we literally have paid for
our sin. He was able to pay for it because He was now so indistinguishable
from us. In the greatest demonstration of love ever, justice was satisfied
because Jesus *became us and died as us, for us, with us*. He had to, so He could
die for our sin without it being the greatest demonstration of injustice! The
guiltless One had to become the guilty one to pay for the guilty one's sin.

The great depth of the love of Christ is that He loved us and gave
Himself for us (Galatians 2:20). The innocent One in love, as Love, was
willing to become so completely one with us that He took us upon Himself,

became us and stood in our place *as the guilty One*. Mercy met truth, our sins were brought into the light and justice kissed peace, because the Prince of Peace stood in our place as us.

The Father accepted Christ's death as your death because Jesus really was you when He died. Your debt is paid. You died with Christ. Oh, the height and depth and width of the love of God in Christ Jesus! Perfect justice was truly satisfied by the most perfect manifestation of love: sacrifice.

We've seen that Jesus experienced every sin ever committed, as both the victim of that sin and the perpetrator of that sin. It is incomprehensible what that must have been like for the Son of God, who Himself had never experienced sin.

Now that we understand that He died *as us*, we are ready to see how He became every individual tragedy and atrocity in the history of humanity. He is intimately acquainted with it all because He experienced it *live* at the Cross as it came upon Him. This is why he is able to sympathize perfectly with our weaknesses, why He is able to relate perfectly with all that we ourselves go through as the victims of others' sin done to us, no matter how devastating.

He is able to relate to every global disaster and every mass tragedy and devastation. He knows *exactly* what it is like, because that *exact* event is what He became at the Cross. All sin, of all humanity, throughout all time and in all creation, Jesus Christ became it at the Cross. He didn't just become the sin as it is as a principle, which He did too, but He became our exact and specific sin—each and every single sin of all people, throughout all time, in all places. Every individual sin! All sin! This answers the cry of every human heart concerning why God seemingly allows tragedy in this world. He gave us our free will, then He became every tragic consequence of our free will throughout all time, becoming each of us, the victims and perpetrators of sin, then He paid the price of it all by His perfect free will.

I shared this with our youngest daughter Nathania, who was thirteen at the time. Like each of our precious daughters, Nathania just loves Jesus with all her heart. She responded, "All of our hurts too Dad! He experienced each one of our hurts too."

I was stunned as I realized she was absolutely right about this. He experienced every single hurt and pain as well as every single sickness and disease in His bruised and torn body, so that we could be healed from them all.

Carlos Rodriguez shares how he had sprained his ankle jumping in a puddle, while at the School of Ministry in Toronto leading a trip to Niagara Falls. As he collapsed on the sidewalk in excruciating pain, He saw a vision of Jesus stumbling, carrying His Cross—and His ankle turned over. The Lord looked right at Him and whispered into his heart, *"Carlos, I became this very sprained ankle at the Cross for you so you can be healed."*

Carlos shares that as he took hold of that truth by faith, he was instantly healed. The substantial swelling immediately vanished and he was able to walk again without pain.

At the Cross, Jesus Christ became all of our sin and all of our sicknesses so that we could be His righteousness and free from all sickness, both in this life and of course forever.

This is enormous and demonstrates the unending love of God in Christ. Never again can anyone truly accuse God, as we all too often do, of being responsible for all the tragedies or sicknesses in the world. We cannot blame God. He has never committed one sin. Has not caused one disaster, one atrocity, or tragedy. Humanity, together with the demonic realm is responsible for all the abominations, genocides, horrors, monstrosities, obscenities, violations, crimes, brutalities, savageries, inhumanities, evil, wickedness, barbarous acts and so on that have been done throughout our history. Instead He chose to become it all, and as it all, pay the ultimate price, giving His perfect Life to pay the ransom price of it all.

One day, I was talking with a young friend of ours from London, England, who worked on the streets pouring out the love of God to the women in prostitution. This wonderful young woman lays down her life for them day after day, relentlessly showing them the love of the Father. In doing do, she has seen some terrible atrocities committed by the pimps and the men that come for the girls. She has lived among the horrors of that world. She shared with me how one of her friends who had been living a lifestyle of prostitution had been brutally burned, murdered and butchered. As she shared this with tears flowing freely in that tender moment, she told me how hard it was for her to see where the love of God could possibly be in those kinds of tragedies.

I shared with her that the Lord Jesus Christ loved the world so much that at the Cross, He was willing to become that *exact situation*. Jesus became the terrible tragedy of being the victim of sin in that terrible event and He also became the terrible tragedy of being the ones who brutally murdered her. He became sin for us, all of us. Sin is sin; there are no little ones and big ones, terrible ones and less terrible ones. Sin is sin and it is terrible enough for us all to have spent eternity burning in Hell, just punishment for our sin, had He not been willing to become our sin and become us at the Cross. He consumed sin through His death forever!

As we discussed previously, God did not make Hell for humanity. He made Hell to destroy sin forever, together with the source of all sin, the devil himself and all the fallen angels. However, if anyone rejects the Son of God, the One whose perfect sacrifice provided the means for our eternal separation from sin, then they remain in their sin, one with their sin and their sin's eternal destiny becomes their eternal destiny, burning in Hell—separated from God.

The ultimate good news for all humanity is that by simply believing in the Son of God, Jesus Christ, all our sin is separated from us *eternally*. Sin's destiny, Hell, is no longer our destiny. Our destiny is our union with Christ forever.

The ancient Jewish leaders so badly wanted Jesus to be crucified because they knew the scriptures. Deuteronomy says that everyone who is hung on a tree is accursed.

If a man has committed a crime punishable by death and he is put
to death, and you hang him on a tree, his body shall not remain all
night on the tree, but you shall bury him the same day,
for a hanged man is cursed by God.
Deuteronomy 21:22-23

Paul picks up that thread in the Book of Galatians.

Christ redeemed us from the curse of the Law, having become a curse
for us for it is written, "Cursed is everyone who hangs on a tree."
Galatians 3:13

They wanted Jesus crucified so that the entire nation would think He couldn't possibly be the Messiah. No one who had been hung on a tree could be anything but a curse! But they completely misunderstood the purpose of the Cross, that unless the Messiah was willing to actually become the curse for us all, we would have remained the curse ourselves forever.

Our champion Savior has forever fully squared up every injustice ever committed by humanity throughout all history. This means that He is able to comfort all peoples for all time in all places through the most terrible circumstances and tragedies, the most terrible atrocities and seeming injustices. He is right there in the middle of it all demonstrating the greatest love imaginable. He Himself became the exact victims of the tragedy and became the exact perpetrators of the same tragedy, so that justice has been Eternally satisfied.

In that state, He took the fire and was melted forever in union with us all. He died as us. He was irreversibly one with us in death so that we could be one with Him in His life. Burning at the Cross, one with us, He thrust Himself entirely upon the mercy and goodness of His Father. Whatever happened next happened to Him and us, at the same time.

CHAPTER 11

HIDDEN IN CHRIST

*Now not for his sake only was it written that it was credited to
him, but for our sake also, to whom it will be credited, as those who
believe in Him who raised Jesus our Lord from the dead, He who was
delivered over because of our transgressions, and was raised
because of our justification.*
Romans 4:23-25

"It is finished!" And He bowed His head and gave up His spirit.
John 19:30

Jesus so loved us that He was willing to be made our sin, and in becoming
our sin He became us. As He hung on the Cross He looked like a snake.
We have seen how the consequences of this unquenchable love meant Jesus
was roasted alive in the fire of God's wrath as the roasted Passover Lamb of
God. He was forever "melted" into us and we were forever 'melted' into Him.
Over and over, I've been so wrecked, overwhelmed by the indescribable and
incalculable love of God revealed by Christ through the Cross.

While Jesus was hanging on the Cross, something beyond our
comprehension happened for the first time in all of eternal history. The

Son of God experienced the Father turning His face from Him. There are some who teach that the Father never turned His face from Jesus. Matthew and Mark tell us that Jesus cried out on the Cross just before He died.

> *At the ninth hour Jesus cried out with a loud voice,*
> "E'loi, E'loi, Lama sabachthani?" *which is translated,*
> *"My God, My God, why have you forsaken me?"*
> *Mark 15:34*

The extreme love of God within the Son was perfectly manifested. Jesus, now fully bonded to us in love, was one with us. That love for us sustained Him as He embraced the unimaginable consequence: He was forsaken by the Father. Forsaken! The dictionary defines "forsaken" as *abandoned, deserted, left high and dry, turned one's back on, cast aside, break up with, jilt, strand, leave stranded, disown, disclaim, disavow, discard, wash one's hands of* and finally, *do away with.*

This is inconceivable. We cannot imagine what that must have been like for Jesus, the Son, who had been in the bosom of the Father for eternity. At any moment on the Cross, He could have called upon twelve legions of Angels and they would have rescued Him instantly. In that moment in which He fully became us, He was *exactly* you and me and the sin of the entire human race, for all history. The full wrath of the righteous fire of God had been poured upon Him. In that terrible condition, the Father had to turn His face from the Son. He looked like the snake.

"I Thirst!"

The greatest sacrifice of love Jesus paid, as He allowed Himself in extravagant love to be one with us, was that the Father could no longer look upon Him. The Father turned His face from Him. Jesus' cry, *"I thirst!"* (John 19:28) may well have been Him thirsting for the very presence of the Spirit. Moses cried out in desperation to the Lord,

> *If Your presence does not go with us, do not lead us up from here.*
> *Exodus 33:15*

The Lord then assured Moses that He would go with them and Moses asked the Lord to show him His glory. Then the Lord spoke to Moses,

> *But He said, "You cannot see My face, for no man can see Me and live!" Then the LORD said, "Behold, there is a place by Me, and you shall stand there on the rock; and it will come about, while My glory is passing by, that I will put you in the cleft of the rock and cover you with My hand until I have passed by. Then I will take My hand away and you shall see My back, but My face shall not be seen."*
> *Exodus 33:20-23*

This passage has such amazing prophetic insight in it. The Lord spoke with Moses face to face as a man speaks with his friend (Exodus 33:11) and yet here just a few verses later, we read that the Lord says that no man can see His face and live (Exodus 33:20). This seems contradictory, but the Lord's heart has always been for all humanity to know Him face to face. But this could not be achieved without the sacrifice, without Jesus being willing to go to the Cross.

The Spiritual Rock

Paul says the ancient Israelites drank from the spiritual Rock, and that spiritual Rock was Christ (1 Corinthians 10:4). We know that Moses brought water from a physical rock and yet Paul says that the Rock was Christ. The natural reveals the spiritual. The natural rock represented the spiritual Rock Himself.

Here in Exodus 33, the Lord says, *"Moses, there is a place that you can stand upon the rock..."* (Exodus 33:21) Prophetically, this Rock is none other than Christ Jesus.

He goes on to say, *"...And I will put you in the cleft of the rock"* (Exodus 33:22).

What a statement about the Cross, where one day, the Father would open up the Son, the Rock and place us all in the "cleft" of the Rock. Paul powerfully reinforces this when He says,

> *But by His doing you are in Christ Jesus, who became to us*
> *wisdom from God, and righteousness and sanctification,*
> *and redemption, so that, just as it is written,*
> *"Let Him who boasts, boast only in the Lord."*
> *1 Corinthians 1:30-31*

Paul says here, it was the Father who placed us in the Son. At the Cross, the Father placed us all in the cleft of the Rock that is Christ. There was not one square inch of Jesus' body that was not ripped open by the flaying at the whipping post. He was opened up so the Father could place us in Him forever.

It wasn't just that His perfect, dying body became a gigantic vacuum cleaner of our sin and us; the Father Himself *placed* us in His Son, through His wounds. He gave you access to the place prepared for you in the Son, in the Father, since before time began (John 14:2).

The Lord then says to Moses, *"I will cover you with my hand until I have passed by. Then I will take my hand away and you shall see my back, but my face shall not be seen"* (Exodus 33:22-23).

I have always struggled to understand this verse since Moses had already seen His face (Exodus 33:11). I have always simply understood that somehow Moses was getting to see God in a greater measure than before, with greater glory than ever before.

When Jesus met the two disciples on the road to Emmaus, Luke says,

Then beginning with Moses and with all the prophets, He explained
to them the things concerning Himself in all the Scriptures.
Luke 24:27

He clearly states that all the scriptures are written concerning Jesus. Could it be that in Exodus 33 the Lord is speaking directly to Moses about there being a place on the Rock? A place where he can stand, and that the Lord would then place him in the cleft in the Rock and cover him with His hand. He is speaking prophetically to Moses, to all Israel and to all humanity.

Then the focus shifts and for the rest of the verse, it appears that he may now be addressing the Rock Himself. This would mean He was saying to Jesus, *"Son, in that day, when they are hidden in the cleft that I will open up in you, the Rock, I will seal them in you with My hand. You will lose sight of My face for a moment, so that they will see My face forever."*

The first Adam, together with Eve, sinned, and they were removed from the Garden. They experienced abandonment and rejection and all the effects of the curse of sin. We've been experiencing that rejection and abandonment one way or another in each of our lives ever since. The Last Adam, Jesus Christ, became our curse and sin and experienced our abandonment and rejection upon the Cross, as us. By doing so, He made a way for us who had become orphans to be brought home as sons forever of the Father.

Jesus was willing for the Father to hide us in Him, the Rock of Ages, here in time and space at the Cross, as He hung and died, so that we could see the Father's beautiful face for all Eternity.

For you have died, and your life is hidden with Christ in God.
When Christ who is your life appears,
then you also will appear with him in glory.
Colossians 3:3-4

We are hidden in Christ forever. If you're "hidden," it implies that someone is looking for you—and someone is (1 Peter 5:8). But Satan can't find us anymore now that we're in Christ; it would be like looking for a light bulb in the sun!

What a Savior Jesus is! His abandonment here on earth into our death, secured our adoption in the Father's house and family forever. He was the Forsaken Son so that we could forever become the adopted sons and daughters. He was cursed, rejected and forsaken, so that we could be blessed, accepted and adopted, kept forever. You are blessed and accepted by the Father forever because you believe in His Son who made that possible at the Cross.

"It is Finished!"

When Jesus cried out, *"It is finished,"* He had become so fully one with us, our sin, our death and our very nature that He literally was us. Love Himself consumed us. At this point He stood before the Father as us, for us and with us. He was fully one with us. He was one with our very sin. His destiny was utterly one with ours.

If this is true, then *it was impossible after Jesus said, "It is finished," for the Father to ever raise Jesus from the dead without raising you and me from the dead with Him!*

Three days later the Father raised Jesus from the dead, just like He promised. The Holy Spirit filled that tomb with galaxy creating power and *Boom!* Jesus' dead body was raised from the dead for all Eternity. Eternal

Life Himself was raised bodily, no longer made in the likeness of sinful flesh, but now clothed in His glorious resurrected body.

> *The immeasurable greatness of his power toward us who believe,*
> *according to the working of his great might that he worked in Christ*
> *when he raised him from the dead and seated him at his right hand*
> *in the heavenly places ... and raised us up with him and seated us*
> *with him in the heavenly places in Christ Jesus.*
> *Ephesians 1:19, 2:6*

Jesus Christ was raised from the dead on the third day, just as the scriptures said. Death could not hold on to Him, because none of the sin was His own. He had died as our sin, but He Himself had triumphed over sin. His perfect life had triumphed over all temptation, without ever sinning. Death could not hold Him because none of the sin He carried at the Cross was His own. He had perfectly fulfilled the Law throughout His life and was without sin.

His resurrection was proof of His sinless life. His resurrection was the testimony for all Eternity that he has lived a sinless, perfect life, the one life that the Creator was worthy of the created living. The life we each owed God, but could never pay Him. Jesus gave the Father that perfect life, so that the Father has credited each of our lives with the very life that Jesus Himself lived, as if it was us who lived it. The Father has already credited you with Jesus' perfect life, lived out on earth. The life Jesus lived has been credited to the account of your life as if it was you that had lived it, literally!

Let's summarize this mind-blowing mystery. In His love for the Father and His love for us, Jesus was willing to become so completely one with us that He literally was us. He took our place so perfectly because in dying, He took our sin, and in taking our sin, He took us too. He became sin for us; in becoming sin, He became us. You can't separate the sin from the sinner. This meant that He had to drink the cup of wrath, which He finished so completely there was not even a drop left. He was roasted alive in the Fire of God and was made like the bronze snake.

The two metals of tin and copper that are melted together to make bronze is such a powerful picture of what happened to us and Christ in the Fire of God's wrath, poured out upon the Son of God on the Cross. The two trees were set ablaze. The Tree of Life was on fire, yet it didn't burn. But the Trees of the Knowledge of Good and Evil, you and me, were burned up forever. I say it again, when Jesus said those incredible words, *"It is finished,"* it was impossible for the Father to raise Him from the dead without raising us too. Mission accomplished!

When the Holy Spirit raised Jesus from the dead, He also raised you and me from the dead with Him. Our spirits are alive in Christ Jesus, one with Him forever. We are one Spirit with Him forever (1 Corinthians 6:17). Paul goes so far as to say in the book of Romans that the Father raised Jesus from the dead to get us!

It will be counted to us who believe in him who raised from the dead
Jesus our Lord, who was delivered up for our trespasses
and raised for our justification.
Romans 4:25

In this incredible verse, Paul says that the Father raised Jesus from the dead because He loved you and wanted you. Of course, He loved Jesus, but He could not raise Jesus from the dead without raising you from the dead with Him. At the same time, He could not raise you from the dead without raising Jesus from the dead. May this awesome truth that speaks of the eternal love of the Father forever burn in your heart. The Father raised Jesus from the dead to get you.

The resurrection is proof that Jesus fully obeyed the Father in all things, lived His whole life without sin as the Spotless Lamb of God. If He had sinned once, He could not have saved Himself, and therefore certainly could not have raised us. He would have broken the Law and been condemned to eternal destruction in death together with us all.

Paul says to the men of Athens at the Areopagus,

> *Because He has fixed a day in which He will judge the world in*
> *righteousness through a Man whom He has appointed,*
> *having furnished proof to all men*
> *by raising Him from the dead.*
> *Acts 17:31 (NASB)*

The resurrection is living proof that the Father accepted Jesus' body as a perfect sacrifice for all humanity. It is also proof that the Father has accepted us together with Him, because we are one with Christ forever. The Father's acceptance of Christ is His acceptance of us.

He was raised in His body. Our resurrection bodies are waiting for us after that great Judgment Day, when our new bodies will be our Eternal dwelling places with the Father and the Lamb as our Eternal Home forever, on the New Earth that will be the New Heaven. We have not yet been raised bodily, but our spirits have been raised with Christ, joined with Him forever (Ephesians 2:6). We are, right now, seated in the current Heaven, reigning with Him, while we wait for our bodily resurrection one day.

Let's recall the moment of Jesus' baptism, when the Father spoke His words of love and affirmation over Jesus, saying,

> *You are my beloved Son; with you I am well pleased.*
> *Mark 1:11*

The Father did not speak as the Son went down into the waters of the river Jordan. He said them when Jesus came up out of the water, representationally covered in us! It was not when He went into the river that the Father spoke. If He had done, representationally He would have only been speaking of the Son, alone. Jesus before death and burial was alone the Son of God, utterly distinct from all others. However, after He said, *"It is finished"* and hung His head and died, as us, for us, with us, He was now fully one with us.

After He came up out of the water, the Heavens opened and the Spirit descended like a dove and the voice spoke. Representationally this was the moment of His resurrection. That glorious day when Jesus' death would rend the heavens open, symbolized by the temple curtain being torn in two after Jesus' death, the Spirit would come and fill the tomb and raise the Son and the sons from the dead. The Father then spoke the words of love and affirmation over both the Son and the sons, you and me, that He was raised eternally one with. That means that the Father says over you and me, *"You are My beloved son, whom I love, in whom I am well pleased."*

How incredible is that? The Father raised His Son to get you, and He loves you as much as He loves Jesus.

Paul says in Galatians that because of His love for us, Jesus gave Himself for us. It was not only because the Father loves us that Jesus went to the Cross. Jesus went to the Cross, because He too loved us.

I have been crucified with Christ. It is no longer I who live, but Christ who lives in me. And the life I now live in the flesh I live by faith in the Son of God, who loved me and gave himself for me.
Galatians 2:20

Jesus Himself loved you so much that He gave Himself willingly to die at the Cross in your place, eternally separating you from your sin and eternally joining you to Him. It was the greatest demonstration of love by the Father, who gave His Son and by the Son, who willingly laid down His life for His friends. By this great act of love, we've all become the sons of God in the Son forever.

It is only because of our finite experience of love we have a difficult time understanding that the very reason the Son gave His life for us, is so we could enjoy the love of His Father forever, just like He Himself has. Imagine what you and I could achieve in this life if we really knew we are *one life* with Christ. We are consumed by love, one with Christ forever. *One with Him forever*, all that is His is ours and all that is ours is His.

The Devil Lost it All!

The final aspect of the price of Oneness is that the devil, having thought he'd won, lost it all. Hallelujah!

Created by God for God, we have always belonged to God. When Satan deceived Adam and Eve into becoming one with sin by eating the fruit of the Tree of Knowledge of God and Evil, he attempted to permanently steal us from God. Jesus said Satan is a thief, who comes to steal, kill and destroy, but that Jesus came to give us life and life in abundance (John 10:10).

I learned years ago when I was a police officer that when property is stolen, a thief never becomes the rightful owner of the property that they have stolen. Stolen property still belongs to the rightful owner it was stolen from. A thief can never own the property they steal and therefore they can never legitimately sell it either. A person who buys stolen property never becomes the legitimate owner of that property. It remains stolen goods even if another person buys it in good conscience. If the property is found in their possession they have to return it to the original, rightful owner and they lose everything they invested in purchasing the goods.

When Satan stole humanity from God by deception, he never became the rightful owner of humanity. We all belong to God, each one of us. God has remained the rightful owner of all humanity throughout history. Jesus restored us back to the rightful owner when He gave His life and paid the Father the ransom price of our rebellion with His own precious blood. We owed that price to the Father but could never pay. He gave the

Father what we could never give Him, a perfect human life and spotless blood. Jesus took back from the devil what rightfully belonged to Himself and the Father, all of humanity, and to those who would receive Him, who would believe in His name, He gave them the right to become children of God (John 1:12).

The devil lost everything he had "invested" in humanity whilst humanity was in his possession. He lost it all. He is the great loser. He will lose even his own life for his rebellion and the author of sin will be thrown into the everlasting lake of burning fiery sulfur (Revelation 20:10). Hallelujah! We belong to Jesus forever. One with Christ, we have been returned to our rightful owner, His Father and our Father.

PART THREE

THE POWER OF ONENESS

CHAPTER 12

MATURING IN ONENESS

The same glory you gave me, I gave them, so they'll be as unified and
together as we are—I in them and you in me.
Then they'll be mature in this Oneness.
John 17:23 (The Message)

In Christ, you are dead. You no longer live. The "old man" you were born in, Adam, died with Christ at the Cross. The perfect life of the Son of God is your life now. Christ dwells in you so you can resist and overcome all the temptation of the devil and this world. In Christ, you are the righteousness of God.

We Have a Powerful New Identity

Just like most Christians, I used to think righteousness was hard and sin was easy. Now we are one with Christ, His righteousness is our new nature, so *righteousness* is easy for us. *Sin* is really hard!

Our new identity in Christ Jesus is so powerful. In the "old nature" of Adam, we had to rely on our own finite strength for everything, even to sin. One with Christ, we have infinite, resurrection power in us to do the right thing. The very same Holy Spirit that raised Jesus from the dead is our nature now, not sin. The Kingdom of Heaven is our natural passion. The Kingdom of Heaven is righteousness, peace and joy in the Holy Spirit (Romans 14:17).

We are the righteousness of God in Christ. Once we were sin, in sin. Now we are righteous, in righteousness. Righteousness comes more naturally to us in the Spirit than sin came to us in the flesh. Peace comes more naturally to us now than stress and anxiety came to us in the flesh! Joy is easier in Christ than grumpiness was in the "old man." Why don't you say goodbye once and for all to Mr. Grumpy! Don't keep him around as your excuse crutch any longer! As a man thinks so he is (Proverbs 23:7).

Just as we once produced the fruits of unrighteousness we now even more easily can produce the fruits of righteousness. The Spirit Himself living in us produces His righteous fruit: love, joy, peace, patience, kindness, goodness, gentleness, faithfulness and self-control. It is His fruit! We are not the producers of the fruit, the Holy Spirit is. Our lives in Christ Jesus are the gardens for His fruit to grow. Just as the Father prepared a body for Christ, so He could do His will (Hebrews 10:5-7), so too now we are Christ's workmanship, created in Him, to do good works that have been prepared in advance for us to do (Ephesians 2:10). Our life now is not about *trying* to serve Him, but letting His Spirit serve us as we live our lives obeying our Father's will.

Knowledge of the Law Leads to Consciousness of Sin

Before we put our faith in Christ our life was dominated by sin. The Law was introduced, so that sin would be exposed as utterly sinful (Romans 7:13). Knowing the right thing to do from a religious mindset, because one knows the Law, allows sin an even greater opportunity to cause every kind of temptation, stumbling and then hold us in guilt (Romans 7:11).

This is especially true for a person who becomes a believer without being taught the truth about their Oneness with Christ. Assuming they join a church, they will quickly become aware of "right and wrong." This is so dangerous if they are not taught they are righteous in *Christ's* righteousness and holy in *His* holiness.

Satan, seizing the opportunity afforded by their new consciousness of the laws of God, will try to cause them to feel even more condemned than they ever did before they came to Christ, accusing them in their hearts of every minor "sin." The believer soon lives in a mentality of defeat and shame. The enemy will then undermine all their understanding of the goodness of God and their ability to stand before Him in His presence. They will quickly feel unworthy of all Jesus had done for them and spiral downwards into discouragement and disappointment. Many Christians live in this defeated state.

We all have times where it feels that we are overwhelmed by sin in all its various guises, whether it's sexual lusts or lust for some new house, car, motorcycle or article of clothing, or whether it is temper tantrums, gossip or jealousies.

Many times in our dealings with sin, we go around what I call "the merry-go-round of sin." You know what that looks like. You fall into temptation, then you realize that you have sinned again. You go before the Lord, confessing and repenting again of the same old sin, promising, "I will never do that again Lord Jesus!" only to fall headlong into it again, meaning you're back in the same old place full of shame. Many times we go round and round this cycle. Our problem is we are focusing on the sin and trying our best not to fall into the sin. This only leads to defeat.

The enemy, knowing this, works hard to keep us focused on our sin. He is happy for us to keep trying to fight our sin, because as long as he can keep our eyes on our sin, we will never live in the truth that at the Cross, Jesus took our sin *and* our "old man of sin" to the grave as the Last Adam, thereby forever freeing us from the power of sin. Paul says in Romans,

We know that our old self was crucified with him in order that the
body of sin might be brought to nothing, so that we would no longer
be enslaved to sin. For one who has died has been set free from sin.
Romans 6:6-7

A slave must always keep their eye on their master. When we were alive in our "old man" state in Adam, we were slaves to sin. Our eyes were constantly on sin and serving sin as our master. Whatever sin told us to do or say we obeyed. We were sin's slaves.

When Christ died He set us free from our slavery to sin. We were never meant to be sin's slaves. We were not created to be slaves to sin and Satan. We were created to be sons of God and joyful slaves of righteousness.

Rather than focusing on our sin, in Christ we focus on Him, asking Him to take all desire for the sin we are struggling with. We are in union with Him. He has forever defeated every sin for us and therefore He is able to keep it from us and us from it.

I've realized there is something better than trying hard not to lust and that is not to notice the object of lustful desire in the first place. God made you for righteousness, and it is your normal passion to desire it rather than sin. The Spirit of God will help you find sin utterly repulsive. Ask Him.

Fixing our Eyes on Jesus

Knowing who we are in Christ and fixing our eyes on who we will be one day in Him for all eternity, looking just like Him, causes us to treasure purity. Being filled with the burning love of God for the poor and being overwhelmed with God's love for every human being is so all consuming it keeps us far from sin. Being occupied with Christ and His heart of righteousness is the best way of staying free from temptation.

Once you become used to a diet of the finest filet steak, you will never be tempted to change it for a tin of dog food.

In Christ, our lives are no longer ruled by trying to live according to what we think is the "right thing to do." Rather, it is living by faith in our Oneness with Christ, who, because He lives to please His Father, is constantly right. Our life is one with Him. In Him we walk by the Spirit and instead of breaking the law of God, we are the very righteousness of God in Him and His will is our greatest privilege and passion. He has done it all for us, now and for eternity.

When our hearts are burning with the passions of righteousness, we notice the things that captivate God's heart, righteousness and its passions, instead of sin and its passions. We become immersed with what righteousness burns for: justice, hope, love, setting the captives free, and ministering in the power of the Spirit through astonishing miracles, signs, and wonders.

The enemy Satan knows if he can keep us focused on *trying* to overcome sin, he will keep us from our true mission. He will keep us defeated and depressed because we are constantly focusing on our failures against temptation, instead of focusing on Jesus and His victory over all our sin and temptation.

Our mission is not focusing on sin. It is finished. That battle is eternally won. Christ has already overcome all the power of the enemy. He has conquered sin and set us eternally free from its power. The power of sin is finished. Christ has done it all for you. Our part is to focus our faith and set all the affections of our hearts on Christ. Our mission in Christ is bringing His love, grace and righteousness to our world by His Spirit and, by the Spirit, doing His supernatural works, so that the world can truly know the power of the Spirit and the joy of the King and His glorious Kingdom, full of love and goodness for them.

So Why Does it Seem so Difficult?

"That all sounds fantastic," I hear you saying. "But why am I struggling so much?"

If we are one with Christ why do we still struggle so much with ourselves, our sin and the sins of others? Why do we believe many lies in our hearts still? Why is our life not manifesting the perfection of Christ? Why doesn't my wife think I'm perfect?

One morning Kate and I were sitting in bed with our cups of tea in hand, having a leisurely quiet time with the Lord together. Kate was reading from The Message, a translation of the Bible in modern, everyday English. Eugene Petersen, the author of The Message writes,

> *The same glory you gave me, I gave them, so they'll be as unified and*
> *together as we are—I in them and you in me.*
> *Then they'll be mature in this Oneness.*
> *John 17:23 (The Message)*

Suddenly in that moment, we realized this verse holds a great key to understanding our walk in the Spirit in Christ Jesus. The words leapt at us: *"Then they'll be mature in this Oneness."*

Paul says, first comes the natural and then the spiritual (1 Corinthians 15:46). When a man and a woman consummate their marriage the Bible tells us that the two become one flesh.

> *Therefore a man shall leave his father and mother and hold fast to his*
> *wife, and the two shall become one flesh. This mystery is profound,*
> *and I am saying that it refers to Christ and the church.*
> *Ephesians 5:31-32*

When Kate and I married we became one flesh. If you had met us on our honeymoon, you would have been left with no doubt we were one flesh. We were so in love and mindful of each other.

However, when we got back home we had our first major argument and before we knew it we were hurting each other verbally and emotionally, for ten years, until we got to Toronto and we were both revolutionized in the Father's love and began the journey of getting our hearts healed.

Throughout those ten years of arguing and bickering, we never once ceased to be one flesh. Our fights never altered our union with each other; however, they did prevent us from manifesting our union because we were so immature in our Oneness.

In exactly the same way, our union with Christ is absolute. However, just as a husband and wife do not always manifest their union, so we do not always manifest the fullness of our union with Christ. *We have to mature in this Oneness* in the Spirit, just as Kate and I have had to mature in our Oneness in the flesh.

Our sin never altered our Oneness in the flesh, but it masked our Oneness. In the same way our sin never alters our Oneness with Christ through the Spirit, yet it masks our Oneness and hugely prevents us from living in the full joy of our Oneness.

We're one with Christ but we're still living in a world full of sin. We are not responsible for the sins that others do to us and we have little choice over whether they sin against us or not. We are more often than not, the innocent victims. However, what we do have responsibility for in every situation is our responses to the sins of others. This we do have complete choice about.

Strongholds of the Heart and Mind

Unfortunately, unlike Jesus Christ, who never reacted in sin to the sin that was done to Him, we react badly to the sins of others. We most often react in unforgiveness and judgments that lead to bitterness and we close our hearts to love. We form self-determined vows in our hearts we can't possibly uphold. They usually start with, "I will never..." or "I will always..." in this way giving the enemy all manner of legal rights to keep us in bondage. We compound this by believing the lies the enemy sows into our hearts in these times of bitterness. They are "lies of the heart."

What gives so much power to the enemy is our will agreement, the exercise of our own will to agree with the accusations of the enemy. The lies the enemy sows into our hearts when we are hurt can only find a foothold if we place our will agreement around them. We can liken these to a house made of bricks and mortar. The lies of the enemy are the "bricks" he sows into our hearts when we are hurt. Our will agreement is the "mortar" that binds those lies into our minds and our emotions. They become part of us because our will holds them in place. They become a stronghold of the enemy in us.

The scriptures tell us that after failing to tempt Jesus, Satan left him until an opportune time. He never found that opportunity with Jesus, but he looks for an opportune time in each of our lives.

When I was a young boy at boarding school, nasty spirits of abandonment, rejection and unworthiness jumped on the opportunity to whisper into my heart, "You're abandoned and rejected, because you are unworthy. Even your own parents have abandoned you and rejected you, because you are nothing and nobody. You will always be rejected and find yourself abandoned, because you are utterly unworthy."

I readily believed these terrible lies and the result was these spirits were able to build their strongholds in my mind and heart. These spirits came and occupied the stronghold they had built because it was their "house" in me. They brought their friends, shame, fear, control and many false comforts. The enemy builds these strongholds in the minds and hearts of every human being one way and another.

Thankfully, with help from loving ministry counselors, I've been able to get free of these strongholds and the nasty "friends" that once lived in them!

The Soul is the Battleground

The demons cannot *possess* a human being, as we often mistakenly give them credit for. All human beings are created by God alone and are His possessions. Some translations say "possessed by a demon," but it is more accurately "oppressed by a demon" as the English Standard Version translates this word. God alone is the possessor of our souls. The enemy is the oppressor.

The demonic is able to gain access to the lives of human beings through our minds and hearts. Our sin gives the enemy legal grounds to access our lives and oppress us as we agree with his lies. Because the strongholds that are built in us are in the realm of the soul the enemy is able to continue operating in the life of a human being, even after they become a born again Christian.

Jesus spoke about these strongholds, or "houses," in Matthew 12,

When the unclean spirit has gone out of a person, it passes through waterless places seeking rest, but finds none. Then it says, "I will return to my house from which I came." And when it comes, it finds the house empty, swept, and put in order. Then it goes and brings with it seven other spirits more evil than itself, and they enter and dwell there, and the last state of that person is worse than the first.
Matthew 12:43-45

Notice the unclean spirit says, *"I will return to my house from which I came."* I always thought Jesus was referring to the human being when the unclean spirit said, "my house." The Holy Spirit showed me I was wrong. Jesus knew that every human being belongs to God alone. So what "house" is the unclean spirit calling "my house"? The strongholds they have built in the realm of the soul, the mind, the emotions as well as the flesh.

When a person gives their life to Christ and is born again their spirit is united to Christ and their spirit man is alive in Him. The soul is the battleground, where the "old man" has been crucified with Christ (Galatians 2:20, Romans 6:6). The enemy tries to make us think the "old man" is still alive. The flesh, or old nature, the old man, is at war against the Spirit.

For the desires of the flesh are against the Spirit, and the desires of the
Spirit are against the flesh, for these are opposed to each other.
Galatians 5:17

The battle is over the will. Our will is one of the greatest gifts God has given to us. It is part of the soul. It can be influenced and controlled by the mind, the heart, our bodies and our spirits. We can control our will, or be controlled through our will.

Before a person is born again their will is controlled by the sinful nature. Through the will, their entire soul is controlled by the sinful nature and any evil spirits occupying the strongholds that have been built over the lifetime of the individual. Sin is natural and the will is bent upon sin. The enemy sows the lies into the mind and heart of any human being. These lies are like a "brick" of a house. The will's agreement with the lie is the "mortar" that surrounds the "brick" and keeps it in place in the minds and hearts. This becomes the basis for the stronghold or house that the demonic uses to oppress that individual.

Once a person becomes born again, they are no longer controlled by the flesh or the sinful nature, but rather have crucified the flesh. Paul says to the Galatians,

Those who belong to Christ Jesus have crucified the flesh
with its passions and desires.
Galatians 5:24

The soul can now be entirely given over to the Spirit as we walk by the Spirit and not according to our sinful nature (Galatians 5:16, 25). The power that sin once had is broken through our union with Christ, but our minds must be renewed so our wills may be occupied fully with the will of God. We must choose the mind of Christ and not allow our minds to be controlled by the lies of the enemy, like our old fleshly mind was before we came to Christ. We have the mind of Christ now (1 Corinthians 2:16).

Three passages of scripture show us how this works.

For those who live according to the flesh set their minds on the
things of the flesh, but those who live according to the
Spirit set their minds on the things of the Spirit.
For to set the mind on the flesh is death, but
to set the mind on the Spirit is life and peace.
For the mind that is set on the flesh is hostile to God.
Romans 8:5-7

Do not be conformed to this world, but be transformed by the
renewal of your mind, that by testing you may discern what is the
will of God, what is good and acceptable and perfect.
Romans 12:2

For the weapons of our warfare are not of the flesh but have divine
power to destroy strongholds. We destroy arguments and every lofty
opinion raised against the knowledge of God, and take
every thought captive to obey Christ.
2 Corinthians 10:4-5

The spirit is joined to Christ and one with Him but the strongholds the enemy has built in the mind and the heart remain in place as long as our will continues to agree with those old lies, even if we are Christians. We renew our minds when we confess our sin of believing the enemy's lies, withdraw our will from those lies, forgive those who may have contributed to us forming those lies and finally align our minds with the truth of God's word. This removes the mortar from the stronghold so now all that remains are loose bricks that are easily pushed over with one puff of wind. The demonic spirit, which had such a hold on us, now has no stronghold to live in and we can command it to go at once out on the breath. "Better out than in," that's what I say!

Healing of the Soul

This dynamic of conquering the mind and the heart is not automatic. Paul is very clear that whilst the flesh is crucified, it is our responsibility to bring our minds into full alignment with this reality. He also calls it "warfare" and refers to the "strongholds" being "destroyed" so we can be "transformed." This is not the means of our salvation; this is the process of maturing in our salvation. Christ has won our salvation for us, but we must appropriate the fullness of the spiritual reality of our union with Him, so it is manifest into every area of our lives through the faculties of the soul.

This works in the same way physical healing works. We know that because of the finished work of Christ at the Cross, our physical bodies can be healed as we apply the power of the Cross to our lives. The presence of sickness has not yet been removed from the earth; that will happen at the last trumpet when even death is finally destroyed (1 Corinthians 15:25-26, 52-57). Every living human, including Christians, can still suffer sickness or injury; however, through the Cross provision has been made by Christ for us to be healed and delivered, as long as we appropriate the power of the Cross.

In exactly the same way we must appropriate the power of the Cross to every area of our hurting, sick or injured hearts and minds. The event of the finished work of the Cross gives us the power to conquer every area of our souls and bodies, it does not absolve us of our responsibility to partner with the Holy Spirit as we walk the way of the Cross bringing all things into the light.

The grace that saved us through faith, from the power of sin and death through the Cross, is the same grace that is available for us to overcome all temptation of sin and all symptoms of sickness in the presence of sin and sickness on earth.

Grace is never permission to do whatever we want. *It is the power to do the right thing.* Grace never gives us license to sin. Righteousness is the manifestation of true grace in our lives. Grace never endorses our choices to walk into sin. Grace never allows sin to be counted as righteousness. That would be an insult to the Spirit of Grace (Hebrews 10:29).

Because the Holy Spirit Himself is the Spirit of Grace, He gives us the power to keep walking on paths of righteousness, if we say no to sin and yes to Him. Grace does not excuse us from repentance, which means "turning around" if we are walking in the wrong direction. Grace is the power to turn around. Yesterday's grace never excuses today's unconfessed sin. Grace gives us the power to confess and repent so that we can receive forgiveness today for today's sin.

Under the Law, there is no forgiveness of sins without the shedding of blood (Hebrews 9:22). However Christ secured for us an eternal redemption through the shedding of His own blood at the Cross.

But when Christ appeared as a high priest of the good things that have come, then through the greater and more perfect tent (not made with hands, that is, not of this creation) He entered once for all into the holy places, not by means of the blood of goats and calves but by means of His own blood, thus securing an eternal redemption.

Hebrews 9:11-12

Eternally, we are already forgiven for all our sin once and for all, past, present and future. The blood of Jesus Christ has paid for all our sin and sanctified us all. By grace, His single sacrifice has paid for us all for all time. According to the will of our Father, Christ has made us all perfect forever in our Father's sight.

And by that will we have been sanctified through the offering
of the body of Jesus Christ once for all.
Hebrews 10:10

But when Christ had offered for all time a single sacrifice for sins,
he sat down at the right hand of God, waiting from that time until
his enemies should be made a footstool for his feet. For by a single
offering he has perfected for all time those who are being sanctified.
Hebrews 10:12-14

Notice in verse 10 the writer of Hebrews says that by the will of the Father we have all been sanctified. Then verse 14 confirms this by declaring that we have been perfected for all time. The writer then says these perfected ones are being sanctified. This seems at first to be a contradiction, yet it is another way of saying we are maturing in this Oneness.

Before the presence of our Father in the Heavens, we are already perfected forever. We are eternally redeemed and sanctified, or made holy as some translations say. We are made one with Christ forever and are perfect in Him in the spirit. However, here on earth in time and space, in our daily lives, we are being sanctified as we mature in this Oneness.

There are those who preach that Christians have no need to repent because we are no longer sinners. It is true that before the Father, we are no longer sinners, however in this world we can still sin because we are still open to temptation in the presence of sin. Sin is still sin. There is no such thing as sanctified, righteous sin! Therefore if we sin, we must confess it and repent from our sinful ways and receive the forgiveness of sins that Christ achieved for us through his shed blood on the Cross. The Apostle John is very clear that we must confess our sins and if we say we have no sin, we deceive ourselves.

> *But if we walk in the light, as he is in the light, we have fellowship with one another, and the blood of Jesus his Son cleanses us from all sin. If we say we have no sin, we deceive ourselves, and the truth is not in us. If we confess our sins, he is faithful and just to forgive us our sins and to cleanse us from all unrighteousness.*
>
> *1 John 1:7-9*

We are responsible for cooperating with the Holy Spirit in the process of maturing in our Oneness.

We've learned from John and Carol Arnott to open our hearts so they can be healed up, regularly taking a week or so to allow trusted counselors to help us through our issues and wounds in our hearts. This allows the Holy Spirit to shine His light on the dark areas of our hearts, our wrong reactions, our secret sins and ambitions. The fruit of this is tremendous. Our marriage is so much healthier and our lives manifest so much more of the reality of our Oneness with Christ.

Every member of the Catch The Fire senior leadership team across the world is required to commit to having regular healing weeks for the heart. We have so much more fun working together as a result. We are all maturing in this Oneness.

The Lord showed me a powerful scripture one day. Paul tells us succinctly that Christians can be defiled in body and spirit, which by implication includes the soul because it is the realm where the body and the spirit meet. He says,

Since we have these promises, beloved, let us cleanse ourselves from
every defilement of body and spirit, bringing holiness to
completion in the fear of God.
2 Corinthians 7:1

Paul includes himself here. He doesn't say to the Corinthian church, *"cleanse yourselves from every defilement."* He says *"let* us *cleanse* ourselves *from every defilement."* This means even the Apostle Paul believed he needed to cleanse himself regularly from the things that defiled him. He says this only one and a half chapters after he wrote we are therefore new creations in Christ. The old has gone and the new has come (2 Corinthians 5:17).

We cleanse ourselves by confessing our sin, repenting of our sin, forgiving those who have hurt us and choosing to align our minds with the truth of God's word, setting our minds on things above where we are seated in Christ (Colossians 3:1), taking captive every thought and making it obedient to God. We deceive ourselves if we think we no longer can be defiled or we have no need for repentance, or healing from life's hurts, especially our wrong reactions to those hurts.

We are new creations, made just like Him forever in the spirit, but we must mature in the manifestation of our Oneness with Christ here on earth. The world around us will see this truth shining in every area of our lives. Thankfully the Gospel is so complete that even in our maturing, the Holy Spirit is the power in us bringing us to maturity. He will complete the good work that He has started in us.

I am sure of this, that he who began a good work in you will bring it
to completion at the day of Jesus Christ.
Philippians 1:6

CHAPTER 13

A NEW PARADIGM

You sent to John, and he has borne witness to the truth. Not that the
testimony that I receive is from man, but I say these things so that
you may be saved. He was a burning and shining lamp, and
you were willing to rejoice for a while in his light. But the
testimony that I have is greater than that of John.
John 5:33-36a

The words of the Apostle John leapt off the page. I saw something I'd never seen before. I sat stunned, realizing that the church across the world today seems to be modeling itself on the ministry of John the Baptist, rather than sharing in and manifesting the ministry of Jesus Christ.

Jesus said John the Baptist was a *"burning and shining light"* (John 5:35) because he testified about the True Light who would come to give light to the entire world. John's ministry was to reveal Jesus, to point us to Him. His job was to preach that the Kingdom was coming, because the King was coming.

Jesus came as the King to *reveal His Father* and to manifest His glorious Kingdom. He changed absolutely everything! He came to give us the Holy Spirit. He came to show us who we truly are as sons in the Son. He came to show us that the Father wants to do the same miracles through us, by the very same Holy Spirit. He came to give us the means to live a life on earth that only He can live. He came to make us one with Him so we could live eternally in His Father's heart and be filled with His Spirit.

John the Baptist was a mighty man; even Jesus called him the greatest man who had lived up to that point.

> *Truly, I say to you, among those born of women there has arisen*
> *no one greater than John the Baptist. Yet the one who is least in the*
> *kingdom of heaven is greater than he.*
> Matthew 11:11

I greatly honor John the Baptist in the Lord. However, his ministry model was never meant to be our model. Jesus came to save us, bring us directly to the Father, fill us with the Spirit and send us out into this world with His supernatural love.

I've noticed that many people believe in Jesus so they can go to Heaven, as though they have their "fire insurance" in their "back pocket," hoping to avoid Hell when they die. However, James says even the devil believes in God and shudders (James 2:19)!

People *go to church* instead of *being the church*. Many Christians are trying to *go to Heaven* one day instead of realizing they are already in Heaven, one with Christ so they can have the joy of going to the world, manifesting Heaven today, right now!

Preaching that everyone must believe in Jesus to be saved so they can go to Heaven is true, but it is just the beginning. It is so far short of the fullness of the Gospel. There is much more! The whole world is waiting to know they've been saved into a new paradigm. Not old religion but a vibrant relationship of endless unlimited power over all darkness through their Oneness with the King of a glorious Kingdom that's within their reach here on earth. A Kingdom that Jesus wants to give us to rule over with Him.

The Gospel is not about humanity trying to get to Heaven. That was Lucifer's ambition. He said, *"I will ascend into Heaven"* (Isaiah 14:13).

All the religions of this world are based on their followers trying to get to Heaven somehow, by their beliefs in some god, their own good works, sacrifice or spirituality. The good news of the Gospel as we've seen is that God came to us as a Man. Jesus Christ came into this world, fully God and fully Man. God loved the world so much He gave His only Son, Jesus Christ, that whoever believes in Him will not perish, but will have eternal life (John 3:16).

Jesus Christ lived the perfect life for us and is the only worthy Savior of humanity, because He loved us and gave Himself for us on the Cross, fully paying for all of humanity's sin with His own precious blood and the sacrifice of His body when He died. At the Cross, Jesus who knew no sin was made sin for us and we died with Him. He died one with us, for us.

The Father raised Jesus from the dead on the third day because He lived the perfect life, including dying for our sin, and none of the sin He paid for was His own. In raising Him from the dead, the Father raised *all those who believe* in Jesus Christ from the dead with Him. Because we were one with Him in His death, the Father raised us up one with Him in His life. Whoever receives Jesus, who believes in His name, Jesus gives them the right to become sons of God (John 1:12).

When Christ ascended into Heaven, 40 days after His resurrection, we also ascended into Heaven with Him in Oneness with Him, the many sons led to glory (Hebrews 2:10). Having returned into the Father's presence, Jesus was glorified with the glory that He has always had from Eternity with the Father, and we are glorified in Him. We are seated with Him right now in the Heavens (Ephesians 2:6, Colossians 3:1-3)!

The Son of God became the Son of Man so that the sons of men could become the sons of God. Jesus became one with us in our humanity and death, so that we could become one with Him in His divinity and eternal life.

Our lives are not about trying to get to God; the good news is God came to us. We are in Heaven, right now! As sons of God, we have the joy of bringing Heaven to earth, manifesting Jesus, so He can reveal the Father through us and change the world.

All of creation is waiting, longing for the sons of God to be revealed (Romans 8:19). The Father is unfolding His plan that Heaven and earth will be one forever, a place to dwell with us—sons just like His eternal Son—living for all eternity in and with Christ. Since we are one with Christ, we can enjoy so much of that future reality today.

> *John the Baptist came preaching in the wilderness*
> *"Repent, for the kingdom of heaven is at hand" ...*
> *the voice of one crying in the wilderness.*
> *Matthew 3:1-3*

Matthew says that John came *preaching*. The church today really loves *preaching*. John preached a message centered on repentance. As pastors, we love to *preach*, especially a message of repentance. As congregations, we love to listen to preaching, especially if it makes us feel like we've been beaten up, reminded of all our terrible sin and then empowered to do better and be more successful in life.

John came baptizing in water, but referring to Jesus, He said,

> *One is coming that is mightier than I...*
> *He will baptize you in the Holy Spirit and with fire.*
> *Luke 3:16*

The church baptizes people using water in different ways, yet the very Oneness that water baptism represents, our sharing in Christ's death, burial and resurrection is rarely taught. Few Christians understand they are one with the Mighty One who baptizes with the Holy Spirit and with fire!

John was a *"voice of one calling in the wilderness."* The church today is in a "wilderness" of its own in its relationship with the world. It's even in a "wilderness" in its relationship with God and other churches! Most of the church around the world is dry and waterless, and religion abounds everywhere. Our religious best efforts are our trusted "fig leaves" of our own righteousness. People are trying to be righteous and "do the right thing" so they can go to Heaven, even using money for righteous acts to appease their consciences. Jeremiah summed this condition up when he prophesied against the Moabites.

> For because you have trusted in your works and your treasures,
> you also shall be taken (into captivity).
> Jeremiah 48:7 (addendum mine)

We easily replace relationship and friendship with the invisible God for a set of rules and regulations on which to anchor our hope, because we can't see Him and we're not sure if He really loves us and is pleased with us. We comfort ourselves that even though we're not perfect according to our own religious rules, at least we're better than those other Christians over there in that other denomination. At least we're better than all the other religions because we're right and they're wrong. And how we love to be right as humans! We hate being wrong, so we do our very best to show everyone how wonderfully right we are, whether in matters of religion, worship practices, politics, etc.

Not only is the church on the whole in a "wilderness," but also like John the Baptist, our leadership models are often a "voice of one." Most churches revolve around one leader, who preaches every week as a "voice of one." Their ministry is almost exclusively based on their preaching and teaching gift, expounding the scriptures each week in Sunday services and weekly Bible studies. It's a pulpit or platform ministry, with sound expository, inspirational, empowering or revelatory preaching, week after week.

Imagine what the world would look like if every Christian sitting in those seats week after week knew they were sons of God, one with Christ, filled with the Spirit—individually and corporately—and immersed in Love Himself. Imagine if they knew their mission was boldly going to the world with miracles, signs and wonders, bringing Heaven on the earth, instead of "going to church" week after week. Imagine if every Christian on earth today knew they were one with Christ and were burning with love.

What would the world look like if the sons of God began to truly live as sons in our Father's Kingdom? Sons, living from His presence and resources, manifesting Jesus through our lives instead of trying to tell the world we've got the "right" message? People don't need a great deal of being "preached" at to give their lives to Jesus when we show them their loving Father, demonstrating the Spirit's power, healing their sick, injured or broken lives and the lives of those around them.

Jesus' ministry could not be more different from John's ministry. We were never meant to copy John's. We're in a New Covenant that is a new paradigm of Oneness with God. Jesus came to reveal the Father. The Father sent Jesus to show the Father's love for the world. He sent Jesus to save the world, not condemn it (John 3:16-17), now Jesus is sending us to show the world what love looks like among a people embracing the Cross and resurrection.

For those who believe in Jesus, He came to give everlasting forgiveness, reconciling us to God through His shed blood and His death on the Cross, so that we could have His Spirit in us. He made Himself one with us in our sin and death so we could be one with Him in His righteousness and life.

Jesus desires to send us to show the world the Father through sharing in His ministry of reconciliation, bringing forgiveness to the world, so that whoever's sin we forgive is forgiven (John 20:21-23). We are now filled with His Spirit, the Holy Spirit, so we can reveal the Father just like He did, through amazing signs, wonders and miracles.

We are not to live under condemnation, nor are we to condemn anyone in this world. Paul says that God is making His appeal to the world, not counting their sin against them; He is making that appeal through us as His ambassadors.

> *All this is from God, who through Christ reconciled us to himself and gave us the ministry of reconciliation; that is, in Christ God was reconciling the world to himself, not counting their trespasses against them, and entrusting to us the message of reconciliation. Therefore, we are ambassadors for Christ, God making his appeal through us.*
> *2 Corinthians 5:18-20a*

Our mission is to the world, carrying the message of God's heart and love, that He does not treat anyone according to what their sins deserve. We are not to condemn. The Holy Spirit's role is to convict the world regarding sin, righteousness and judgment. Jesus said that it was better that He go, because when He did He would send the Counselor, the Comforter to us. He goes on to say,

> *When he comes, he will convict the world concerning sin and righteousness and judgment: concerning sin, because they do not believe in me; concerning righteousness, because I go to the Father, and you will see me no longer; concerning judgment, because the ruler of this world is judged.*
> *John 16:8-11*

Carlos Rodriguez, my friend and Lead Pastor at Catch The Fire Raleigh, says, "The sin of the world is not what it does or doesn't do; the sin of the world is not believing in Jesus."

The Holy Spirit convicts the world that it doesn't believe in Jesus. The Holy Spirit convicts the world that its righteousness is not true righteousness, but that true righteousness is found only in Christ.

In Christ, we are the righteousness of God because Jesus has gone to the Father. He has returned to the Father with us, because He became one with us at the Cross, so that we are one with Him in His resurrection. The Holy Spirit will show the world that Satan is judged. His joy is to show the world that there is therefore no condemnation for those who believe in Jesus. It is Satan and sin that are condemned.

Jesus didn't just come to preach repentance; He came to destroy the works of the devil. He took our sin upon Himself and destroyed it forever when He died with our sin, for us, as us.

> *The reason the Son of God appeared was to*
> *destroy the works of the devil.*
> *1 John 3:8b*

When we live in the truth of who we are in Christ, one with Him forever, filled with His glorious Holy Spirit, resting in His Father's presence and love, our passion is walking in God's love and giving it away to the world. We live in our union, or Oneness with Christ, bringing Heaven to earth. The Father is able to do His works in us so that miracles, signs and wonders are our daily experience.

I preached this message at our home church. Carlos Rodriguez came afterwards and said, "Duncan, it's incredible. I couldn't help thinking that Herod slammed John in prison because John was outspoken about Herod's sin of having his brother Philip's wife. The church today loves to point out societies' sins—and pays the same price John did. It gets shut up in 'prison' by the government and the powerful people within society. The church has many enemies today because it spends so much energy pointing out societies' sins."

Stunned, I realized that Carlos was right. There is no record that Jesus ever pointed out to Herod his sin regarding his brother Philip's wife.

Jesus said that the Son of Man came to seek and save that which was lost (Matthew 18:11). Jesus' mission was not to judge the world, but to save it (John 12:47). Much of the church today, like John, has lost its authority in the world because it continually points out societies' sins in judgment. The church that accuses the world in judgment has lost its right to change the world.

Although John preached a message of repentance, there is no record of John the Baptist ever doing a miracle or healing the sick. He did not raise the dead; he did not cleanse the lepers or drive demons out of anyone, as far as we know. I'm not saying this to discredit John. His mission was not to do those things. His mission was to make way for Jesus, who would do all those things.

When Jesus came, He healed the sick, raised the dead, cleansed the lepers, drove out demons and preached the good news to the poor. Our model was never supposed to be John the Baptist's ministry. We were not meant to preach sermons about Jesus, call people to repentance, baptize them, drawing them to ourselves, and then make sure they go to church every Sunday.

When John was in prison, sadly, he sent some of his disciples to Jesus asking if He was really the Messiah or should they look for someone else (Matthew 11:3). I have often wondered what it was that caused John to doubt whether Jesus was really the Messiah at that point. He started off so well, pointing out Jesus as He walked past him while John was baptizing at the River Jordan,

> *Behold the Lamb of God, who takes away the sin of the world.*
> *John 1:29*

Could it be that John heard in prison, perhaps from his own disciples that Jesus had given his power and authority to Jesus' disciples and they were doing miracles?

*Jesus called to him his twelve disciples and gave them authority over
unclean spirits, to cast them out, and to heal every disease and every
affliction ... "And proclaim as you go, saying, 'The kingdom of heaven is
at hand. Heal the sick, raise the dead, cleanse lepers, cast out demons.'"*
Matthew 10:1,7–8

John had been the *"voice of one, crying in the wilderness,"* and now he
was in prison. He heard that Jesus' disciples were going to all the towns and
villages and preaching the good news of the Kingdom, doing miracles, signs
and wonders, something neither he, nor his own disciples had ever done.

He was from the line of priests. But these men, Jesus' disciples, were
simple fisherman like James and John or Peter and Andrew. Even worse,
Matthew was an ex-tax collector. All of them were now ministering in the
power and authority of Christ, doing things that John had never done. John
was the voice of one; they were the 'voice of many waters.' He may have felt
that he came to make way for Jesus, not a bunch of fisherman!

I can't help thinking how much the church today behaves this way
in its attitude towards those who are manifesting Jesus' ministry of signs,
wonders and miracles. Sadly, rather than being thrilled about hearing how
God is using people, their friends, or a different church than the one they
attend or lead, they become critical of what others are doing, sowing doubt
about whether or not it is a true work of God.

Jesus' response to John the Baptist was very simple. He summarizes
his ministry this way,

*Jesus answered them, "Go and tell John what you hear and see:
the blind receive their sight and the lame walk, lepers are cleansed
and the deaf hear, and the dead are raised up,
and the poor have good news preached to them.
And blessed is the one who is not offended by me."*
Matthew 11:4-6

John never followed Jesus. He could have done so. There was nothing stopping him following Jesus, just like Andrew, one of his disciples, did. He could have abandoned his ministry that day with Andrew and decided to follow Jesus instead (John 1:34-42).

Today we preach about Jesus, but are we truly following Him? Or are we holding on to our own ministry, rather than being willing to follow Christ? What would John's life have been like if he had decided to follow Jesus? Perhaps he would have gone on to become one of Jesus' twelve. Maybe he would have become one of the greatest apostles. In the end, his choice to carry on in his own ministry cost him his life. He had a following, but was unable to follow Jesus.

In Christ Jesus, our joy is to bring the love of God to the world by the Holy Spirit: healing the sick, raising the dead, cleansing the lepers and delivering them from demons, as well as preaching the good news to the poor. As we do this, we will reveal the Father. That's what it truly means to follow Jesus.

Jesus, speaking of John the Baptist, says, *"He was a burning and shining lamp"* (John 5:35). He *was*. Not he *is*—he *was*. John was a burning and shining light, but Jesus is the light of the world.

He says in John 8, *"I am the light of the world"* (John 8:12).

He doesn't say, "I *was* the light of the world," or, "I *will be* the light of the world."

He says, "I *am* the light of the world."

He was, He is and He will always be the light of the world. He is the everlasting light of the world that has burned and shone for all eternity.

In the Old Covenant, the priests were to keep the lamp with its seven lights burning in the Holy Place, throughout the night (Leviticus 24:1-4, Exodus 25:31-40). The Ancient Israelites were to provide pure olive oil to the priest to keep that hungry lamp burning continuously. If they didn't work hard to provide the oil, the lamps would burn out.

Their light was not eternal. It was dependent on their works. They had to clear land, cultivate the soil, grow olive trees and harvest the olives once a year, then carry the olives to the press, press them and eventually produce a few gallons of olive oil. They had to be willing to give the precious oil, which they also used for eating and cooking, and take it to the priest who would burn it to keep the seven-branched lamp burning in the Holy Place. It was hard work. Israel had to produce its own light in the Holy Place. They had no light of their own. The Lamp was a prophetic statement that their Messiah, who was coming, was their true, eternal lamp.

Everlasting Supply

One day when I was preaching in Puerto Rico, I had a rest before the evening meeting. I fell asleep and the Lord spoke to me through a dream. I dreamt I was preaching on Zechariah 4, a chapter full of mystery. The prophet Zechariah records a vision he was given. He saw a seven-branched golden lamp burning brightly, which had a golden bowl above the seven lamps, full of golden oil flowing straight into the lamps. Golden pipes fed the golden bowl from two olive trees behind the lamps. Zechariah says,

> *A second time I answered and said to him,*
> *"What are these two branches of the olive trees, which are beside the*
> *two golden pipes from which the golden oil is poured out?"*
> *He said to me, "Do you not know what these are?"*
> *I said, "No, my lord." Then he said, "These are the two anointed ones*
> *who stand by the Lord of the whole earth."*
> *Zechariah 4:12-14*

In my dream I knew the two olive trees represented the Law and the Prophets, which Jesus said were written of Him (John 5:39). Moses and

Elijah symbolized this when they both appeared on the mountain when Jesus was transfigured. The disciples saw the glory of Jesus Christ as His face suddenly shone like the sun and His clothes became as white as light (Matthew 17:2). The Apostle John saw with his own eyes the revelation of Jesus Christ, God over all. He saw the True Light that was come into the world (John 1:9).

Luke records that they spoke about Jesus' soon-coming departure in Jerusalem, meaning His death on the Cross. The word for "departure" literally means "exodus." That was the moment when the Messiah, the Anointed One of whom the Law and the Prophets testified, the ultimate Passover Lamb, would give His life to save the world. The moment when He gave His life to bring His people out of slavery and bondage, into the Promised Land of the Kingdom of Heaven. When the only Son of the Father allowed Himself to be beaten and put to death so that murderers, thieves and sinners could become sons of the Father by a free gift of incredible love and grace. The Father spoke from the bright cloud and testified to the glory of His Son, giving an emphatic command to the disciples to listen to His Beloved Son, whom the Law and the Prophets testify.

He was still speaking when, behold, a bright cloud overshadowed them, and a voice from the cloud said, "This is my beloved Son, with whom I am well pleased; listen to him."
Matthew 17:5

Jesus is the Light of the World. As the One who was crushed for us, He is the everlasting supply and supplier of golden oil, the Holy Spirit Himself. Whoever would receive Him and believe in His name would be given the right to be sons and daughters of God just like Him (John 1:12). As children of God, we too are the light of the world, and our lamps are supplied with the same golden oil Zechariah saw.

Zechariah saw the day when the church—both the Messianic Israelites and the Gentiles—would be an everlasting lamp, the very light of the world themselves. Jesus confirmed this Messianic promise when He told the disciples in the Sermon on the Mount in Matthew 5, *"You are the light of the world"* (v 14).

Jesus Christ, the Son of God, came into the world as the light of the world, so that those who would believe in Him would be sons and daughters of God, just like Him. One with Him, they too would be the light that would burn brightly like stars forever, because they would be given the Spirit without measure, the Spirit of Sonship (Galatians 4:6).

> *For He whom God has sent utters the words of God, for He gives the Spirit without measure. The Father loves the Son and has given all things into his hand. Whoever believes in the Son has eternal life; whoever does not obey the Son shall not see life, but the wrath of God remains on him.*
> *John 3:34-36*

Whoever *believes* in the Son has eternal life and is given the right to become a son or daughter of God himself or herself. As sons and daughters of God we are filled with an everlasting supply of oil from within. We are united with Him forever through His Spirit so that we can do the supernatural works, or miracles, that testify to Jesus' magnificent presence. Paul illustrates this saying,

> *Does he who supplies the Spirit to you and works miracles among you do so by works of the law, or by hearing with faith?*
> *Galatians 3:5*

The miracles that were being worked in the early church were not happening because they were doing the works of the law under the

Old Covenant, but because the Holy Spirit was supplied to them. He is the miracle worker in us.

> *You are the light of the world. A city set on a hill cannot be hidden.*
> *Nor do people light a lamp and put it under a basket, but on a stand,*
> *and it gives light to all in the house. In the same way, let your light*
> *shine before others, so that they may see your good works and*
> *give glory to your Father who is in heaven.*
> *Matthew 5:14-16*

Jesus is referring to the works He Himself will do in us. Our works alone are like a light that is hidden under a basket, no matter how charitable the works. The good works that allow His light to shine are the *supernatural* miracles that only the Holy Spirit can do through us. The Apostle John tells us John the Baptist was not the light, but he came as a witness to the light. He was to bear witness to the True Light: Jesus Christ the Savior of the world.

> *There was a man sent from God, whose name was John. He came*
> *as a witness, to bear witness about the light, that all might believe*
> *through him. He was not the light, but came to bear witness about*
> *the light. The true light, which enlightens everyone,*
> *was coming into the world.*
> *John 1:6-9*

Now, it is our privilege in this new paradigm to learn to wield the eternal power of the Kingdom as ever maturing sons of God so that the world can be consumed by love. The world is waiting for us, the sons of God, to manifest Jesus wherever we go as we live our lives from a place of Oneness with Him in the Father's love. It is His joy that we steward the infinite treasures of His Kingdom serving all humanity with passion and joy.

In Christ, we are the light of the world, burning brightly with an everlasting supply of the oil of the Holy Spirit so that our flame of love will never go out. We can show the whole of creation what the sons of God really look like. We can overcome the world with Jesus and plunder the dominion of darkness, setting people free from all the works and power of the devil.

Like Jesus we can say, "We do nothing of ourselves." Rather, it is Christ living in us by His Spirit, who is doing the Father's works in us and through us. What Jesus said about Himself is also true of us in Him.

The testimony that I have is greater than that of John. For the works that the Father has given me to accomplish, the very works that I am doing bear witness about me that the Father has sent me.
John 5:36

The miracles the Father has given us to accomplish will bear witness to who we are in Christ and who Christ is in us. Knowing that you are one with Christ absolutely changes everything. From this place of Oneness, you can set the whole world on fire with the love of your Eternal Father as the light of the world.

CHAPTER 14

INFINITE TREASURE

Son, you are always with me, and all that is mine is yours.

Luke 15:31

Our Oneness with Christ gives us direct access to the infinite treasures of God as sons of God, from which we can make endless withdrawals. There is no demand that we could place upon God that will ever diminish His resources. He has given us all things and there's *nothing* left out of *all* (1 Corinthians 3:21).

Oneness is the key to enabling us to accomplish all that God has planned in advance for us to do in this life, whatever our calling is (Ephesians 2:10). With the revelation of Oneness with Christ burning in our hearts, Kate and I were ready for the next great challenge in our lives.

After eight wonderful years in Toronto, we moved to Raleigh, North Carolina, USA. We knew God was calling us to extend the TACF family by starting the first Catch The Fire church outside of Toronto, called "Catch The Fire Raleigh." This launched our entire ministry into an exciting new phase of intentionally starting Catch The Fire churches around the world; whole communities filled with the presence and power of God manifesting Oneness in burning Love Himself. At the same time, TACF became "Catch

The Fire Toronto".

In Raleigh we faced giant trials of many kinds, learning quickly that only Jesus can build His church, but that one with Him, He is able to do it through little ones like us.

In the January of our fourth year as a church, my cell phone rang. It was our Jewish landlord. "Duncan, my partner and I want to sell the building you're leasing from us right away. Can we do lunch as soon as possible?"

My mind raced.

You want to sell our building? You have to be kidding! I thought to myself.

Things are going so well right now, we're growing and we love the building we're in. It's our Catch The Fire Center, where we've had so many promises from God that a great move of God is going to explode in our church: in that exact building and on that exact piece of property in Raleigh, North Carolina. There's no way you're selling the building. That's not in the master plan!

"Sure Eli, we can do lunch." I replied, fully determined that I would dissuade them over lunch from selling the property, as I had done whenever they had mentioned the idea before. We had been leasing their building for two years. It was nearly perfect for us in every way. So much better than what we'd had the first 18 months, leasing a banquet center on Sundays for a few hours!

My stomach was churning anxiously as I drove to lunch.

"Surely this is not a final decision," I comforted myself. Sitting in the car with me were Carlos Rodriguez, who we had just appointed Lead Pastor of the church, and Murray Smith. All three of us had "wasted" our lives on this mission with Jesus. Carlos and Catherine and Murray and Ash are all radical lovers of Jesus who passionately embrace sharing in Christ's suffering that they might share in the power of His resurrection. They're champions of walking the "Way of the Cross," living for Jesus only, considering it pure joy to lay down everything, so that Christ would be made famous in them. Jesus has pulled together an awesome senior team with a

singular passion for His name and His fame.

By the time we reached the lunch venue, peace had begun to fill my heart. The Holy Spirit whispered to me, *"Don't forget I said to you before you moved to Raleigh, Stand back and watch what I'm going to do through you!"*

The Holy Spirit had sustained me through every fiery trial on this incredible journey of starting Catch The Fire Raleigh. Repeatedly, we had come to the end of ourselves and the beginning of Christ. Every time we learned to step back into Him, He would step forward in and through us and do extraordinary things.

Throughout my life, I'd thought life in Christ was about having the same attitude that John the Baptist had when he said about Jesus' ministry,

He must increase, but I must decrease.
John 3:30

It had always seemed so humble to think of Jesus increasing and me decreasing. And yet the more I asked the Holy Spirit to teach me the Gospel the more I began to realize this wasn't the New Testament way Jesus came to show us. It was true for John under the Old Covenant, but not for us in the New Covenant.

It wasn't even "all of Jesus and none of me," which sounds even more humble. No, I've learned that in the Gospel of Jesus Christ true humility is "all of Jesus and all of me, in Jesus." All of us, in all of Him. *We are one with Christ.*

I shared with Carlos and Murray and we all agreed: if they were determined to sell the building, there was no other option for us but to buy it.

My heart was perfectly at rest. Our Oneness with Christ was the key to all the impossible becoming possible in our lives. I was ready for anything as we began ordering our food, making all the necessary small talk that those kind of awkward moments seem to require with everyone skirting carefully around the elephant in the room.

Eli, our landlord, opened the conversation. "Gentlemen, we've decided we are going to put our building that you're leasing from us on the market. We want to sell it fast and so we'd like you to let us know in two weeks whether you'd like to buy it. You must put down a nonrefundable earnest deposit of $65,000 and sign a purchase agreement contract to close in three months. We have three other buyers wanting to buy the building if you can't for any reason. We like you guys, so we're giving you first opportunity to buy it. The purchase price is $1,400,000 and we think you're getting a great deal because we've made huge improvements to the property since it was valued two years ago at $1,600,000."

As I sat listening, it just would not sink in. I was watching him talking, his lips were moving, sound was coming from his mouth, but his words were not computing in my mind. I couldn't get my mind around those figures.

$1,400,000! Okay that's an impossible amount of money for us as a church. For crying out loud, we've only got $15,000 in our building fund! I thought to myself, assaulted by fear. Even if we were able to persuade a bank to give us a mortgage, we would still need to raise the 30% equity, which was $420,000. *This is impossible!*

"What do you think, Duncan?" Eli's question jolted me right back to the conversation.

Without hesitation, faith rose up on the inside of me and I said boldly, "Eli, Yeshua, your mighty Messiah, who you don't believe in, is our Savior as well as yours. He will absolutely enable us to buy this building. Absolutely! If you will include the $50,000 that we gave you as a deposit on signing, we will give you $15,000 earnest money, sign the purchase agreement and our champion King Yeshua, Jesus Christ, will give us the $1,335,000 so that we can buy this building in three months' time. We'll pray about it, share it with our wives and some of our people and we'll get back to you within two weeks."

Full of faith, I held out my right hand to him to shake on that deal. Eli looked into my eyes and shook my outstretched hand. We struck the deal and I jumped out of the boat right there. We were walking on water. I'd never felt so much faith coursing around my heart, quashing so much fear in my mind. Perfect love was driving out sheer terror.

During the next few days, Kate and I went into the secret place with God, as did each of our team. There was nowhere else to go. This crisis was really an invitation to discover a greater dimension of our union with Christ, a deeper revelation of the Cross of Christ, and the power of His resurrection. The Father was inviting us to join Him in the way of the Cross. He wanted to show us that the Holy Spirit was our inheritance, the very Spirit of the Father and the Son, dwelling in us and with us. Impossibility is the playground of Oneness. It was for joy that Jesus endured the Cross! Joy!

Buying this building was really all about plumbing the depths of the love of God in Christ Jesus. It was the necessary environment to discover, through the Holy Spirit, dimensions of the Gospel of Jesus Christ and the love of the Father that can only be discovered in the face of impossibility.

"Look up, son. Look at Me. Keep your eyes steadfastly on Me," the Holy Spirit urged me gently, yet firmly. Paul knew the importance of not looking at the world around us.

> *If you then be risen with Christ, seek those things which are above,*
> *where Christ sits at the right hand of God. Set your affection on*
> *things above, not on things on the earth.*
> *Colossians 3:1-2*

The Holy Spirit longs for us to learn to live in the bigness of God, rather than the smallness of man. In Christ, our inside world is so much bigger than the world on the outside of us. Greater is He that is within you, than he that is in the world (1 John 4:4). He loves to wean us off trusting in our own strength or the strength of others, and most especially the strength of money.

When we have God, we have everything. Jesus' words in the story of the Prodigal Son (which should be called "The Loving Father") sum up our life in Christ perfectly.

> *Son, you are always with me, and all that is mine is yours.*
> *Luke 15:31*

What an extraordinary verse. All that the Father has is ours. The Father is always with us. What an answer to every crisis. What an answer to the crisis of needing $1,400,000. We already have all that belongs to the Father. We can look to our own meager resources, or even the banks' meager resources or we can let impossibility be our playground of Oneness in the Father.

Crisis in Africa

During that time, I got an email from my friend Rolland, one of my heroes in the faith, which shook me to the core of my being. He forwarded a special news bulletin from the United Nations, alerting the world of a pandemic, human catastrophe that was looming on the horizon. The report stated that, due to repeated drought year upon year throughout the past decade and the associated failed crops during the last growing season, 10 million people were facing death across the entire region south of the Sahara Desert known as the "Sahel," stretching from Mauritania in the West, to Sudan in the East.

Rolland and Heidi Baker are the founders of IRIS Global, one of the greatest ministries on planet earth today. They are based in Mozambique, working among the poorest of the poor. Their international ministry is full of love and God does the most incredible signs and wonders among them, winning whole villages to Christ as the blind see and the deaf hear. Their ministry cares for thousands of children and has planted thousands of churches.

As I read the words of the report Rolland sent me, tears welled up in my eyes. Our friends, especially in Niger, many of whom we had won to Christ and shared so much fellowship with, were facing starvation and possible death. These beautiful Fulani and Tuareg converts, were the first believers in the true and living God in their entire generational line, going all the way back to Noah and the flood. I cannot begin to imagine how precious they are to Jesus.

I knew it was terrible timing for me to be gone, as we were having our own "crisis" with the building sale, but there was no way I could ignore the desperate plight of our friends in Niger. How could we lead them to Christ and His Kingdom and then abandon them in their great time of need? It was either stay in Raleigh and help develop a carefully thought out fundraising strategy, or head to Niger for two weeks to feed the poor.

It was a no-brainer. I shared the Niger crisis with Murray and we both decided to book our flights to Niger with Carlos' and our wives' blessing. I knew if we took care of Jesus' business feeding His precious Fulani, He would take care of our business in Raleigh.

We decided to take my eldest daughter, Jessie Faith. She is an awesome woman of faith. She was 18 years old at the time, and freshly back from Pemba, Mozambique where she had graduated from the IRIS Harvest School. She had been wrecked by the Love of God and experienced so many Heavenly visions and personal encounters with Jesus and the Father. Her heart is broken for the lost and the poor. It was such a joy for her to come.

Two days before we left for Niger, one of John Arnott's friends invited the Catch The Fire global senior team, as part of our annual retreat, to join them on their sport fishing boat for the day in Florida. It was huge fun, but while we were cruising I became increasingly agitated.

All around us were $100 million houses and boats. Here I was, about to leave for Niger with $30,000 that had been given in a special offering to enable us to buy food. I knew from experience it wouldn't go far towards feeding the hundreds of families among our people facing starvation and death.

I was also facing having to make the decision to sign on the dotted line, that we would close on our building in three months. Something began rising up in my spirit. I climbed the steps to the lookout tower on the fishing boat to get alone with God. The Holy Spirit reminded me that I'm one with Christ in the Father. Oneness gives me access to infinite treasure!

I cried out to the Lord, "Father, clearly there is a lot of money in this world. My problem is that I don't have access to any of it! All around me is extravagant wealth, being used largely for self-indulgent opulence. I don't resent that per se; however, God, if these people can spend hundreds of millions of dollars on houses, cars and boats, then how much more should I trust You to provide us with $1,400,000 to enable us to purchase what is really Your building?"

I continued praying, "Father, Your word says in Psalm 24:1 that the whole earth is Yours, everything in it and all the people who live in it. I am Your beloved son, one with Your Beloved Son, Jesus. I am always with You and everything that You have is mine."

Suddenly, the Lord gave me a huge gift: His supernatural faith in my heart for everything we needed in Raleigh and in Niger. I sensed He wanted me to reach into the invisible atmosphere of His Kingdom, just above my head, take hold of what we needed and pull it down by faith.

Jumping to my feet, with my right hand in the air, I grabbed a fist full of what we needed, declaring, "In the mighty name of Your Son Jesus Christ, who I am one with, and with whom I am seated in the Heavens, I reach into the invisible atmosphere of your Heavenly Kingdom reality that is all around me and pull down $1,400,000 into Catch The Fire Raleigh's account!"

In that instant, I knew that if one more word was said to the Lord on the subject, it would be sin! It would be an expression of doubt. I climbed down to the main deck below and rejoined my friends. I knew that it was done. The Lord would give us the finances for it all. It was His building and He was going to pay for it and bless our Jewish landlord's socks off, despite the fact that he was an atheist! No one knew what I had just done except the Lord.

Back at home in Raleigh, getting ready to leave that night for Niger, my phone rang. It was Jim, the Vice President of the eighth—and last—bank we had approached. All the others had said a flat out "no"; some of them even laughed at Murray. It had been a tough and sometimes humiliating journey for him. Every bank refused to lend us any money because we were a church; and on top of that, we were a non-denominational church, only three and a half years old.

My heart leapt. Surely this was the moment we had all been waiting for. Surely Murray's hard work was about to pay off.

"Jim, how are you?" I greeted him.

"I'm great thanks Duncan, but I have some bad news for you I'm afraid," he said in his deep Southern drawl.

"I know I'd said a while back that we might be able to help y'all out. But in fact, our Credit Loan Officer has decided that y'all are too high a risk for us at this time, with the economy the way it is. I'm so sorry."

It should have been devastating news, but I was filled with faith and found myself thanking Jim for giving us the opportunity to really see Jesus shine. I'd come to realize that impossibility is really the only place that God can really, truly shine. Everything that we do in our lives that is possible is where we get to shine, but when it comes to the impossible, only God can shine.

We met together as a team and despite the gravity of the situation, we decided that if the Lord didn't come through for us, we would still sign the contract binding us to buy the building in three months or lose the $65,000 deposit. Never before had I faced such a critical decision, yet perfect peace flooded my heart and mind. We were sons of God, one with Christ. He is all we need.

We decided to hold on to all the prophetic words He had spoken to us through the Holy Spirit: "Revival will come to Raleigh. God wants to give us the building and the land for His purposes for this city. He has earmarked this building and land to be His and to be the place where He would manifest His glory in and through us."

We knew we must partner with Him in faith and believe that He will come through for us. I closed the meeting saying, "Carlos, please sign the purchase agreement and hand over the $15,000 earnest money this week to Eli and his partner, while Murray and I are in Niger. We will accept the Lord's invitation to believe Him to do the impossible and reveal His majesty to us."

Despite the impossibility of the situation, I could see that our team all came to the same conclusion. Jesus is our great hope!

Before I knew it, Murray and I were on the airplane to Paris. There was no turning back; we were way out of the boat, walking on the water with Jesus. On one hand I felt utterly helpless, with no opportunity to make any meaningful contribution to resolving one of the largest crises I had ever experienced as a leader. On the other hand, I felt absolute peace and confidence in the magnificence of the Father to come through for us, most especially for the fame and renown of His glorious Son.

My thoughts began to turn towards the Lord Jesus, the power of His death on the Cross and His resurrection. I realized how easily we miss experiencing the fullness of the power of the Gospel, because we see the Cross and resurrection as an event that happened to Jesus for our salvation. We miss the incredible invitation to join Him on that journey of the way of the Cross and resurrection, living in the truth of our Oneness with Christ.

There's something about facing impossibility that creates the necessary environment for us to enter into greater experience and revelation of our union with Christ and the fullness of our life being hidden in Christ in God, fully immersed in Love Himself.

Staring at what I felt was a gigantic mountain, needing $1,400,000 million to buy our building in three months, with no opportunity now to fundraise in time, coupled with knowing that in a few hours I would be on the edge of the Sahara in incredibly challenging spiritual, physical and emotional circumstances, I pressed deeply by faith into the revelation of my Oneness with Christ. His life in me, and my life in Him.

Transported in the Spirit

Sitting on the airplane, my thoughts drifted back to two years earlier, when I went to Niger on our first emergency-feeding trip. The whole nation of Niger had been in a severe drought that year too. I had learned about it from Terje, and the two of us determined we had to help them.

On arriving in Niger, Terje and I planned our trip to maximize our effectiveness. We knew one of our dearest friends, chief of large numbers of nomadic Fulani people, might be at Adgeri, a market town in the deep bush. We had no way of contacting him and had to trust the Lord would put it in his heart to be at the market when we arrived.

We had a deadline. The once-a-week-only market started the next day at 8 am and the traders would begin leaving at 2 pm. It would be completely over by 4 pm. It was a minimum of a five-hour drive off road in our 4x4.

Due to several reasons beyond our control, it was 2:30 pm before we could leave our city. I was so frustrated. I was driving and knew the difficult journey ahead of us, especially at that time of year because the sand is the deepest. Unless we reached the market town by 4 pm our entire trip was futile. Hundreds of our friends would risk starvation and even then, there was no certainty the chief would be there that day.

Leaving at 2:30 pm meant arriving at 7:30 pm, long after dark. The traders and our friend would be long gone.

As we pulled out of the outskirts of the city, I was so righteously angry. With great passion I banged my fist onto the dashboard yelling loudly, "In Jesus' mighty name we shall enter Adgeri at 4 pm!"

Everyone was startled by my sudden outburst, but there were the sounds of a confident "Amen!" coming from everyone in the vehicle. We all knew the impossibility of the situation.

We drove through endless thorn tree bush in 120° F. Suddenly, one of our Fulani pastors started pointing excitedly at a town appearing through the Acacia trees a few hundred yards ahead of us.

"Ga Adgeri, Mun zo, Mun zo, Mun zo!" he shouted in the Hausa tribal language, which I speak fairly fluently, having grown up in Nigeria.

"There's Adgeri, we've arrived, we've arrived, we've arrived!"

Everyone was in total shock. We looked at the time: *it was exactly 4 pm.* Joy exploded in the Land Cruiser as we all simultaneously realized we had experienced our first transportation in the Spirit.

The Holy Spirit had picked up our entire Toyota Land Cruiser and transported us at some point without any of us noticing. The five-hour journey took one and a half hours!

It was the strangest feeling to know that, even though I had been driving with maximum concentration because of the severe terrain, I had not been aware of the moment when we had been entirely transported by the Holy Spirit. It was totally miraculous and impossible outside of Christ, but all things are possible in Christ.

With exceeding joy, we walked into the town. Around the very first corner, we came face to face with our dear friend, the chief. He was overcome with joy and wonder. In tears, he shared how he was riding to market on his camel at 3 am that morning, having left 70 of his people at his nomadic camp with just one bowl of millet between them all. He had cried out to the Lord, "Heavenly Father, with all my heart I ask You that somehow You would send Duncan and Terje to meet me in the market to help us, please, Father. I don't know how that could possibly happen, but I trust You because all things are possible for you."

We were all overwhelmed by the great love of God and His mighty power towards those who believe, whose hearts are set upon Him. What a champion Savior Jesus Christ is! We were able to buy enough millet for him and his people to make it through to the next harvest. I will never forget that moment. It marked me forever.

Lower in the Dirt, Higher in the Heavens

Now sitting on the airplane, heading back to Niger two years later, my heart was filled with so much joy and confidence as I faced one of the most challenging two weeks of my entire life. Our life in Christ is a constant invitation from the Holy Spirit to embrace by faith the sufferings and death of Christ, because through sharing in His death, our life is truly finished. His resurrected eternal Life is able to completely fill us and occupy us. This is not just a theological statement, it is our reality to experience and dwell in. Truly, Christ lives in us and we live in Him!

When we get lower in the dirt with Him, we soar higher in the Heavens with Him. The way up is truly downwards. Our life in Him is about embracing the will of the Father in the strength and power of the indestructible life of the Holy Spirit. The One who raised Jesus from the dead lives in us. The invitation is always to come to the end of ourselves and the beginning of Christ. In that realm all things are possible, because the life we now live is no longer our own, we live by the faith of the Son of God (Galatians 2:20).

We arrived in Niamey the next day. Sitting in the evening dusk as the sun went down over the vast, lazy Niger River, I sensed the affectionate invitation of my Heavenly Daddy to hold on tightly to Him. My life was no longer my own. I'm one with Christ, hidden deeply in the Father, filled with His mighty Spirit.

He whispered again, "Stand back son, and watch what I'm going to do through you!"

I realized right then that the Holy Spirit had fully prepared me throughout my entire life for just this moment. I was fully surrendered. All that I am is in Christ, all that He is, is in me. The reality of my Oneness with Christ, which the Holy Spirit had been teaching me for years, was the anchor in my heart as I faced these gigantic mountains of impossibility. The $1,400,000 we needed in Raleigh, which seemed so far away, and all the tons of food we would need to feed hundreds of families in Niger in the next few days, *was all in Christ*. Everything we could ever need is found in Him. My eyes were on Him and Him alone. No bank, no church, no employer, no sponsor, no human entity could possibly compare to the greatness of Christ.

We drove hundreds of miles through the desert bush in our 4x4 Land Cruiser, going from town to town buying as much food as we possibly could and placing it in the hands of the chiefs to give to their people. We prayed multiplication over the huge bags of millet in every place we went. Our friends were overjoyed as we manifested the love of God to them. We heard the Niger Muslim Fulani chiefs saying over and over, "We've never experienced love like this!"

The Holy Spirit filled us all with joy unspeakable: His joy in our lives laid down for those He deeply loves in one of the poorest nations on earth.

On our long drive home through the desert, we were arrested and detained for several hours by the Niger military because they thought we were spies. With all that was happening in Libya to the North and Mali to the West, we could see why the Niger military arrested us. No one else from a western nation would have been crazy enough to be driving around the Niger desert then! There was war all around us, and militant Islamic extremists everywhere.

Murray and I both had soldiers thrust their AK-47 semiautomatic assault rifles directly into our faces. Murray had to open the rear doors of our beat-up old Land Cruiser for the soldiers, while one of them aimed the anti-tank machine gun on their jeep directly at him, finger on the trigger.

After several hours of wrongful detention, they eventually let us go. We were shaken up by the whole experience, but it was worth it all. We had been there for our friends in their time of great need.

We flew home to Raleigh the next day, exhausted yet with our love tanks full and a deep sense of satisfaction in the Lord. We knew without any shadow of a doubt what Paul the Apostle meant when he said that we are hidden in Christ (Colossians 3:3).

Coming home to Raleigh, we were immediately faced with the reality of our desperate need of $1,400,000 dollars; yet more than ever I understood my Oneness with Christ. Perfect peace and excitement filled my heart. We found the team excited too, knowing that God was about to do something special. We were all full of hope in the Holy Spirit. It felt strange to be so at peace in the face of absolute impossibility.

I've realized now that's what supernatural hope feels like. It's the absolute assurance that God will for *sure* do what He alone is able to do. It is faith, combined with perfect peace, anchored in joyful expectation of the goodness of God. It causes a deep settled-ness in our hearts in the midst of the crisis. It is what enabled Jesus to sleep in the bottom of a boat in the middle of a raging storm, when everyone else in the boat was terrified for their lives.

A few days after we arrived back in Raleigh, my phone rang again. It was Murray. "Dunc, I've got something to show you. Are you at home? I'd like to come over right away." Within a few minutes he drove to our house from the church and stood in our kitchen.

"This arrived for you," he said, handing me an already opened envelope addressed to "Duncan Smith, Catch The Fire, Raleigh."

"Murray, what's this letter addressed to me doing already opened?" I asked. "It's a good thing for you, you're my brother!" We both laughed.

"I couldn't help opening it, Dunc. I knew in my spirit that it was something exciting. Have a look."

I pulled out the letter, written on letter-headed paper with the name of a charitable giving fund at the top of the letter. The first few lines of the letter read,

Dear Colleague,
Please find attached below a check in the amount of $1,200,000 from one of our donors who wishes to remain anonymous, but wants you to know that you may use the funds as you see fit...

Attached to the letter was a check. As I read the words and saw the check at the bottom of the page my whole body started shaking with intense excitement and joy. I fell onto our kitchen floor yelling at the top of my lungs, "Oh God, You are so great! You are so awesome! Thank You with all my heart. You've overwhelmed us with Your love. You're good, God. You're good!"

I felt as though the Father had kissed me smack on the top of my head and knocked me over with outrageous love. This was way beyond anything we could have dreamed of.

In an instant, we went from having virtually nothing to buy our building to having almost all we needed. It was such an incredible parallel of the Gospel of Jesus Christ. We were so impossibly far short, we were without hope in the natural. On top of that, eight banks had told us they would not lend anything to us. Our only hope was Jesus, and He did not disappoint us.

As I lay there stunned on my kitchen floor, rolling around with extreme joy, the Holy Spirit reminded me of what He had said to me two years earlier when we first started leasing the building.

"Remember Duncan, I told you that I would do a miracle so great for you with this building, you will all laugh for two years every time you remember what I did for you."

Murray and I laughed uncontrollably as we recalled what God had said. We were forever changed in those moments, both of us. Our sky has never been the same since. We were elevated into the greatness of our God, into His big, big sky.

It was with great joy that we walked into our local bank in North Raleigh and asked to see our branch manager.

Michael had become a good friend since the first day I walked into the branch and opened our bank accounts for Catch The Fire Raleigh, both personal and corporate. He knew very well the ups and downs, the highs and lows and the struggles of faith that we had endured. He knew our accounts.

His bank was one of the ones that had turned us down, even though he so badly wanted to help us.

"Hi Michael, we'd like to make a deposit please," I said, handing him the check.

He stood there holding the check with his mouth hanging open, staring blankly at the check, simply unable to believe what he was looking at.

"What? Is this real?" he asked, looking up at me after a few seconds.

"Michael. I was hoping you would tell me that it is real," I said, laughing. "Of course it's real," I said boldly. "It's from Jesus!"

He burst out laughing with great joy. "I'm so happy for you guys. I'm just so happy for you. In my wildest thoughts, I never imagined you guys from Catch The Fire Raleigh would walk into our branch with a check for deposit that was over a million dollars!"

The entire branch came to a standstill. People were shaking their heads and laughing, hardly able to believe the story. Everyone was overjoyed for us and we all gave thanks to Jesus, our great champion Savior.

When Carlos made the announcement to the church family the following Sunday the whole church went into exceedingly joyful celebration. Murray then preached one of the greatest messages on Christ's strength being made perfect in our weakness. Carlos shared with the church that we would be taking a special offering to give us all a chance to have some "skin in the game," as we say in America. It was unforgettable.

The following Sunday the church gave $75,000! It was one of the most joyful offerings I've ever been a part of.

That night when we went to bed, I whispered to Kate, "Darling, tonight, with all that has come in, we are only $25,000 short of the purchase price. We have $1,375,000 *cash*! The last bit is so small for Jesus!"

Kate reminded me of a vision that a man had given us when we were ministering in Cape Town, South Africa, just before we moved to

Raleigh. He shared that the Lord had taken him into Heaven, as He often did, and this time, the Lord took him into a vast, endless room, filled with great riches and treasures. The Lord told him this was the storehouse of Heaven and he could come anytime to the storehouse and help himself to whatever he needed. Suddenly, he was aware they were not alone in the room. As he looked over to his side, he said he saw Duncan and Kate Smith merrily helping themselves to the riches of heaven and putting them in the large sacks they were carrying as if it was the most normal thing in the world to do. Then he heard the Lord say, *"Tell Duncan and Kate, I'm giving them great resources. Buildings, people and nations!"*

The very next day, we were sitting at one of our favorite cafés in Raleigh, enjoying the warmth of the bright April sunshine, sipping a sensational Dopio (a double espresso, the nectar of Heaven). My cell phone buzzed, alerting me to a new text. It was Murray.

"Dunc, another envelope has arrived from the same charitable giving fund addressed to you. Would you like me to open it or bring it to you?"

I chuckled to myself, thinking about how hilarious Murray can be. "You go ahead and open it and let me know," I replied. *After all it's probably just a receipt or something,* I thought to myself. It's amazing to me how often our initial response is doubt rather than faith!

Next thing I knew, Murray was calling on the phone again. "It's another check with a letter in exactly the same wording as the first letter."

Dear Colleague,
Please find attached below a check in the amount of $100,000 from one of our donors who wishes to remain anonymous, but wants you to know that you may use the funds as you see fit...

"Kate, It's another enormous, anonymous check, this time in the amount of $100,000! This is just over the top goodness from our Heavenly Daddy!" I yelled out in front of everyone walking into the café. We were staggered by the greatness and goodness of our Heavenly Father towards us all.

Our Father has made us sons in the Son. Now that we're sons, we
too have the choice Jesus had. He did not consider equality
with God something to be grasped, but as a Son,
emptied Himself and became a servant of all.
Philippians 2:6

But there is an invitation for a deeper level of relationship even than sonship in the Kingdom.

In the natural, we didn't choose to be our earthly father's son or daughter. He chose us, one way or another. The choice we have is whether we want to be his friend.

In the same way, we did not choose to be our Heavenly Father's son or daughter. He chose us in Christ before the foundation of the world and placed us in His Son at the Cross (1 Corinthians 1:30, Ephesians 1:5). This sonship was made active in our lives the moment we became born again through faith in Jesus Christ (Galatians 3:26). But now, one with Christ, immersed in Love Himself, we have the choice to be His friend.

The pathway to sonship was "upward" in Christ through our sharing in His ascension, when He led many sons to glory as we have seen (Hebrews 2:10). The invitation that leads to friendship is laying down our lives and becoming servants of all, as sons in the Son forever. The pathway to friendship with God is "downward," being willing to embrace servanthood by going lower in this world. As sons and daughters in union with Jesus, we can choose to be servants of all, serving humanity, bringing God's infinite treasures to a broken world.

As we do this, we enter our Father's business as He confides in us the secrets of His heart so that we can obey His will and serve the broken and lost ones that His heart so loves. In Oneness, we have access to all we need. Our service is not from our own finite and limited resources, but is supplied from an endless resource of treasures in Christ Himself. We don't get tired, we don't get used, we don't run out, we don't run dry. We're our Father's best friends and colleagues. We know the Father has given us all things in Christ. In Him, we've come from the Father and are returning to the Father one day (Psalm 25:14, John 5:19-20, John 13:3, John 15:15).

As a servant of all, we have unlimited access to infinite energy, passion, supernatural power, finances, wisdom, knowledge, joy, peace and most of all, Love Himself. As we serve up our Father's limitless resources, revealing His Kingdom, we discover that being a friend of God makes us a colleague of God in the "Family" business!

We called Eli that afternoon and asked to have lunch with him and Bill the next day. Murray and I joyfully asked them at lunch if we could close on the building two months early so we didn't pay two extra months' lease of $18,000.

"Did the banks give you a loan after all then, Duncan?" Eli asked quizzically.

"No," I replied. "As you know, 8 out of 8 banks all said "no" to lending us a million dollars because we're a church. We decided not to look to them anymore."

I paused, and then looking straight at him across the table, I said, "But Yeshua, your Messiah, who you don't believe in, has given us $1,480,000 *cash* so we can close immediately with $80,000 left over!"

Eli laughed as he always does with a twinkle in his eye. He is not a follower of Jesus yet, but I know one day he will give his life to his beautiful Messiah Yeshua. He could not deny the greatness of this miracle. He has become my friend.

We agreed to close that week, and Catch The Fire Raleigh became the proud owners of their very own center, entirely debt-free. It was just such a joyful moment. What a glorious Savior Christ is!

Life in Oneness

To be in Christ is to have all things. To share in Christ's suffering has always been my greatest privilege, and now more than ever, it is my joy to walk in the way of the Cross. The way of the Cross is the way of resurrection, ascension and glorification with Christ, in Christ. Our union with Christ enables us to live a life that only Jesus can live on the earth.

As sons in the Son, we are hidden forever in the Father, filled with His very Spirit, in perfect union, inheritors of all things, including most especially God Himself (Genesis 15:1). Everything else is easy in Him. We have His faith working in us, enabling us to access His endless resources! There is no demand that we can ever place upon God that will diminish Him. He is infinite and has infinite resources. We're His sons in His Son and as sons, we're colleagues in our Heavenly Daddy's family business. We've got the business checkbook, called faith, and we have direct access to infinite resources! Nothing is impossible. One with Him, we can do all things the Father has planned in advance for us to walk in from before time began (Ephesians 2:10).

Jesus is inviting you, in Oneness, to reach up with your arms right now into that glorious atmosphere of His Kingdom that is within your reach just above your head. Take hold of a fist full of Heaven's abundance by faith and pull it down. Put it into your bank account here on earth and expect great things. You're one with the richest person in the universe and He is burning with love for you. The more you ask, the more He's glorified in the world as He does the impossible through you.

CHAPTER 15

THE FULLNESS OF DEITY

For in Him all the fullness of Deity dwells in bodily form,
and in Him you have been made complete.
Colossians 2:9-10a (NASB)

And behold, I am sending the promise of my Father upon you.
But stay in the city until you are clothed with power from on high.
Luke 24:49

My friend Steve Long, Senior Pastor of Catch The Fire Toronto, was listening to me preach on Oneness through the Cross and resurrection while we were on a missions trip in Malawi together. He suddenly exclaimed from the front row, "Wow! Our Oneness with Christ means that we are the living headquarters of the Trinity on the earth!"

Steve was exactly right. Nothing is impossible for you and me in Oneness with Christ. *God* Himself dwells in us!

Peter says God anointed Jesus of Nazareth with the Holy Spirit. Jesus came to show us His Father, and He also came to show us who we really are. He came to show us what it truly means to be human and what we can do in Oneness when we are anointed with the Holy Spirit.

God anointed Jesus of Nazareth with the Holy Spirit and with power.
He went about doing good and healing all who were
oppressed by the devil, for God was with him.
Acts 10:38

Jesus did not consider equality with God something to be held on to, but emptied Himself (Philippians 2:6-7). Though He was fully God, Jesus chose to live in this world from His "Man-ness" rather than His "God-ness." He chose to be confined completely to his humanity rather than live from His divinity. As a Man, He relied entirely upon the Holy Spirit in Him and on Him.

In this way, He showed us what it really means to be human: sons, one with God and anointed by God with the Holy Spirit and power. If Jesus had done everything He did from His divinity as God, rather than by the Spirit as a Man, He could not have been a worthy Savior.

Jesus had to be willing to be made exactly as you and I are, so that in the likeness of us and even ultimately as us, for us, He could triumph over all sin. As a Man, He triumphed over the devil and the dominion of darkness.

There is nothing Jesus did on earth that He did not do as a man. Therefore there is nothing we can't do that He did. All He did, He did by the Holy Spirit and we have been anointed with the very same Holy Spirit. By that one Spirit, we can do all the Father wants us to do. We can heal the sick, we can walk on water, multiply food, raise the dead, open the eyes of the blind, open the ears of the deaf, loose the mute tongues, cleanse skin disease—just like Jesus did. Matthew says,

Jesus was going throughout all Galilee, teaching in their synagogues
and proclaiming the gospel of the kingdom, and healing every kind of
disease and every kind of sickness among the people.
The news about Him spread throughout all Syria;
and they brought to Him all who were ill,

those suffering with various diseases and pains,
demoniacs, epileptics, paralytics;
and He healed them.
Matthew 4:23-24 (NASB)

Notice Jesus healed *every* kind of disease and *every* kind of sickness. What is excluded from *every* kind of disease and *every* kind of sickness? The answer of course is nothing. That means there is not a single type of sickness or disease we will ever come across in ourselves or another human being that has not already bowed the knee to Jesus and fled from His presence.

No matter what condition is in front of us, it has already come face to face with Jesus Christ as a human being. It has been defeated by the same Holy Spirit in Him and on Him that now is in you and on you. One with Christ, we are always the winning team!

Understanding different operations of the Holy Spirit in our lives as sons of God is a key to living a life of fruitfulness in the Kingdom, releasing the supernatural miracles, signs and wonders the Father wants to do through us, so He can make Jesus famous among us.

There are two distinct aspects to the Holy Spirit's work in the life of a believer: the inner work and the outer work.

The Inner Work

The inner work comes from the innermost being just like Jesus said:

On the last day of the feast, the Great Day, Jesus stood and cried out,
"If anyone thirsts, let him come to me and drink.
Whoever believes in me, as the Scripture has said,
'Out of his heart will flow rivers of living water.'"
Now this He said about the Spirit, whom those who believed in Him

were to receive, for as yet the Spirit had not been given,
because Jesus was not yet glorified.
John 7:37-39

When we receive Jesus Christ into our lives through faith and we are saved by grace, the Holy Spirit, the very Spirit of the Son and the very Spirit of the Father, comes and dwells in us. The Spirit joins us eternally to Christ, giving us new birth, and through that union He joins us to the Father. We are one spirit with Him (1 Corinthians 6:17). He springs up as living water flowing from within us, up and out of us into eternity.

The Holy Spirit's presence in us is forever if we are one with Christ. We don't need "more" of the Holy Spirit *in* us because we have the fullness of God dwelling in us already, since we are born again. The Spirit transforms us from the inside out. He is in us to transform us. He is the golden oil in us (Zechariah 4:12).

When Jesus rose from the dead, the He appeared to His eleven disciples and gave them the Holy Spirit.

Jesus said to them again, "Peace be with you. As the Father has
sent me, even so I am sending you." And when he had said this, he
breathed on them and said to them, "Receive the Holy Spirit. If you
forgive the sins of any, they are forgiven them; if you
withhold forgiveness from any, it is withheld."
John 20:21-23

Jesus gave His disciples His supernatural peace, which is a work of the Cross and resurrection. He commissioned them into His mission as sons filled with the Spirit, sent to the world to save it, by revealing the Savior's forgiveness, through mighty works only God can do.

Jesus breathed on them saying, *"Receive the Holy Spirit!"* I believe it was at this point that they were "born again." They were born of the Spirit, alive in His resurrection life in the Spirit forever. The resurrected Messiah, the Life-giving Spirit (1 Corinthians 15:45), breathed on them just as He breathed on Adam when he became a living being in the Garden of Eden (Genesis 2:7).

The Holy Spirit in them was the evidence in that moment that they were one with the resurrected Jesus standing in front of them, the evidence that Jesus was God and that His resurrection was real. The Spirit of Christ came in them through His breath.

They were given the Spirit in them and from that moment the fullness of the Deity was dwelling in them, because they were in Him. In Christ Jesus, we who are born again have the fullness of God dwelling in us. Christ in us is our hope of glory. Paul puts it so powerfully in Colossians,

> *The riches of the glory of this mystery,*
> *which is Christ in you, the hope of glory.*
> *Colossians 1:27*

> *For in Him the whole fullness of deity dwells bodily,*
> *and you are in Him.*
> *Colossians 2:9*

Jesus' disciples in that moment became participators in the Divine Nature (2 Peter 1:4). They had the indwelling Spirit, the very Spirit of God, the Spirit of Christ in them. So do we now. Paul says it like this,

> *You, however, are not in the flesh but in the Spirit, if in fact the Spirit*
> *of God dwells in you. Anyone who does not have the Spirit of Christ*
> *does not belong to him. But if Christ is in you, although the body is*
> *dead because of sin, the Spirit is life because of righteousness.*
> *Romans 8:9-10*

The Spirit lives within, coming up and out, into eternity. This is the indwelling Spirit for our salvation and the very Spirit who bears His fruit in us, the fruit of the Spirit (Galatians 5:22). This is not our fruit. We can't bear this fruit. It is the fruit of the Spirit. The good news is that if He dwells in us, He produces His fruit in us without us having to try. This is the inner work of the Holy Spirit.

The Apostle Paul writes,

> *You are all sons of God through faith in Christ Jesus.*
> *Galatians 3:26 (NASB)*

He goes on to say we have received our adoption as sons on the inside of us, in our hearts,

> *And because you are sons, God has sent the Spirit of his Son*
> *into our hearts, crying, "Abba! Father!"*
> *Galatians 4:6*

> *For you did not receive the spirit of slavery to fall back into fear,*
> *but you have received the Spirit of adoption as sons, by whom we cry,*
> *"Abba! Father!" The Spirit himself bears witness with*
> *our spirit that we are children of God.*
> *Romans 8:15-16a*

We are sons of God, just like Jesus and we have an inner witness, the Holy Spirit Himself, the Spirit of Adoption, so we can cry out, "Daddy!" We have received the Spirit of Adoption within us.

Blasted

I wonder what it looked like when Jesus Christ, the Eternal Son of God, freshly risen from the dead, breathed on those eleven disciples and said, *"Receive the Holy Spirit!"*

Did they stand there politely and say a quiet, *"Thank You Jesus, thank You very much! That was nice of You to share Your wonderful Holy Spirit with me."*

Can you imagine John, a couple of disciples down the row, whispering to Peter, "Hey Pete, what was that like?"

Then Peter answering, "Warm, and a little moist, but not too bad!"

No way! They had no chance to chat about it. I think when Jesus breathed on them and said, *"Receive the Holy Spirit!"* they flew backwards and were laid out on the floor, overwhelmed by the power of the living God. It was a miracle those eleven men lived through that moment!

Jesus then tells them something extraordinary, revealing just how perfectly one we are with Him now that He has given us the Spirit in us. In Luke 5, we read the story of the paralyzed man, whose friends lowered him through the roof to place him before Jesus. Jesus said to him, when He saw the faith of his friends, *"Son, your sins are forgiven"* (Luke 5:20).

This caused a real theological explosion in the minds of the teachers of the law and Pharisees who were in the room. Their problem was that a mere man, Jesus of Nazareth, was telling someone that their sins were forgiven, which is something only God has authority to do. Jesus, knowing their thoughts, said to them,

> *Why do you question in your hearts? Which is easier, to say,*
> *"Your sins are forgiven you," or to say, "Rise and walk"?*
> *Luke 5:22b-23*

The answer to Jesus' rhetorical question is that neither is possible unless you are God. However, if you are God you can do both. Then as a man He demonstrates that He is fully God by healing the paralyzed man with a word of command. He establishes His absolute authority to pronounce the man's sins forgiven by healing him.

Sharing in His divine nature means we now, one with Him, have His mission to announce forgiveness of sins, because of His sacrifice at the Cross for all people, for all time. We prove our authority to forgive the world their sins, by doing miracles only God can do in Jesus' name.

The Holy Spirit in us gives us the authority of Jesus as God, to pronounce forgiveness to whomever we forgive and heal their bodies. One with God, we now walk the world just as Jesus did. We are meant to be as good news to the world as Jesus was. The world will know Jesus is able to forgive their sins because Jesus does His miracles through us. In order to do those miracles though we need power!

The Outer Work

Jesus told the same disciples, who now had the Spirit in them, to wait in Jerusalem for the promise of the Father. He told them they would be *clothed* with power from on high.

> *And behold, I am sending the promise of my Father upon you.*
> *But stay in the city until you are clothed with power from on high.*
> Luke 24:49

Clothing is something we wear on the outside of us, not the inside. Jesus is referring to the second work of the Holy Spirit.

> *Do not leave Jerusalem but wait for the promise of the Father ...*
> *you will be baptized with the Holy Spirit not many days from now ...*
> *but you will receive power when the Holy Spirit has come upon you*

and you will be my witnesses both in Jerusalem and
in all Judea and Samaria and the end of the earth.
Acts 1:4,5,8

Clearly Jesus is referring to an outward work of the Holy Spirit, saying that they would be *baptized* shortly after He ascended to Heaven. The word *baptidzo* in Greek means to be *immersed, submerged or made fully wet.* It refers to an outer work. It is the same word we use for baptizing someone in water.

The disciples would be drenched in power when the Holy Spirit came upon them. They already had the Holy Spirit in them. His presence in them was the evidence of their union with Christ. His presence on them would enable them to do the miracles that only Jesus could do. John the Baptist had already prophesied that Jesus would give them the Holy Spirit and fire. They had the Holy Spirit in them, now they needed fire on them!

I baptize you with water for repentance, but he who is coming after
me is mightier than I, whose sandals I am not worthy to carry.
He will baptize you with the Holy Spirit and fire.
Matthew 3:11

When the Holy Spirit came a few days later on the day of Pentecost, they were all baptized with the Holy Spirit and with fire.

Divided tongues as of fire appeared
to them and rested on each one of them.
And they were all filled with the Holy Spirit.
Acts 2:3-4a

Tongues of fire entered the room, divided above them, and then a tongue or flame of fire rested on each of their heads and they were each filled with the Holy Spirit. It was a baptism of Love Himself, the very Spirit of God. Fire lit the "Oil" on the inside of them! They each became the light of the world, the witnesses of love to their cities and the whole world. Without the power of the Spirit on them, they could not have been effective witnesses. Oil needs fire and fire needs oil.

After the Spirit came upon them, they became totally different men who reached the entire known world in one generation with the good news of the Kingdom of Heaven, demonstrating their bold message with extraordinary miracles, signs and wonders.

Jesus also said the power they would be clothed in would come "from on high." It would come down and rest on them. The inner work He said would "well up into eternity," implying it would come up and out.

The Holy Spirit falling on them on the day of Pentecost was the evidence that Jesus' death, resurrection, ascension and glorification was not just His own. It was the evidence of the disciples' death, resurrection, ascension and glorification in Him. The Holy Spirit coming on them was the evidence of their Oneness and immersion in the Trinity forever.

Matthew says that some of them doubted even after He appeared to them giving them the great commission.

And when they saw him they worshiped him, but some doubted.
Matthew 28:17

I've often wondered about that little statement there. Surely they did not doubt His resurrection. By then they were all convinced of Jesus' resurrection. He had stood right there in front of them.

No, I've realized they doubted that Jesus' resurrection was their resurrection. They had no evidence of their ascension and glorification with Him.

His Father would not have accepted Jesus if He had come into Heaven without us, the many sons led to glory (Hebrews 2:10). The Holy

Spirit would not be given until Jesus had been glorified (John 7:39). When the Holy Spirit was given, it was the evidence that Jesus was glorified in the Heavens, the evidence of our Oneness with Him. His glorification meant our glorification in Him. He couldn't have been glorified unless He brought us with Him. He would have failed in His mission.

To understand this, let's look at it in reverse. The Holy Spirit coming on Pentecost on the disciples was the evidence they needed that Jesus was glorified in the Heavens, which was the evidence of their glorification in Him in the Heavens too. This meant His ascension was our ascension, His resurrection was our resurrection, and His death was our death on the Cross, with Him. No wonder the disciples were able to change the world in one generation. They *knew* they were *one* with Christ.

If you are born again today, the Father wants to give you the Holy Spirit on you so you can transform the world you live in with His supernatural power just like they did. All you have to do is ask the Father right now to receive that glorious promise.

The inner work of the Spirit, whose presence in us is the earnest deposit of our inheritance in Christ, is the very assurance of our salvation (Ephesians 1:13-14). The Spirit transforms us from glory to glory from the inside and bears His fruit in us (2 Corinthians 3:18). The outer work of the Holy Spirit on us is the anointing by which we become effective witnesses, gain access to the gifts of the Spirit and transform the world around us, filling the whole earth with the knowledge of the glory of God. The Holy Spirit in you transforms you; the Holy Spirit on you transforms the world around you.

The outer work of the Holy Spirit is not a "once and for all" work in the way that the inner work is. The Spirit in us is without measure because we are one with Christ (John 3:34, John 7:37-39, Colossians 2:9-10a). The Holy Spirit on us is given to us in ever increasing measure as we ask God for more.

I meet people who believe the baptism of the Holy Spirit is a once in a lifetime experience. They'll say, "I was baptized in the Holy Spirit 25 years ago. I don't need any more."

Their understanding of the two works is that they are *both* a once and for all work. But this was not the experience of the early church. The very disciples who experienced the Holy Spirit on the day of Pentecost asked God for more a few days later when they came under heavy persecution from the authorities for preaching Christ. God gave them more all right— He gave them so much the entire building shook! I want a building-shaking baptism of the Holy Spirit. I haven't had that yet, so there must be more, so much more.

And when they had prayed, the place in which they were gathered together was shaken, and they were all filled with the Holy Spirit and continued to speak the word of God with boldness.

Acts 4:31

This level of outpouring on them resulted in them preaching the word of God with even greater boldness. The second baptism came as a result of them asking for more boldness, not for more of the Holy Spirit. To give them more boldness meant giving them more of the Holy Spirit.

The Lord places such a high value on humility and intimate relationship, which is why the measure of the Holy Spirit we have *on* us, is related to the measure we *ask* for. We receive more by asking in the secret place, waiting on the Lord, and we also receive more when we humble ourselves by asking others to lay hands on us. Our humility honors others and is the doorway for more from God.

The measure of the Spirit we carry varies according to our waiting, our asking and our willingness to humble ourselves. We do this by submitting ourselves to gain from others what we don't have ourselves by asking them to lay their hands on us, to receive more of the Holy Spirit on us through impartation. The neat thing about the Lord is we can gain more anointing by asking *any* believer to lay hands on us, not just the "superstars" of our day. The measure He gives us from others is not dependent on how much they carry. It is the Lord who gives from Himself through the person we're asking to receive from, not the person themselves. They are the oil lamp and as long as they have fire, they can give us more fire.

The best part of all is that we grow in relationship with the Holy Spirit, touching His heart more intimately through asking and waiting. We also get to know others in the Kingdom through the dynamic of impartation. It's a win/win. I love it!

The Holy Spirit Among You

There is a third dimension of the Holy Spirit's work beyond the inner and the outer work. The Holy Spirit wants to come among a community under the open Heaven above them. When a community begins to hunger corporately for more of the Holy Spirit on them, He comes in a massive outpouring among them. This is what happened in 1994 in Toronto and thrust us into 20 years of revival all over the world, as has happened many times throughout history among hungry communities.

This is what we're so hungry for in Catch The Fire across the world. We're individually and corporately, in our communities, crying out to the Lord for the Holy Spirit among us. We want to arrest His gaze as a people so He comes in His manifest power and glory among us in unprecedented power, the likes of which have never been seen in any generation. Any church can ask for this.

When Jesus came up out of the water, symbolizing His and our resurrection, the Heavens were torn open. The voice spoke from Heaven and the Spirit descended upon Him. The Heavens were never shut again above Jesus' head. He lived under an open Heaven from that moment when He rose from the dead and we were made alive in Him. The Heavens are still open over Jesus' head—above you! You are one with Christ, so you live under an open Heaven. Christ is in you, the hope of glory (Colossians 1:27) here on earth, and you are in Christ in the Heavens (Ephesians 2:6). So if you are in Christ in Heaven and Christ is in you on earth, how can there be anything but an open Heaven above your head?

When you moved into your town, you brought an open Heaven. When you visit anywhere on earth, you bring an open Heaven to that place. This is awesome! The only thing is, the pipe above your head is not as wide as it would be if there were two of you Christians. Gather three, and it's even wider. Imagine how fat the pipe must be over your church with 200 or 2,000 members. What would the world look like if every Christian knew the Heavens were open above their heads, not because they've spent hours in prayer rending the Heavens, but because they're one with Christ? We say many unnecessary things in prayer meetings.

We don't have to plead with the Lord to open the Heavens as we worship and minister to Him. Instead, we can simply thank Him that Heaven is open above our heads because of Oneness. When we meet together under that open Heaven to give ourselves in abandoned worship of Jesus, we can ask the Father to pour on us unprecedented levels of the Holy Spirit among us.

In revelation of our Oneness with the Son of God as sons, we are drawing His gaze, moving His heart, hungering and thirsting for Him, thanking Him for His great love for our cities and nations and expressing our deep love for Him corporately. Most of all we're enjoying the riches of His grace and His ever-increasing manifest presence among us, because Heaven is invading us together.

When the Holy Spirit comes among us as a community we become a gigantic combine harvester of souls instead of being lone harvesters with a sickle. We become a giant ocean going fishing vessel, instead of a small boat at best, or a single fisherman on the bank at worst.

Imagine carrying so much of God's presence and power on you

that people who have no clue who Jesus is could literally sense Him on you individually or your church community. We are especially pressing in to God asking to carry His presence at that level. This is the third dimension of the Holy Spirit's work, the Holy Spirit *among* you. His corporate anointing radically changes a city, a region, and eventually, a nation.

The Father wants to give us so much more. He wants us to have an ever-increasing measure of His Spirit on us. He wants us to continually come back to Him and ask Him for more of His Spirit on us. Then we can live extraordinary lives, fully empowered by the very same Holy Spirit that Jesus Himself was anointed with when He walked this earth doing such incredible signs, wonders and miracles. It is our privilege as sons to come to our Father and ask Him to pour out more of His glorious Spirit, who is Love Himself upon us. We have unlimited access to the Father, who delights to give us the Holy Spirit and the Kingdom. We can come any time and ask Him for more. We're not asking for more *within* us, we already have the fullness of the Spirit in us. But we are coming to ask for more *upon* us and *among* us, so that we can use all that is ours in Christ to the fullest. Then we're ready to enter the greater works.

CHAPTER 16

MEGA WORKS

Truly, truly, I say to you, he who believes in me,
the works that I do, he will do also; and greater works
than these he will do; because I go to the Father.

John 14:12

One of my favorite sayings I learned at Catch The Fire Toronto is, "More, Lord!" Day in and day out at our Toronto church, people have said, "More, Lord!" and He has answered, pouring out His Spirit in unprecedented measure on everyone who has asked. But there are those who have been offended by this simple prayer.

"Why do we need to ask for more when we already have Christ?" they ask.

They are well meaning, yet they are missing out on so much that the Lord wants to give us. He wants us to enter the realm of the "Mega Works."

In America, we use the expression "Awesome!" to describe anything and everything that impresses us. The English have their version too: *"Mega!"*

Jesus used that word too to describe the kind of things that you and I would do because He's gone to the Father. He used the Greek word, *megas ergons*, meaning *mega works*—or *greater works*.

Truly, truly, I say to you, he who believes in me, the works that I do,
he will do also; and greater works than these he will do;
because I go to the Father.
John 14:12

Jesus is giving us an incredible invitation here into the full measure of what is possible for us through our Oneness with Him, which will come through His death, resurrection, ascension and glorification as He returns to the Father.

And the Father wants to take us even further: He wants us to have an ever-increasing measure of His Spirit on us so we can do *mega works*. It is our privilege as sons to come to our Father and ask Him to pour out more of His glorious Spirit, who is Love Himself upon us. We have unlimited access to the Father who delights to give us the Holy Spirit. We can come anytime and ask Him for more. We're not asking for more within us, since we already have the fullness of the Spirit in us, as we've seen. But we are coming to ask for more upon us so that we can use all that is ours in Christ to the fullest. I like to ask for the double portion.

When I was at university, I would listen to messages by Reinhard Bonnke, the evangelist and founder of Christ For All Nations (CFAN), one of my all-time heroes in the faith. My father-in-law gave me a couple of Reinhard's messages on cassettes, and I listened to them over and over again, until I could quote them word for word. I even mastered a fairly convincing Reinhard Bonnke accent. I loved him and I loved his preaching. I wanted more than anything to have an anointing like his anointing and to preach the Gospel of Jesus Christ with signs and wonders like he did.

One day as I listened to one of Reinhard's messages in my bedroom, I felt an overwhelming hunger for more of the Holy Spirit and I lay prostrate on the floor, with my face pressed to the floor. I asked the Lord, "Father, I ask You in the mighty name of Jesus, that You would give me a double portion of the anointing that rests on Your servant Reinhard Bonnke so that I can make Jesus famous my whole life. I ask You that it would be a sign You have given me what I've asked for, that I would meet this great man somehow and he would lay his hands on me and say those words: 'I give you a double portion.'"

I firmly believe Reinhard's anointing is his anointing and we must all ask the Lord for our own anointing, but I also understood impartation. I was asking the Lord to give me the "double portion," just as Elisha asked Elijah.

Elijah said to Elisha, "Ask what I shall do for you, before I am taken from you." And Elisha said, "Please let there be a double portion of your spirit on me."
2 Kings 2:9

Smith Wigglesworth, a great English preacher, once said, "There is something about believing God that will make Him pass over one million people just to anoint you!"

I had no way of ever meeting Reinhard Bonnke in this huge world, filled with billions of people, but I knew God finds our hunger for Him and our faith in Him irresistible.

Seventeen years went by. Throughout that time I hung pictures of Reinhard Bonnke's huge campaigns in Africa on my office walls in Toronto, Canada, to remind me of the ocean of souls in this world that need Christ. I understood by then that my calling was to reach the "crowds" by raising up disciples to become leaders and teaching them to do the same, according to Paul's mandate to Timothy (2 Timothy 2:2).

However, I loved the pictures of the huge crowds, one of which was a large picture of the single biggest crowd CFAN has ever had in one single meeting, well over a million people. The pictures were a constant reminder to me of the millions of people we can reach through the power of multiplication, as every believer reaches one and then disciples that one into a champion who can win others, who then in turn wins others.

One day John, Carol and I were having lunch together at the church. One of our colleagues called to let me know that Reinhard Bonnke was having lunch at another table in the same restaurant as he was, very close to the church. I told John and he immediately jumped up and told Carol and me we should go right away to see if we could greet him.

We headed over to the restaurant and John and Carol waited in the car while I went into the restaurant, doing a quick bypass to make sure it really was the great man of God at the table. Sure enough, there he was, sitting with a couple. I went back to his table and with apologies, greeted him and his friends. I told him he was one of my lifelong heroes of the faith and that my father-in-law had given me his preaching on cassettes years ago. I explained that I was now a pastor at the Toronto Airport Christian Fellowship and that John and Carol Arnott were outside and wished to greet him as well.

He was very kind and burst into a huge smile assuring me he would join us outside when he had settled the bill. Within a very short time, Reinhard came out of the restaurant, striding across the car park towards us with his friends. He gave John and Carol a huge hug.

Then straight away John, who is hilariously playful sometimes, gave me such a shock by saying, "Reinhard, you are one of Duncan's heroes in the faith. He can do your accent really well, can't you Duncan? Why don't you show Reinhard and his friends how you can take off Reinhard's accent?"

I was floored, but this was not a time to be shy, so with my best impersonation of Reinhard, I preached a few lines from one of his sermons I used to listen to repeatedly. He immediately burst out laughing and said in his husky German accent, "Oh Duncan, when you were speaking just then, you had no accent at all! Not at all! I haven't preached that message in a very long time! I must preach that one again!"

John, who clearly hadn't finished having the maximum fun said,

"Reinhard, you minister a lot in Nigeria. Duncan can do a perfect Nigerian English accent too, because he grew up in Nigeria with missionary parents. Duncan why don't you show Reinhard your Nigerian English accent too?"

Without hesitation I preached another line or two in a perfect Nigerian English accent. Reinhard laughed very hard; he loves Nigeria and instantly recognized the authenticity of my accent. He mentioned that he was going to Lagos, Nigeria about six weeks later, to do a large campaign—and invited me to join him as a guest. I was so thrilled.

Then John did one of the most incredible things only a true father in the faith can do for a son. He said to Reinhard, "It would be the greatest honor in Duncan's life if you would lay hands on him and give an impartation of the anointing. Would you be willing to do that?"

Reinhard looked at me with his piercing eyes and said, "It would be my pleasure!"

I had never shared with John my secret prayer all those years ago. The Holy Spirit completely orchestrated the perfect moment.

I knelt down in front of Reinhard right there in the car park, silently asking for the double portion. He laid his hands on my head and prayed Heaven down on me, asking the Lord to gloriously anoint me.

He ended by saying, "I give you the double portion in Jesus' name!"

I fell onto the pavement of the car park as the Holy Spirit fell on me in mighty power. I was pinned to the ground by the weighty glory of God.

From that day on, I noticed a powerful increase in the level of effectiveness and fruitfulness in the Kingdom through my life and ministry.

The Lord had heard my prayer all those years ago. He gave me the answer when I was willing to seize the moment by faith and humble myself before another man, honoring the anointing, by honoring Reinhard and allowing the Lord to use him so mightily to impart a greater measure of the Lord's anointing onto my life.

I have asked many people to give me an impartation, and each time

I've seen an increase. The more I use the anointing, the more it increases.

Use what you have, and always be hungry for more. No matter how anointed we are, there is always more. There are billions of souls still trapped in the dominion of darkness and it's our privilege as wise sons, one with Christ, burning with Love Himself, to win them by the anointing (Proverbs 11:30).

Power for Greater Works

Terminal cancer, paraplegia, quadriplegia, multiple sclerosis, cerebral palsy, Down's syndrome and Parkinson's disease are a few of the many conditions and diseases that I long to see people healed instantly from. There is a burning fire in my heart to see the victory of the Cross of Jesus Christ being manifested through us as we lay hands on the sick and they are fully healed. I'm longing to see Jesus' power and authority being fully evidenced through all His people, myself included. Jesus invites us into His works—and even greater works than He did, if we believe in Him.

There is so much more for us to press into. There are endless supernatural adventures in God. There is power in the name of Jesus to destroy all the works of darkness and we are one with Christ. The Bible tells us that for this reason the Son of God was revealed: to destroy *all* the works of the devil.

> *The Son of God appeared for this purpose,*
> *to destroy the works of the devil.*
> 1 *John 3:8b*

One day, I asked the Lord why I don't see everyone healed of every condition that I minister to. His answer was amazing. He simply reminded me of His word in Malachi,

But for you who fear my name, the sun of righteousness
will rise with healing in its wings.
Malachi 4:2

As the sun rises at dawn, it seems weak in its strength. The same sun gets hotter and hotter and stronger and stronger as it rises. In exactly the same way, the Lord showed me that when the Son rises in this world as we make Him famous, His power will grow increasingly powerful. The key is holding on to the truth of our Oneness with Christ, until we are ourselves are manifesting the "noonday sun." We must press on and not give up, ever!

There is a deep longing in me to see the greater works and to see those with incurable conditions totally healed by Jesus through us, His ordinary people, who are called by His name and filled with an extraordinary God. Go for it! Let's let our "failures" lead us to the secret place with God, where we can cry out to Him for more of His anointing and power for the "noonday sun" to rise in our generation.

I want to share some of the hundreds of stories of Jesus' power. My hope is that these stories will stir your heart to begin asking God to enable you to do the greater works like Jesus promised because He has gone to the Father.

During my time at TACF, I went to Kyrgyzstan to lead a weeklong school with 300 Kyrgyz pastors and leaders. This trip was very special to me, because my father, Colin, came with us. He loved being part of the team and ministered tirelessly, despite being the oldest member of the team. Each night at 10 pm we did a head count; my father was always missing. We'd find him in the middle of a huge group of Kyrgyz people. He'd be laying hands on them, praying for them and pouring out the Father's love on them, filled with the burning, fiery love of God. He could not help giving it away to those precious Kyrgyz people.

During one of the sessions on the importance of forgiveness, I noticed a woman in the middle of the crowd. Every time I looked in her direction, she would point to her ears and then her mouth, and then shake her head. She seemed a little weird, honestly, and I kept hoping she would stop. It was distracting me while I was preaching!

At the end of the message we always had a huge response as the people dealt with their forgiveness issues. I asked the team to wade into the crowd and minister healing, as we often see a healing explosion after such a message. I waded into the crowd myself, laying hands on people to heal them in Jesus' name. As I turned around, I came face to face with this woman. She repeated her routine action of pointing to her ears and then to her mouth and shaking her head.

My interpreter was working with me and I asked her to find out what was going on. She quickly ascertained in Russian that next to the woman was her 16-year-old daughter and her elderly mother. They both told my interpreter that the woman had been deaf and mute since birth, 40 years ago. I realized that was what the woman had been trying to tell me!

Without hesitation I put my fingers in each of her ears and commanded the Kingdom of God to come and the will of her Father in Heaven to be done on earth in her body, just as it is in Heaven. I commanded the deaf and mute spirit to leave her immediately.

The woman looked right into my eyes and put both her forefingers on each hand to her ears and then to her mouth and shook her head as she had done, so many times. My heart sank as I had thought my words of command sounded really good and powerful! I felt very aware of my failure and her straight faced glare. I did it again, exactly as I did the first time. She repeated her ritual and shook her head. By this time, the level of faith and excitement in the crowd around us started rapidly leaking out of their shoes. All of my faith leaked right out of my boots!

I repeated my prayer of command about seven times and each time with no change. I was about to use my usual statement when nothing happens: "I'm really sorry you haven't been healed, let's put this one down to the fact I'm still learning."

However, I remembered that the sun is rising and I am truly one with Christ. Everything I did, Jesus did, and vice-versa.

Jesus' faith was mine.

Suddenly, after I said it one last time, she gave a look of utter surprise, broke into a broad grin and pointed enthusiastically at one of her ears, repeatedly jabbing her finger upwards. Then she pointed at the other ear and shook her finger as if to say "no," pointed at her mouth and shook her head.

I was stunned. I realized right away she was telling us she could now hear in the one ear, but not the other yet. I excitedly and authoritatively commanded the other ear to open in Jesus' mighty name. She jumped again with surprise and started pointing excitedly upwards at that ear too, then quickly pointed at her mouth and shook her head again. I knew she was letting me know both her ears were open but she still couldn't talk. The crowd was all murmuring excitedly.

In that moment the Holy Spirit whispered into my heart, *"Duncan, spit on her tongue!"*

I went into conniptions!

Spit on her tongue Lord? I can't do that! I might miss and hit her in the eye and she's not blind! I thought to myself. I was desperately trying to remember exactly how Jesus had spit on the deaf man's tongue in the story (Mark 7:33).

I couldn't remember, so I did what spontaneously came to mind (which, by the way, is always a good thing to go by when you're not sure of what to do). I carefully put my right two forefingers up to my mouth and spat on them both, fully loading them up with my spittle, till they were dripping. Then looking straight at the woman, I opened my mouth and stuck out my tongue. She looked extremely hesitant at this point to copy me, and I didn't blame her. After a second or two, she opened her mouth and stuck out her tongue.

I thrust my two fingers onto her tongue and my slimy fingers hit her doubly slimy tongue and skidded off to one side. The instant my fingers hit her tongue and slid off, her tongue was loosed and she started shouting, "Slava Bogu, Slava Jesu! Slava Bogu, Slava Jesu!" Which is Russian for "Thank You God, thank You Jesus!"

Then she put her hand to her mouth as people often do when they feel they've said something wrong, then she took it away instantly and started shouting again, "Slava Bogu, Slava Jesu! Slava Bogu, Slava Jesu!"

Her mother and daughter stood, stunned, with their hands over their mouths. They were astonished. So was the crowd—and so was I. I had a thought that I should ask her to say something "normal" to her mother, something unspiritual. I didn't want her to think the only time she could speak was when she was praising God. I wanted her to know she really could speak. I asked my interpreter to tell her that, which she did.

The woman turned to her mother and rattled something off in fluent Russian. Her mother and daughter both screamed in complete shock, their hands over their mouths. The crowd went wild and my interpreter just stood there with her mouth covered by her hand in amazement.

I asked her what in the world the woman said to her mother and when the interpreter recovered enough to speak, she told me the woman had turned to her mother and said, "Mom, when are you going to take me and my daughter home for dinner? We're starving hungry!"

My first thought was to wonder why in the world she would say those as her first words in her life. Then I realized, I probably would have said that too if I had been trying to tell my mother I was hungry for 40 years!

The woman was given fluent Russian instantly, as if she had spent her whole life speaking. It was just an absolutely electric moment. The people went wild with joy; the "lid" on all our lives was blown off. Truly, nothing is impossible for God! We can do the works of Jesus because we are one with Him. All glory to Jesus!

Another time, I was in Norway, spending a few days with my friend Terje Liverød. He had invited me to a barbecue with some of the leaders from his church. While I was there, one of Terje's friends shared how Terje had invited him and his wife to join them at a Catch The Fire conference in Vennesla, Norway, where I was one of the speakers. Apparently, Terje had introduced him to me on the first day of the conference but I didn't say a word to him. Instead, I had jabbed my clenched fist right at his stomach at close range without touching him, yelling, "Boom!"

I then fixed my gaze on him rather piercingly, before turning around and walking off! He told me he was immediately outraged and offended by my strange and inappropriate behavior. He was about to tell his wife to get her coat so they could get out of there because we were all crazy.

However, as he turned to his wife, who looked shocked as well, he realized the pain he had been constantly suffering with every day since he had had surgery some years earlier for cancer in one of his organs was gone. It had instantly vanished the moment I had air "punched" him. He told me he was absolutely floored and gave glory to Jesus. He stayed for the rest of the conference pain-free, and had been pain-free ever since, which at that point was over a year. Hallelujah!

He told me that as a result of that experience, he brought one of his friends to another Catch The Fire conference in Oslo, Norway several months later. Again, I was one of the speakers. He brought his friend because he was suffering with Stage 4 cancer and had been sent home to die, with only a few weeks left to live. Apparently, I didn't recognize him or remember him; but after he had briefly introduced me to his friend, I "punched" his friend in the direction of his stomach at close range without touching him, making a sweeping fast chop across the air about six inches above the man's head.

I said in a loud strong voice, "Kingdom of God come and will of my Father be done! I command the spirit of death to leave this man now! Boom!"

Apparently I then turned around and walked off. His friend looked at him with an astonished voice, as if to say, "What in the world was that?"

Instead, he said words to the effect of, "Wow! There's no more pain, it's just instantly vanished! I think I'm healed!"

Sure enough, he made an instant and total recovery from that moment on and almost a year later was back at work and living a healthy and normal life. Hallelujah!

Recently a young woman came to Catch The Fire Raleigh. She had two small children but looked like "death warmed up." She was dying of Stage 4 cancer. Her friend, who brought her, introduced me to her at the end of the service and asked if I would minister to her, explaining the situation.

Knowing that people who are dying are not looking for nice prayers, they need healing, I unashamedly "punched" her in the stomach area without making any physical contact. I made a "chop" in the air above her head, also without touching her. I prayed the same prayer of command, commanding the Kingdom of God to come and the will of her heavenly Daddy be done, and the spirit of death leave her! When I had finished, she turned around with her friend and left. I've never seen her again.

But several weeks later, I received an email from some close friends of the same woman. They were students at the Bethel Supernatural School of Ministry, in Redding California. They filled me in on the story. Knowing their friend lived in Raleigh, they had encouraged her, "Get down to Catch The Fire Raleigh and ask them to pray for you to get healed." It was her last hope because the doctors could no longer help. Her friends told us that after she visited our church that day, she had contacted them to let them know she had been completely healed that morning, when the pastor had prayed for her. They reported she had no trace of cancer in her body! I was stunned reading their email. All glory to Jesus our Champion Messiah!

The Father wants to increase the level of power on our lives so that He can use each of us effectively in bringing the Kingdom of God on the earth. My longing is that each of you will be inspired to go into the secret place and ask for more, so much more, of the glory of Jesus. The Lord is so moved when we are willing to humble ourselves before others that have gone ahead of us and receive an incredible impartation of so much more.

The very first time we experience the Lord when we are saved, being baptized in the Holy Spirit and fire is just the beginning. He wants us to ask Him for all He is longing to give us, if only we will draw near to Him and ask Him.

We have His fullness within us and there is a broken world out there waiting for the sons of God to be revealed. They are waiting for someone to show them what the Father is truly like by doing the very miracles Jesus did and even greater miracles in His mighty name.

I'm convinced there is no limit to what we can ask the Father for. Jesus' invitation of John 14:12 is without conditions for those who believe in Him, and I think Jesus is inviting us to take that verse so literally we could potentially experience the very same transfiguration Jesus experienced (Matthew 17:1-5). The Father could literally show us Christ in us, the hope of glory dwelling within us, the glorious Treasure streaming through the earthen vessels (Colossians 1:27, 2 Corinthians 4:7).

Imagine being in a prayer meeting with a group of friends. Suddenly, one of your friends starts pointing at you with their mouth hanging open because everything that happened to Jesus on the mountain of transfiguration is happening to you as you are literally transfigured in front of their eyes. Then it happens to all your friends. I think if that happened, our prayer meetings might be jam-packed from then on! I'm pressing in for levels of glory so great among us, that we live in perpetual awe.

Anointed Shadows

Peter walked with such an awesome level of the Holy Spirit's presence and power on him, 2000 years ago, that huge numbers of people brought their sick relatives and friends to him convinced they would be healed.

They even carried out the sick into the streets and laid them on cots
and mats, that as Peter came by at least his
shadow might fall on some of them ...
and they were all healed.
Acts 5:15-16b

The crowds were so big many couldn't reach him. But the anointing was so tangible on him that someone got the idea even his shadow might carry the presence and power of God! They laid their sick relative where Peter's shadow would be sure to hit them. When it did, the power of God hit their relative and they were instantly healed. Suddenly everyone had the same idea. Maybe his face was radiant with so much glory that his shadow was filled with the rays from the light of his face!

Imagine having so much anointing on you that even your unsaved friends start coming up with ingenious ways of making a draw on the power of God on you! That's what happened to Peter. I'm longing for God to release so much power on us that the world rediscovers that even our shadows are anointed. By the way, it really helps if you go outdoors. Our shadows are much stronger in the daylight than in the church! The church that leaves the four walls is far more likely to help the world rediscover the shadow healing ministry. How anointed does the world think your shadow is?

I can't help thinking that if Peter discovered his shadow could heal the sick a few short months after Jesus went into Heaven, what was His expectation of the greater works we would have discovered 2000 years later? I think he might be very disappointed with where the church is at generally across the earth! It's time to press in to God, asking Him to unleash unprecedented levels of His manifest presence and power on us. My prayer lately is, "Father, would You please give us the maximum possible level of power we can have on us and among us before we die. Anoint our shadows again. Give me a mighty shadow!"

We want the kind of power that causes the world to flock to us to meet Jesus. The kind of power that enables an entire generation to be saved, becoming the greatest harvest of souls ever witnessed on planet earth. The kind of power that causes the world to dream of ways they can place a draw on our anointing. It's time for the church to come out of the shadows and into the sun, rising with healing on its wings, so that the church can cast its shadow on the world and see Jesus heal it of all its pain and suffering. Rise up church, you are one with your Savior. There is *fire*, even in your shadows, to do mega works!

CHAPTER 17

THE FIRE OF LOVE

God is love.
1 John 4:8,16

Love is ... the very flame of the Lord.
Song of Songs 8:6

See how great a love the Father has bestowed on us, that we would be
called children of God ... and we know that when He appears,
we will be like Him, because we will see Him just as He is.
1 John 3:1-3

The greatest part of Oneness is our immersion and union with Love Himself. The Apostle John tells us in his first letter, God is Love (1 John 4:8, 16). What a statement! So absolute and compelling and he tells us twice in relatively quick succession in chapter 4 of 1 John. Whenever the Word of God states something twice it means it is very important. God is love. John does not state that God is merely loving or lovely, but that He *is* love.

The God of the Bible is the only God who claims to be Love and who has demonstrated that love in the only way to demonstrate love perfectly: by laying His life down for His friends. To make the claim, "I am Love," God must be telling the truth, being love for all people, throughout all time and eternity, in all places and be able to exhibit that love perfectly, hindered by no one else. He must be the only God.

The only God who is Love is the Trinitarian God revealed in the Bible. No other god is able to make the claim to be love and no other god has ever demonstrated perfect love.

To be Love, God has to be Trinity. For love to be love, there must be a lover who loves, a beloved who receives that love, and the love itself. The lover has to give and receive love. The beloved receives the love from the lover and gives that love back to the lover. The love has to flow two ways: from and into *both* parties. God is one God who is one essence, one substance, Love, but He eternally exists as three distinct Persons: the Lover, the Beloved and the Love. He cannot be just one singular person. One person cannot be love. Love must be given *and received*.

This is the great mystery of Love. There is constant movement in Love, a glorious eternal dance. Love is a glorious feast of eternal delight between each of the Persons within the Trinity. The Lover has eternally loved the Beloved with Love from His great heart, and the Beloved has eternally reciprocated that Love to the Lover from His great heart. A glorious communion, or community of Love.

Jesus Christ of Nazareth always referred to God as "My Father." The ancient Israelites in His day tried to stone Him because He called the Father, His Father, thereby making Himself equal with God.

*"My Father is working until now, and I am working." This was why
the Jews were seeking all the more to kill him, because not only was
he breaking the Sabbath, but he was even calling God his own Father,
making himself equal with God.*
John 5:17-18

Do you say of him whom the Father consecrated and sent into the
world, "You are blaspheming," because I said, "I am the Son of God"?
John 10:36

Jesus knew that He was the Son of God and rightly called God His Father. In the Psalms, God refers to His Son.

I will tell of the decree: The LORD said to me, "You are my Son; today
I have begotten you."
Psalm 2:7

The Father Himself also testified of Jesus Christ of Nazareth on at least two occasions, as recorded in the Gospels. Once at Jesus' baptism as He came out of the water and once on the mountain when Jesus was transfigured in front of the three disciples.

And a voice came from heaven, "You are my beloved Son; with you I
am well pleased."
Mark 1:11

And a voice came out of the cloud, saying, "This is my Son, my
Chosen One; listen to Him!"
Luke 9:35

This reality leads us into understanding more of the mystery of God. God is utterly unchanging. He has not changed in all eternity and neither will He change in all eternity.

For I, the LORD, do not change.
Malachi 3:6 (NASB)

If God were able to change, then it would mean that at one time, He was not God, but He changed and now He is God. If He is "god" now but He is able to change, then what is He going to be next? Whatever "that" is, it is not God, because God is only God if He is eternally God. Thankfully, God is, always has been and always will be, the same. He exists as God, in the everlasting now, and He does not change. He is the eternal *"I AM who I AM"* (Exodus 3:14). That's why He is God.

The Eternal Father and the Eternal Son

If Jesus called God His Father, and the Father confirmed this, calling Jesus His Son, then God has eternally existed as Father and God has eternally existed as Son, because God cannot change. If Jesus is God's Son, then He has always been the Father's Son, throughout all eternity. If the Father is Jesus' Father, then He has always been the Son's Father, throughout all eternity. Because God is Love, the relationship between the Father and the Son is eternal Love. There has never been a moment in all eternity when the Father and the Son have not existed.

When God calls Israel *"My son"* in Hosea 11:1, He is revealing His Eternal Fatherhood. We know that Israel as a people have only existed since their ancestor Jacob, who God later named Israel, was born of Isaac about 2000 years before Jesus came.

Because God is eternally unchanging, this means He was a Father before Jacob was born and the nation of Israel came into being. Jacob's birth would have changed God into a father, if He had no Eternal Son already. The very fact that the God who cannot change calls Israel *"My son"* is living proof He has an Eternal Son. The same argument goes for Adam, who Luke calls the son of God (Luke 3:38).

A father is only a father once He has a child. Before he has a child he can make claims to be many things, but he cannot claim to be a father.

It's having a son or a child that defines a person as a father.

God, who cannot change, could not call Adam or Israel "My son" unless He was already a Father. The very reason He could call Israel His son, was because for all eternity He has been the Father of His Eternal Son. He did not "become" a Father; He already was one.

For all eternity the Son has been the Son because He has had an Eternal Father. You can only be a son if you have a Father. God is the Eternal Father who loves the Son and the Eternal Son, who loves the Father and the Eternal Spirit, who is the love between the Father and the Son.

Love Needs

A couple of years after arriving in Toronto, I was receiving some healing from life's hurts. My counselors helped me to see that for much of my life growing up, I believed I didn't need anyone. I believed at a subconscious level that I was just fine on my own. I didn't need my wife, my parents, my leaders, my children, my church; I didn't need anyone.

I was convinced that everyone else didn't really need anyone either, unless they were weak individuals that needed help. But in that moment with my counselor, I realized that we all, particularly men, have a tendency to want absolute independence. We reserve the right to need no one, and we project that onto our spouses and our children, trying hard to make sure they know they don't really need us either. They, like us, are fine as long as we have God, or as long as we are being strong!

I suddenly realized this was ungodly, and I yielded to the invitation to deal with the root causes of my independent self-reliance (in my case, 13 years of boarding school). After the ministry time I was able to embrace being needed, and to embrace the reality that I have needs I can share with others in love. I realized that *love needs*. Kate couldn't believe I was the same husband!

However, I have struggled to understand how the infinite, omnipotent God, who is Love, "needs." How can love need, if God is Love?

The answer came as I was teaching our first year students at the Catch The Fire School of Revival in Raleigh.

I was sharing with the class, that about three years earlier, our youngest daughter Nathania, had asked me a very tough question, one evening at the dinner table, as a twelve year old.

"Dad, you know you always have told us that Jesus went to the Cross and not the Father?"

I answered, "Yes."

She went on, "Then you've taught us, Jesus did nothing of Himself, but only what He saw His Father doing? Well, that means the Father must have gone to the Cross first!"

Stunned by the enormity of her question and ability to come up with such a theological conundrum, I told her to eat her dinner up and that her father needed some time to think before I gave her an answer. I also told the class I still was searching for the answer.

Then, right there, as I was teaching on the nature of the Trinity and their Eternal existence as three Persons of one substance as the community of Love, I understood the answer: Love truly "needs."

It is this incredible dynamic of "need" that gives us a glimpse of the eternal selfless revelation and experience of Love, which is the eternal Cross the Trinity have forever been willing to embrace. The Cross has always existed in the Trinity as the way of Love that the Father, the great Initiator of the Love, has always embraced and revealed.

The Father, who is God, could choose to be and to do whatever He wants in and outside of the universe, yet He constantly forsakes all things and instead chooses just one thing and one thing alone: to be known as the Father of His great Son. In choosing this "death" of all things, He embraces His "Cross," His sacrifice. He denies Himself and all self-definition and chooses instead, to be eternally defined by His Son, preferring Him above

Himself. In this, He experiences the "resurrection" of knowing and enjoying the eternal delights of being "Abba," "Daddy," the Eternal Father of His beloved Son.

The Eternal Son, who is God, could choose to be and to do whatever He wants in and outside of the universe; yet like His Father, He constantly forsakes all things and instead chooses just one thing and one thing alone: to be known as the Son of His great Father. The Son has always embraced His own "Cross"—the sacrifice of saying no to all things, denying Himself and all self-definition and choosing instead to be eternally defined by His Father, preferring Him above Himself. In this, He experiences the "resurrection" of knowing and enjoying the eternal delights of His Father, defined, known and enjoyed eternally as *"My Son, whom I love."*

The words of the Father in Mark 1:11 are in the eternal, present tense. He did not say, *"My Son whom I loved"* or *"My Son whom I will love."* He said, *"My Son whom I love."*

Only an Eternal Being can say, *"My Son, whom I love."* And He can only say it to an Eternal Being. Otherwise, He would have to say, *"My Son, whom I love for now, while He is alive."*

The Father, who loves the Son, is the Eternal, Everlasting great I AM. His name is the I AM who I AM. The Son Himself has the same name, I AM who I AM, which in Hebrew is YHWH (Exodus 3:14).

Both the Father and the Son eternally exist as the Eternal I AM. Jesus told the Pharisees,

> *Truly, truly, I say to you, before Abraham was, I AM.*
> *John 8:58*

The name I AM is the eternal name of God, who exists as the Father who is Love and is loved eternally, and the Son who is Love and is loved eternally, and the Spirit who is the eternal Love.

The Eternal Flame of Love

The Holy Spirit is the eternal Love Himself who has flowed from the Father to the Son and from the Son to the Father. Love is a consuming fire. At the burning bush, fire appears and the voice speaks from the midst of the burning bush that was on fire, yet it did not burn. God tells Moses to speak to the leaders of Israel.

> *God said to Moses, "I AM who I AM." And he said, "Say this to the people of Israel, 'I AM has sent me to you.'"*
> *Exodus 3:14*

In both the Old Testament and the New Testament, it is written that God is a consuming fire:

> *For the LORD your God is a consuming fire, a jealous God.*
> *Deuteronomy 4:24*

> *For our God is a consuming fire.*
> *Hebrews 12:29*

Solomon says in Song of Songs,

> *For love is strong as death, jealousy is fierce as the grave. Its flashes are flashes of fire, the very flame of the LORD.*
> *Song of Songs 8:6*

Love is the very flame of the LORD! God is a consuming fire. Love is a consuming fire that cannot ever be quenched. Wow! This is so incredible! I'm just on fire writing this. The Holy Spirit is the very Love of God and He is a consuming fire. He is the flame of Love, the very flame of the LORD, the I AM who I AM. He is the very Spirit of the Father (Matthew 10:20, Romans 8:11) and the very Spirit of the Son (1 Peter 1:11, Romans 8:9, Galatians 4:6) and He Himself is the Eternal Spirit (Hebrews 9:14). God is the burning fire of Love.

Paul confirms this in Romans.

Hope does not disappoint, because the love of God has been poured out within our hearts by the Holy Spirit who was given to us.
Romans 5:5

We cannot have the Love of God without the Holy Spirit. If we have the Holy Spirit, then we have the Love of God. This is so wonderful. The Love of God is not a theology, philosophy or theory. It is not a platitude or wishful thinking. The Love of God is none other than the Person of the Holy Spirit, the third Person of the Trinity.

He wants to be experienced. He delights in the finished work of the Cross, through which Christ became one with us so that we could be eternally one with Him. He delights that we are now sons of God, just like the Son of God. Sons of glory, just like Jesus (Hebrews 2:10). He delights that we are one spirit with Him.

But the one who joins himself to the Lord is one spirit with Him.
1 Corinthians 6:17 (NASB)

To be one spirit with Him means that we are one with the everlasting flame of Love Himself. We are one with Christ; therefore we are one with the Father and one with the Holy Spirit. We are the beloveds in the Beloved! We are the sons of God, brought into the eternal dance and family of Love. We are one in the communion of Love, the community of Love. We are now eternally loved as beloveds in the Beloved forever and ever. There is no distinction. The Father does not love the Son Jesus more than He loves you and me. In Christ we are the sons of God, loved just like Jesus is loved. The very same flame of Love, the Holy Spirit, the Spirit of the Father and the Son, burns in us and we burn with love in Him. In Christ Jesus, we are one with burning Love Himself!

One of the verses in the Bible that is most precious to me is John 17:23. Jesus is about to go to the Cross, where He would reveal the greatest love, the eternal love of the Father and the Son towards us who believe, demonstrated when Christ died for us while we were yet sinners (Romans 5:8).

Jesus prays to the Father saying,

> *The glory that you have given me I have given to them, that they may be one even as we are one, I in them and you in me, that they may become perfectly one, so that the world may know that you sent me and loved them even as you loved me.*
> *John 17:22-23*

I'm sure without exception all of us would agree that Jesus is the Father's favorite Son. Here in this prayer, Jesus reveals the eternal plan the Father and the Son have always had. The Father would have many sons just like His Eternally Begotten Son, each of whom would be loved exactly as he loves His dear Son Jesus. This means the Father loves you and me as much as He loves Jesus, which makes each of us His favorite sons! Come on! Now and forever, the Father loves you as much as He loves Jesus and sees you as His favorite Son.

Look at Jesus' purpose in our Oneness: *"that the world may know that You sent Me, and loved them, even as You have loved Me"* (John 17:23b). Our Oneness with Christ is our greatest soul winning opportunity.

There is no limit to endless Love. Endless Love knows no competition. There is no shortage of love in Eternal Love! Jesus knows, in the Father's gigantic heart of love, the Father can love us all, as if each of us is His only son. Jesus Himself loves us so much that, in His love, He wanted the Father to love you as the Father loves Him. He gave His life so we could experience the same love of the Father for all eternity.

How do we know this is true? How do we know this is true in us—experiential truth, not just abstract theological truth? We know it because the Trinitarian God has revealed it through the Cross and resurrection of Jesus Christ, by the Spirit. The Father, the Lover, loves you as much as He loves Jesus, the Beloved, and He proved it by raising Jesus from the dead to gain you by the Holy Spirit, Love Himself (Romans 4:25).

The proof of His love and our Oneness with Him is His Spirit dwelling in us. The Apostle John knew that, which is why he writes,

> *By this we know that we abide in him and he in us,*
> *because he has given us of his Spirit.*
> 1 John 4:13

He was there in the room when the Holy Spirit fell on 120 people that had gathered and were praying in unity. Suddenly they all heard the sound of a mighty, violent rushing wind that came from Heaven and filled the whole house where they were sitting. Luke tells us in Acts 2 that they saw what appeared to be tongues of fire, individual flames that were together and then separated, coming to rest on each of them. All of them were filled with the Holy Spirit.

Baptized in the Flame

Understanding that God is love, we can see Pentecost so differently now. It wasn't just about being clothed in power; it was a total immersion in Love Himself. What an incredible moment that must have been for all the early believers that morning on Pentecost. Absolutely mind blowing and utterly amazing. When the Holy Spirit came from the Father, just like Jesus had promised before He died and rose again, He came in the form of physical fire. The fire in the burning bush that Moses saw was now on their heads!

John the Baptist had said that One would come after him, whose sandals he was not worthy to untie, and that this One would baptize not with water as John had been doing, but He would baptize with the Holy Spirit and with fire (Matthew 3:11).

Pentecost was a baptism of fiery love. They were filled with the Holy Spirit and the fire of God's great love fell upon them. Their hearts burned with His love. The flames of love were on their heads in the visible realm and love was burning in their hearts in the invisible realm as they were all filled with the Holy Spirit, Love Himself.

God loves us with an everlasting love, because He is the Eternal I AM the consuming fire of Love. He became one with us at the Cross, and through sharing in His death and resurrection we are one with Him in His eternal life. We are forever beloveds in the Beloved Himself, and therefore one with the Father and one with the Spirit. We are literally immersed in the Trinity, forever burning with His fiery love.

Imagine spending three and a half years as one of Jesus' closest friends and disciples. Imagine what it would have been like to be able to witness firsthand the incredible miracles, healing, signs and wonders that He did and listen to the most powerful teachings ever spoken by any human being throughout history. Imagine leaning on Jesus' breast, so close to His heart.

The Apostle John had that very opportunity. By the end of Jesus' ministry he described himself as the *"one whom Jesus loved"* (John 13:23, 21:20), who leaned on his breast at the Last Supper. This demonstrates the amazing level of friendship love between Jesus and John, which must have spoken to the heart of Christ. He had come from the Father's bosom, where for all eternity He had rested, and where He was now returning. He knew that because He was going to the Cross, John and all of us would be able to rest in His bosom, in the bosom of the Father forever.

John was there with Jesus from the very beginning of Jesus' ministry all the way to the Cross. As far as we can tell from the scriptures, he was the only disciple who was there at the Cross. As He was dying, Jesus declared John to be Mary's son and Mary, Jesus' mother, to be John's mother. John tells us that from that moment he took Mary into his home as his own mother and presumably cared for her for the rest of her life (John 19:27). John witnessed Jesus' death. He witnessed the blood and water gushing out of Jesus's side as the soldier pierced Him (John 19:34).

John was one of the very first disciples to witness and believe in Jesus' bodily resurrection. He had run to the tomb and seen the clothes lying where Jesus had been laid. He saw the head cloth that had been wrapped around His face lying neatly folded off to one side. When he saw these things, John believed Jesus had been raised from the dead, just like He had promised (John 20:8).

He had been there when Jesus suddenly appeared to them all when they were all gathered in a fully locked room, for fear of being found and put to death just like Jesus (Luke 24:37-43).

John felt the *physical* body of the resurrected Son of God. Jesus now had a body that looked just like them, yet quite obviously was something altogether more awesome. His body was spirit, yet physical at the same time. This shows us that to be "spirit" in the Kingdom of God does not mean ghostlike, in the way that we tend to naturally think of what it means to be "spirit." This is phenomenal! Most of humanity has associated "spirit" to be nonphysical in the sense that it can't be touched; but Jesus, after His bodily resurrection, shows us being ghostlike is not what it means to be spirit at all. The Uncreated One has a physical body that is tangible to sight and touch forever.

This is amazing, considering He tells us in John 4 that God is spirit.

God is spirit, and those who worship Him
must worship in spirit and truth.

John 4:24

Notice that Jesus says *God* is spirit. God is Father, Son and Holy Spirit. All three Persons of the Trinity are of the exact substance: spirit. Jesus is the exact representation of the Father and the radiance of His glory (Hebrews 1:3). This means that the Father is exactly like the Son and the Son exactly like the Father. This means that the Father Himself has a tangible form that can be seen and touched. Jesus confirms this in John 5.

And the Father who sent me has himself borne witness about me. His
voice you have never heard, his form you have never seen.
John 5:37

It also means that the Holy Spirit too has form, as Luke writes,

The Holy Spirit descended upon Him in bodily form like a dove.
Luke 3:22

The Holy Spirit in this case chose to come as a dove. Jesus' resurrected body shows us that each person of the Trinity has form, and that they relate to each other intimately just like we do, physically, tangibly, through our bodies. They share one substance, spirit. And yet because spirit is not like anything of this world, they can enjoy having a physical relationship with each other bodily, without in anyway compromising their capacity to be everywhere at once.

As spirit, they have form that can be seen and touched. John tells us that he saw the Spirit descend upon Him and remain on Him (John 1:32). This implies touch; that Jesus and the Holy Spirit had a tangible, sensory experience as the Spirit rested on Him. Jesus' resurrected body shows us we too will have the same form of God for eternity.

Spirit is substance that can be felt and seen. Jesus felt dynamite power go out of Him when the woman with the issue of blood reached out and touched the very edge of His garment (Mark 5:30 and Luke 8:46). He could feel the power and substance of the Holy Spirit. He says in John 5:19 and 20 that the Son could do nothing of Himself, but only what He saw the Father doing. The Father was spirit, yet Jesus understood that to be "spirit" means to be tangible and to be visible, even though it is invisible to the natural eye. Its invisibility does not mean it can't be seen, because spirit is substance. It can be seen and felt. Deep calls to deep. The Spirit searches the deep things of God. Sight is implicit in this.

The Key to the Supernatural

Faith is the key to the supernatural realm. It is the 'currency' of the Kingdom. It was true for the disciples when Jesus appeared to them in His resurrected body and they saw Him, heard Him, touched Him, and even watched Him eat a piece of fish in front of them.

Hebrews 11:1 says that faith is the *substance* of things hoped for and the certainty of things not yet seen. True faith is never blind. Later in that chapter the writer says that by faith Moses endured the wrath of Pharaoh, because he saw Him who is unseen.

Faith enabled him to see the substance of God, though God was invisible. He longed to see His person, His face and he pursued God until he saw the brightness of His tangible form and met with Him face to face. He and the elders even ate with God on the mountain.

Then Moses and Aaron, Nadab, and Abihu, and seventy of the elders of Israel went up and they saw the God of Israel. There was under his feet as it were a pavement of sapphire stone, like the very heaven for clearness. And he did not lay his hand on the chief men of the people of Israel; they beheld God, and ate and drank.

Exodus 24:9-11

The elders all saw God. They ate and drank with Him. They saw Him so clearly that Moses could describe God having feet, and under His feet was a pavement of sapphire stone. They saw the very substance of Heaven. They could say forever that God had feet and that He stood on those feet just like we do and that God has made substance in the heavens to walk on, in this case a *sapphire* stone pavement. I cannot even conceive how beautiful that must have been.

All of Israel who have ever loved God since have longed for this tangible experience of seeing and touching God. It has been placed in the very heart of humanity since God created us in His glorious image. God doesn't have a form, a body with feet like ours. We have form, a body, just like His! We have eyes, hands and feet precisely because He does! We are made in His image.

John was on the Mount of Olives when Jesus said His final words and then ascended into the sky until a cloud hid Him from their sight. Jesus flew in a body just like theirs that could be seen and touched, yet was now obviously radically different to theirs. He flew! Those kinds of moments must have made a lasting impression on them all.

John writes in his first letter to the churches,

> *That which was from the beginning, which we have heard, which we*
> *have seen with our eyes, which we looked upon and have touched*
> *with our hands, concerning the word of life.*
> *1 John 1:1*

It was seeing Him and touching Him – the resurrected Christ – that was the evidence and anchor of John's hope in the Gospel. He had done this for three and a half years with Jesus and knew that the evidence of His life and ministry showed He was God, but then the unthinkable for all the disciples happened. Jesus was killed on the Cross. He had watched this man who was the hope of the world die. His hope of God in Christ was dashed.

Then after He rose again three days later, John was able to see and touch this very same Man, who burst out of his grave clothes as the Man of Heaven, fully God and Lord over all the universe, having conquered death forever. What he saw convinced him of the greatest hope of all: that we can see, hear, touch and intimately know forever this Majestic Man, who is God!

For John, this hope of Jesus' tangible substance in His resurrection body was the essence of the hope of all humanity in the Gospel: that we too will have the very same resurrection bodies. This has been the deepest hope in the human heart since antiquity when we were removed from the garden and lost our capacity to readily see and touch God the way Adam could. However, John's hope goes so far beyond what Adam once had.

See what kind of love the Father has given to us, that we should be called children of God; and so we are. The reason why the world does not know us is that it did not know him. Beloved, we are God's children now, and what we will be has not yet appeared; but we know that when he appears we shall be like him, because we shall see him as he is. And everyone who thus hopes in him purifies himself, as he is pure.
1 John 3:1-3

What a glorious hope John had burning in his heart. One day when Jesus appears, John says, we shall see Him and *"we will be like Him"* (1 John 3:2). We will be just like Jesus! We will be able to walk through walls and fly just like Jesus did. More than that, we will be raised from the dead, so that sin, death and Hell will never again ever be able to hold us. We will be glorified with the same glory that Jesus has been glorified with; the Father's very own 'Self' (John 17:5 and John 17:22).

In the great love of God, the Father answers the deepest cry of John's heart expressed in 1 John 3:2. It was the Father's answer to the greatest mystery: what did Jesus look like now that He had returned to the Father?

John knew that Jesus, having returned to His Father, was now glorified in His Father's presence (John 7:39, John 17). John had never seen Christ in the fullness of His majestic glory.

The Glorified Christ

At the very end of John's life, while he is a prisoner on the Island of Patmos for the sake of the Gospel, the Father answers the cry of John's heart and shows him Jesus, as He is, in His majestic, radiant glory.

It is so very exciting. In Revelation 1, when John turns to see the voice that was speaking behind him, that sounded like the thundering of a multitude of many waters, he turned and saw Jesus face to face in all His glory. The resurrected Christ, now ascended and glorified forever. John's reaction, despite being intimately acquainted with Jesus for three and a half years as well as being with Him for forty days after He had been resurrected, was that he fell face down as if he was dead. The majestic presence of the Glorified Jesus Christ, the Son of God, was utterly overwhelming for him. He had witnessed Him as the Lamb on the Cross; now He was the blazing fiery, glorious Lion of Judah!

> *I saw one like a son of man, clothed in a robe reaching to the feet, and girded across His chest with a golden sash. His head and His hair were white like white wool, like snow; and His eyes were like a flame of fire. His feet were like burnished bronze, when it has been made to glow in a furnace, and His voice was like the sound of many waters. In His right hand He held seven stars, and out of His mouth came a sharp two-edged sword; and His face was like the sun shining in its strength. When I saw Him, I fell at His feet like a dead man.*
> *Revelation 1:13-17 (NASB)*

The Lord revealed Himself to John and in showing Himself to John as He is now glorified in the Heavens, He revealed the fullness of the greatest good news to all humanity of those who believe in Jesus: *we will be just like Him.* John is given a glimpse of what we will all look like one day, when Jesus appears.

Our faces will shine like His, our eyes will be blazing fire. We will be dressed in white robes to our feet, with golden sashes across our chests. Out of our mouths will come the word of God, sharp as a two edged sword. In our hands we will juggle stars, and our feet will be like polished bronze. His feet were like burnished bronze and our feet will be like polished bronze. The bronze that He was willing to become at the Cross that testified to His Oneness with our sin and us, now gives testimony of our Oneness with Him in His resurrection and glorification forever. John saw us all in Jesus' feet that walked the earth, and now walked the Heavens!

We are one with Him forever and one day we will be just like Him. That is our glorious hope and the best news a human being can ever hear!

We will not be confined by anything in the natural realm. We'll be able to fly! We'll be able to hear sound, touch and feel, smell, see and taste. We'll enjoy delicious food forever! Everything will stimulate our senses beyond our wildest imagination. The colors will be beyond anything we've ever seen and the fragrances of the New Earth will be beyond our wildest dreams. If you love technology in this world just wait to see the technology of the New Earth we'll be inventing and using with God. I'm excited about that!

We are going to live eternally in our new home that will be His new home, a New Earth, that is the New Heaven, where God will dwell forever, together with us. This temporary world will be transformed into the eternal beautiful home of the greatest love affair in all eternal History. Heaven and Earth as one place, where forever God and Man live together in perfect, glorious union. The streets of our eternal home will be made of gold and its walls will be made of the most precious Heavenly gemstones, sparkling in the everlasting, glorious, pure, radiant light. Hallelujah, we have the brightest, most glorious future that is beyond all possible imagination!

Until that day it is our privilege, in Oneness with Christ, to bring as much of what is reserved in the Heavens for that day, into today. We can now live our lives from Heaven to earth, just like Jesus did.

> *No one has ascended into heaven except he who descended from heaven, the Son of Man who is in Heaven.*
> *John 3:13*

Jesus was in Nicodemus' garden when He said this, yet Jesus knew He was in Heaven simultaneously. This is where we are, seated in the Heavenly realms, walking on earth, One with Christ, the Father living in us by the Spirit. It is now our turn to take up our cross daily and serve the world just like Jesus did. We will live with one glorious passion: to make Jesus incredibly famous doing all that He did and even greater things than He did.

Plunging into the depths of the Cross and resurrection is our privilege on this side of death and is the key to living by the Spirit in the supernatural realm. Oneness with Christ means we can live a life on earth that only Jesus can live. It changes absolutely everything. He dwells in us on earth, and we dwell in Him in the Heavens. Together in Oneness with Christ, we bring Heaven to earth.

CHAPTER 18

ETERNAL FIERY ONES

But I see four men unbound, walking in the midst of the fire, and they are not hurt; and the appearance of the fourth is like a son of the gods.

Daniel 3:25

Since I was a young boy, I have always loved the story of Shadrach, Meshach and Abednego. Three best friends who defied one of the fiercest, greatest and scariest kings that has ever lived on planet earth: Nebuchadnezzar, King of Babylon. The story is an awesome story of God's deliverance.

Nebuchadnezzar had created a golden statue of himself, placing it in the center of the city. He decreed that when all the people, including all the senior leaders of the nation, heard the sound of music, they were all without exception to bow down before the golden statue of Nebuchadnezzar or be thrown into a burning furnace.

Shadrach, Meshach and Abednego were Jewish exiles and senior leaders in Babylon because of the favor of the Lord that was upon them. They loved the God of Israel and refused to bow down to Nebuchadnezzar's golden statue when the music played. Everyone else bowed down, and when they saw that the three men refused, they reported them to the king. The king was furious when he heard about their refusal to obey his royal decree and ordered them brought before him.

The king asked if they would repent and bow down to the statue. They refused, declaring one of the greatest statements of courage ever made.

Oh Nebuchadnezzar, we don't need to defend ourselves before you in this matter. If we are thrown into this blazing furnace, the God we serve is able to rescue us from it and He will rescue us from your hand, O King. But even if He does not, we want you to know, O king, that we will not serve your gods or worship the image you have set up.
Daniel 3:16b-18 (NASB)

The king was furious with the three men, and ordered the furnace to be heated up seven times hotter than usual. He had them bound and thrown into the fiery furnace, which was so hot that the men carrying them to the mouth of the furnace all lost their lives in the fire.

As Nebuchadnezzar looked into the furnace, he exclaimed,

But I see four men unbound, walking in the midst of the fire, and they are not hurt; and the appearance of the fourth is like a son of the gods.
Daniel 3:25

He approached the furnace and shouted to them, asking them to come out of the fire. When they came out and everyone thronged around them, they were unharmed. Not one hair on their heads was singed, and there was no sign of fire damage or smell of fire on them or their clothes. It was a tremendous demonstration of God's power to save us from the fire. It was the literal fulfillment of the Lord's promise to Israel through the prophet Isaiah.

When you walk through the fire you will not be burned; the flames
will not set you ablaze. For I am the LORD your God,
the Holy One of Israel, your Savior.
Isaiah 43:2b-3a (NASB)

What a picture of the Cross. The *"one like a son of the gods"* was without doubt the very same One who is the Son of God, who came into the "fires" of this world of sin and death and rescued us from the fire of a just God: "seven times" hotter than any earthly fire we would have had to suffer. Jesus was melted forever into Oneness with us; the tin and copper became one brand-new metal, bronze.

Jesus Christ rescued us from the eternal fire of Hell when He went to the fire of the Cross. Satan wanted us to bow down and worship him and his image, but Jesus Christ came into the fiery furnace of sin and death and rescued us who believe. When we get to Heaven there will not be even one hair of our heads singed, nor will there be any damage or smell of fire on our clothes. Hallelujah! What a Savior.

This "Fourth Man" who walked in the fire with these three men, is the Man of Fire with whom we are one for eternity. In the Heavens we shall be the ones who walk with the Fiery Three, who are the glorious persons of the Trinity, each of whom have a form that we too will have. This is one of the most exciting aspects of our salvation. Our Oneness with Christ means we are one with the consuming fire of Love Himself.

I've heard it preached that the Father has no body. However, I think this is perhaps not the best way to describe the Father. He does not have a body made of flesh and blood like ours, that's for sure; but as we have seen, He does have form. Jesus said the Father is spirit, but that doesn't mean he doesn't have substance. The Father has form. He has a voice, therefore He speaks from His mouth and He can be seen.

His voice you have never heard, his form you have never seen.
John 5:37

There are glimpses we get in the Bible of the Father's glorious form. Daniel sees a vision of the Ancient of Days take His seat.

As I looked, thrones were placed, and the Ancient of Days took his seat;
his clothing was white as snow, and the hair of his head like pure wool;
his throne was fiery flames; its wheels were burning fire. A stream of fire
issued and came out from before him; a thousand thousands served him,
and ten thousand times ten thousand stood before him.
Daniel 7:9-10

This is a remarkable description of the Father. He has form such that He is wearing clothes. He has a head with hair that is white like wool. He has all the features of a human head, with eyes, ears, nose and mouth. It's not that He is like us. We are like Him! He is not made; we are made in His image.

He can sit and does sit, having arrived from somewhere on his feet to take His throne. This is not the description of someone without a body. He has a body, but not as we know a body, because His body is spirit, not flesh and blood. It's a Heavenly, uncreated body.

The Apostle John sees His form when he is in Heaven in the Spirit.

At once I was in the Spirit, and behold, a throne stood in heaven,
with one seated on the throne. And he who sat there had the
appearance of jasper and carnelian, and around the throne
was a rainbow that had the appearance of an emerald.
Revelation 4:2-3

He sees One who is seated on the throne in Heaven. We know that this 'One' is the Father because, Jesus, the Lamb of God, comes up to Him who is seated on the throne and takes the scroll from His hand, because He alone was worthy to do that (Revelation 5:7).

Look at how John describes God the Father's form. He says that he had the appearance of "jasper" and "carnelian." Some translations say "sardius." All three of these stones are variations of red in their color. Jasper is a red opaque color. Carnelian varies from red to orange and yellow. Sardius is a red precious stone and likely to be what we might call a ruby.

The Father is red! He is indescribably beautiful, beyond our imagination, and He looks like burning, fiery red rubies laced with orange and yellow. He is described in very fiery terms.

Daniel says there is a river of fire flowing from before Him. Not a few flames, but a *"stream of fire"* (Daniel 7:10) that must have looked similar to a molten lava stream. Liquid fire! This is the glorious fiery Father, the first Person of the Trinity.

We know that the Ancient of Days in Daniel's vision is the Father rather than the Son, because a few verses later Daniel goes on to say,

> *I saw in the night visions, and behold, with the clouds of heaven there came one like a son of man, and he came to the Ancient of Days and was presented before him. And to him was given dominion and glory and a kingdom, that all peoples, nations, and languages should serve him; his dominion is an everlasting dominion, which shall not pass away, and his kingdom one that shall not be destroyed.*
>
> Daniel 7:13-14

Here we see distinctly two persons in the vision. One like a Son of Man and one called the Ancient of Days. We know they are two distinct persons in the vision because the one like a Son of Man comes up to the Ancient of Days. He is led into His presence.

We see that this Son of Man is no ordinary man. For starters, He's walking on the clouds, something that no human, no other man, has ever done! The disciples saw Him ascending into the Heavens until a cloud hid Him from their view (Acts 1:9).

Secondly, no other man has ever been given an everlasting kingdom that will never be destroyed. A kingdom is only a kingdom while the king is alive, so for a kingdom to be everlasting, the King must be eternal. This one, like a Son of Man, was an eternal Man, who is the rightful King of an eternal Kingdom.

No other man has ever been worshiped in the presence of the Ancient of Days by every people, nation and language. Only God is to receive that worship. Only He is worthy of that worship. Here we have this worship being given in front of the Ancient of Days to a Man. That this Man was worshiped and adored in the presence of the Ancient of Days is testimony to who this Man really was. He was none other than the King of Glory Himself, the Eternal Son of God, the second Person of the Trinity, the only One who is worthy of the very worship the Ancient of Days Himself, the Father, is worthy to receive.

This Son of Man is none other than Jesus Christ Himself. The One who is the same yesterday, today and forever (Hebrews 13:8), just like His Father who is the *"one who was and is and is to come"* (Revelation 4:8). This is the same Jesus Christ, who says to John, *"I am the Alpha and Omega"* (Revelation 22:13).

His Father calls Himself by the same name, saying to John, *"I am the Alpha and the Omega"* (Revelation 1:8). This Son is the radiance of God's glory and the exact representation of the Father's being who sustains all things by His powerful word (Hebrews 1:3). The One who said to Philip, *"Don't you know me, Philip ... Anyone who has seen me has seen the Father, so how can you say 'Show us the Father?' Don't you believe that I am in the Father and the Father is in me?"* (John 14:9, paraphrase)

This is the glorious Son who said,

He who loves me will be loved by my Father as well and I too will
love him and manifest myself to him. If anyone loves me and
obeys my teaching, my Father will love him and we
will come and make our home with him.

John 14:21

To love Jesus is to love the Father, because He is one with the Father forever. Yet in the glory of this communion of love we call the Trinity, He is a distinct person within the Godhead, of the exact substance of the Father and the Spirit.

The Father is revealed in Daniel's vision in fiery terms. John's description of the glorified Son of God is closely similar when he sees a vision of Jesus Christ on the Island of Patmos.

One like a son of man, clothed with a long robe and with a golden
sash around his chest. The hairs of his head were white, like white
wool, like snow. His eyes were like a flame of fire, his feet were like
burnished bronze, refined in a furnace, and his voice was like the
roar of many waters. In his right hand he held seven stars,
from his mouth came a sharp two-edged sword,
and his face was like the sun shining in full strength.

Revelation 1:12-16

What a glorious, majestic, infinitely beautiful, champion Savior! His countenance is exactly like His Father's. His head and hair are just like the description of the head and hair of the Ancient of Days. Jesus is truly the radiance of the Father's glory and the exact representation of His being. The second Person of the Trinity is described in the same fiery terms as His Father.

We've seen that the Father and the glorified Son are described in very similar terms. For years, I have wondered what the Spirit Himself looks like. I've wondered if it's even possible to use that kind of language about the Holy Spirit. After all, He is the Holy *Spirit*! Just like Jesus referred to the Father as being spirit, yet having form, I began to realize that the Holy Spirit, who is obviously spirit, might have form, as the Father has form.

Some years ago, I was ministering with John Arnott in Bogota, Colombia with two other pastors from Toronto. John spoke one morning in a church of about 15,000 people. At the end, the pastor of the church asked us to lay hands on everyone there for an impartation of the Holy Spirit. We waded into this gigantic sea of people laying hands on everyone.

They were all longing for more of the Lord. For two hours, we each laid hands on endless hungry people. Every person we touched was filled with the Holy Spirit and was overwhelmed by God. They all fell over, hundreds and hundreds of people. The men that were helping to catch people as they fell were working tirelessly with us, but despite their best efforts, the power of the Holy Spirit was so overwhelming they could not keep up. People were literally piling up on top of each other. They didn't seem to mind one bit, though.

What was so remarkable in those two hours was the Holy Spirit seemed keener than I was to touch His people. As I went into the crowd I would feel His tangible presence in me and *with me*. Sometimes He would go before me, an invisible Presence walking in front of me, and the people would fall left, right and center before I even got to them. Then next minute, I would see the evidence of Him moving in a different direction in the crowd near me.

I discovered there were "hot spots," where it seemed like the Holy Spirit particularly wanted to stay in that place in the crowd and really pour out His power on those individuals. If I stayed in the hot spot the level of power became so strong; then I would walk too far and move out of the hot spot into an area of the crowd that was "cool."

I learned that day the Holy Spirit loves to partner with us and He is more hungry to touch His people than we are for Him to touch us.

There is something about hungry hearts that is irresistible to Holy Spirit. He will pass over others to reach the hungriest. I also began to be convinced, through the way He moved through the crowd that day, that the Holy Spirit must have form. I was hungrier than ever to know Him more.

Sometime later, during one of our annual youth camps in Toronto, I had another dynamic experience with the Holy Spirit. During the worship one night, I decided to get my video camera out. I stood off to one side, near the front of the meeting hall, filming every now and then.

My attention was drawn to one of our 13-year-old girls. She was dancing with all her might before the Lord. The level of passion, hunger, unashamed, totally abandoned dancing and worship she expressed amazed me.

Suddenly something astonishing happened. It was as though a door opened just above her head and an invisible Person dropped through landing right on top of her. She yelped as she was mushed to the floor in a heap, shaking violently on the floor. I knew the Holy Spirit had just radically touched her.

Quick as a flash, the teenager next to her fell over, just as if someone had laid their hand on their forehead, like we do when we lay hands on people. Then, down went the next kid and the next and the next. It was the most extraordinary thing I have ever seen.

It looked just as though a person was walking around the room, laying hands on each of the young people's heads. One by one, they were touched. They were filled with the Holy Spirit, falling over, shaking violently, crying, laughing, and many of the other typical reactions to the presence of the Holy Spirit. The difference this time was that there wasn't any human being involved. It looked like a person was there, except that they were invisible. It was totally mind blowing!

This invisible Person did not stop until they had "laid hands" on every one of the hundred or so young people in the room that night. The whole room was in total chaos with bodies strewn everywhere, and all the youth were filled with the Holy Spirit. I caught the whole thing on film and have never shown it to anyone. The moment was so holy, beyond anything I have ever seen in this world. It was a Heavenly invasion as the Holy Spirit Himself took over the meeting.

The glory went on and on and after about an hour or so, I had the thought, *"I ought to make room for the guest speaker to speak."* I was in such a terrible dilemma because I didn't want to cut across anything that the Lord was doing in such a sovereign way.

Eventually, I did ask everyone to take their seats and they all did quite valiantly, picking themselves up and dragging one another back to their seats, some of them scraping each other off the floor.

I introduced the speaker. She said one line and suddenly from the back row, one of the young men jumped to his feet and sprinted to the front of the room, yelling "AGHHH ..." all the way. Then he threw himself onto the floor at the front just next to the guest speaker. In that instant the entire room of young people all followed him at once and there was a mosh pit of bodies lying everywhere of youth expressing extreme hunger for the presence of the living God.

We "lost" the meeting, I'm thrilled to say. For hours we were all overcome by God's presence and glory. Our own daughters each had dramatic encounters with the Lord that night too.

Abby, our middle daughter, who was ten years old at the time, was forever marked that night. She was so filled with the Holy Spirit. She laughed nonstop with her eyes shut, shaking all over for hours. When we decided at about midnight that she really should go to bed, we tried to lift her up but she was too heavy. It took seven of our strong young men to pick up a slim ten year old because the weighty glory of God was so thick on her.

When they eventually managed to get her onto her bed, with my wife supervising the operation, Kate asked Abby, who was still laughing uncontrollably, what had been and was still happening. Abby simply said over and over, "He's so beautiful, He's so beautiful and He's tickling me!"

Her face was shining and she has never been the same since. I don't think our family and many of the youth will ever forget that night.

My experiences with the Holy Spirit pushed the envelope for me. I saw increasingly evidence that He has form. Growing up as a missionary kid in an Evangelical Christian family, I had never thought about the Holy Spirit in any other terms other than He is likened symbolically to wind, fire, oil and water, or perhaps a dove. He was always the member of the Trinity least spoken or thought about. Now after these experiences in Colombia and at Youth Camp, I was getting really excited about the Holy Spirit.

One Sunday at TACF, John and Carol called me onto the platform and shared that they felt the Lord wanted them to commission me to go to the nations. I went up onto the platform and John spoke a few words over me. They anointed me and prayed for me in front of the congregation. As they laid hands on me, the power of God hit me and I went flying backwards onto the floor on my back.

Carol then started soaking me like she's done for thousands of people. John carried on with the meeting. As Carol was soaking me on the platform and praying for me quietly, the Lord took me into a vision.

I was on a vast plain like the ones I grew up around in Northern Nigeria. A wide open plain, with horizons as far as the eye could see. As I looked in one direction I saw in the far distance the figure of a Man shimmering in the midst of what looked like a mirage on a hot summer day. As I noticed Him, instantly He rushed right up to me, taking split seconds to reach me from the far distance. The speed with which He rushed up so that He stood right in front of me shocked me. I was overwhelmed by His presence.

He was shimmering and dazzling. He had the form of a man, but His clothing was fiery light and extremely bright. He Himself was like fire, like glowing fiery, molten metal, except like nothing I had ever seen. He was so forceful and graceful all at the same time. He looked at me with piercing fiery eyes and smiled.

At the speed of light, He reached out His fiery hand and touched me. Instantly He lit me. I caught fire as He touched me. I had the sensation of being on fire and started screaming and vibrating violently on the platform, my shoes nearly flying off. I started rolling back and forth because I was "on fire!" I had the sensation of red-hot fire, yet not the pain I would have had if I were physically burned, just the conscious awareness of tremendous heat.

For over a year, I felt the sensation of heat on me constantly. During the day, going about my daily work, I was burning. Sitting and eating, I was burning. Hanging out with my children, I was burning; and sometimes when I was preaching, the heat was almost unbearable.

Kate would get upset with me when we would go to bed, complaining that I was like a red-hot oven! I would wake up in the night and have to throw the sheets and bedcovers off me because I was just burning.

But during this time, I noticed the anointing in my life really increased. The Lord began to do extraordinary things in the meetings that I was involved in, or when I would minister to people on the streets or in restaurants. Miracles and healings were like a hot knife through butter. Many people I laid my hands on would feel the sensation of intense heat all over their bodies. It was remarkable. Sometimes while I was preaching in the nations, people would be spontaneously ejected out of their seats and roll violently over and over down the aisles as if they were on fire and trying to put the fire out. It was quite shocking at times. This particularly happened in Australia and Great Britain.

I was so intrigued by the vision of the visitation of this fiery Man. Who was it? Was it an angel? Was it a fiery Seraph? Was it the Lord? Which One in the Trinity was it? Was it even biblical? I'm one of those people who like to know these things. It was so dramatic and made such an impact on my life, I needed answers to these questions.

Who had protected me that day all those years ago in Oxford, when I was mugged on the way home that night I was so gloriously baptized in the Holy Spirit? Who was the One leading me around the crowd in Colombia creating "hot spots" in certain places among the people? Who was the invisible "Person" that came in through the "trap door" at the youth camp and who came up to me in the vision as a "Man of Fire" and lit me that Sunday?

Recently, the Lord showed me the answer to all the questions I had been asking concerning the Holy Spirit as I was preparing to preach at Catch The Fire Raleigh.

Ezekiel's Vision

One day, I was reading in the book of Ezekiel and my eyes were opened to a passage of scripture that I had read so many times before, but had never stopped to consider.

> *Then I looked, and behold, a form that had the appearance of a man of fire. Below what appeared to be his waist was fire, and above his waist was something like the appearance of brightness, like gleaming metal, like amber. He put out the form of a hand and took me by a lock of my head, and the Spirit lifted me up between earth and heaven and brought me in visions of God to Jerusalem.*
>
> *Ezekiel 8:2-3a*

The words leapt out at me. I had never seen before that this passage clearly gives us a glimpse of the form of the Holy Spirit. He is described in extraordinary, fiery terms—just like the Father and the Son. He appears to Ezekiel as a glorious "Man of Fire," or a "Fiery Figure," as some translations say; so beautiful, powerful and otherworldly.

Ezekiel is lost for words trying to describe what he saw. He tries his best, but he just can't find the words to exactly describe this glorious, magnificent Being. He has to resort to describing Him using the closest human and other created things.

He first says that he sees a figure *like* that of a man. Most translations have a footnote saying a "Fiery Figure" or a "Man of Fire" because Ezekiel can't describe this Man.

He looks as though He has the form of a man, with arms, legs, a waist, head, hands and so on, but He clearly was not a man, not a human being. Neither was He merely a human that was on fire. He *was* fire! He was a Man *of* Fire, or a Fiery Figure. His "body" looked like He was fire from the waist downward, and molten, glowing metal or red-hot yellow amber upwards. The Hebrew word here is used for polished bronze. None of which is remotely human.

Ezekiel tries again to describe Him using human terms saying, *"from the appearance of his waist downwards ..."* I love that. It's as though Ezekiel is saying,

"I'd like to say from his waist downward, but I can't, because I've never seen a waist like that! I can only say, from the *appearance* of His waist downwards."

Then he goes on to say He was *like* fire. Ezekiel can't say fire because it was fire, but not like fire he'd ever seen before. It was an altogether different fire, so he has to say *like* fire. He says that He stretched out what *looked like* a hand. He can't call it a hand but has to say what *looked like* a hand.

It is so fantastic. Ezekiel saw such a majestic Being and was without words trying to describe the vision.

He goes on to show another remarkable dynamic of the awesome nature of this Fiery Being. He says,

> *He took me by a lock of my head; and the Spirit lifted me up*
> *between earth and the heaven.*
> *Ezekiel 8:3a (KJV)*

This verse stuns me even as I'm thinking about it. The very first part of our anatomy that burns instantly when exposed to fire is our hair.

I had an experience with fire trying to light our barbecue cooker once. The cooker flared in my face and singed my eyebrows and the front of my hair. It was terrible and I was so relieved to have not been badly hurt. Hair burns in seconds in the presence of fire.

I learned firsthand that the very first part of our bodies incinerated by fire is our locks of hair! The weakest part of our entire bodies is our hair. If someone tried to lift you up right now by your hair they would have a handful of hair and you would have a very sore head! Yet here is this "Man of Fire," reaching out a "hand" of fiery glowing amber—and Ezekiel's hair is not damaged in any way.

Not only does the fiery hand not burn the hair, but supernatural strength is instantly imparted to Ezekiel's hair and hair follicles. So much so, the Spirit is able to lift him up by a lock of his hair. *Not just off his feet, but up between earth and Heaven!* This is a supernatural Being, able to impart supernatural strength to the created, something only the Creator can do. This is no human being.

The psalmist says that God makes the winds His messengers; this can be translated as making "angels" and "flames of fire" His servants (Psalm 104:4). I've wondered if maybe this Fiery Being that Ezekiel met was one of God's fiery angelic beings.

However, upon closer examination of the passage, it clearly says that:

> *He took me by a lock of my head; and the Spirit lifted me up*
> *between earth and the heaven.*
> *Ezekiel 8:3a (KJV)*

"He took me by a lock of my head" and *"the Spirit lifted me up"* are describing *the same* action. The one who stretched out what looked like a hand, took Ezekiel by the lock of his hair and lifted him up by it, was one and the same Being.

This Man of Fire is none other than the Holy Spirit himself,

appearing to Ezekiel as the form of the Fiery One that He is. I can never
again go back to thinking of the Holy Spirit in impersonal terms alone like
fire, water, oil or wind. He is like all of those, yes, but He has a form.

He has hands and a body with a waist and legs just like a man,
yet He is no man in the sense of being human. He is God, of one substance
with the Father and the Son. He is the uncreated Creator of all things, just
like the Father and the Son, the glorious third Person of the Trinity. Just
like the other two Persons of the Godhead, He is described in fiery terms,
having aspects of His form that are just like the Father and the Son.

This forever changes my relationship with the Holy Spirit. He is
no longer impersonal. He is no longer distant. The fire that Jesus baptizes
us with is not an abstract fire. It is none other than this glorious Fiery
Person whose very Presence in us, on us, and among us when He touches
us, imparts majestic, supernatural strength to our physical bodies in this
natural world. It explains why I burn with love whenever I'm filled with the
Holy Spirit. He is the Love of God, the flame of Love, the I AM Himself.

Our story is the greatest love story the universe has ever witnessed.
Christ came as the "Fourth" in our "fire" of sin and death on earth, rescuing
us from an everlasting fire. He did this so that we could be the "fourth"
in the eternal consuming fire of Love, the Trinity Themselves. We are now
forever one with Him, one with burning Love, the Eternal God who is a
consuming fire. In this world, that glorious reality is thinly veiled beneath
our skin. May our faces shine with ever increasing glory the closer we get
to that final trumpet call.

We are the fiery sons of God, just like Him. We walk in the fire of
God's love and give it away. We are in the eternal dance of Love , joining
the three Fiery Ones, Father, Son and Holy Spirit. God is our glorious
inheritance. Like Shadrach, Meshach and Abednego, we are not consumed,
burned or harmed, nor do we even smell of fire. God's fiery presence imparts
glorious supernatural strength and might to us, right now and on into
eternity. Our spirit man is fully one with each Person of the Trinity. We

will walk as Four Fiery Ones for all eternity, consumed by Love.

We are the glorious Bride of the Heavenly Man, a fiery, passionate, intimate Bride who is making herself ready, maturing in her Oneness with the Spirit. She is preparing for the ultimate return of the King, her glorious Eternal Bridegroom. Soon, at the end of all time, God's ultimate purpose will be made complete when we are given our new fiery bodies just like Jesus' glorified body. All things will be made one. We will live forever in the New Heaven that will be the New Earth (Isaiah 65:17, Revelation 21:1).

The glory of that day is so far beyond the natural faculties of our minds or our imaginations we cannot even begin to perceive what it will be like. Yet Paul says,

> As it is written, "No eye has seen, nor ear heard, nor the heart
> of man imagined, what God has prepared for those who love him,"
> these things God has revealed to us through the Spirit.
> I Corinthians 2:9

It is the joy of the Holy Spirit to make known to us what belongs to Jesus and therefore belongs to us in Him (John 16:14). We can taste glimpses of the eternal glories to come while we are alive on this earth. There are no limits. These things God has revealed to us. The world is longing, groaning, waiting for the sons of God to be revealed.

Go for it! Consumed with Holy Fire, you are what the world is waiting for. You are the light of the world, the express manifestation of Love in you on the earth! Billions of souls are desperate to discover Heaven's Blueprint and live a life in Christ Jesus full of miracles and power that never ends.

"Until that great day, I ask You Father, let us live in as much of Your manifest Presence as we possibly can in these earthly bodies. In Oneness with Your Son, let us

burn with as much of Your fiery love and power, through the Holy Spirit, the brightest lights we can possibly be in this world. Let us enter in to the greater, mega works. We ask You for the greatest adventure in the supernatural, full of extraordinary miracles, encounters, manifestations of the Spirit and multitudes of souls won by Love into Your Kingdom. Let our beings be so saturated with Your glory that even our shadows can satisfy the draw of the desperate for Your touch. May Your Son receive the reward of His suffering through our lives, the nations as His inheritance, as we learn to embrace suffering and become servants of all. May we know You in the deepest, most intimate friendship, experiencing the fullness of our union, our Oneness with You, in Christ by the Holy Spirit. More Lord, so much more! Amen!"

Now unto Him that is able to keep you from falling and to present you faultless before the presence of His glory with exceeding joy, to the only wise God, our Savior, be glory and majesty, dominion and power, both now and forever. Amen.

Jude 24-25

ABOUT THE AUTHOR

Duncan and Kate Smith are revivalists who carry the fire of God's love and power all over the world. Duncan and Kate are presidents of Catch The Fire World, a global movement of revival churches, missions and ministries, birthed out of the Toronto Revival. Duncan and Kate are senior leaders of Catch The Fire Church in Raleigh, North Carolina, a vibrant, growing church full of the love and presence of God, which they started with their three beautiful daughters. They also founded the School of Revival in Raleigh, which is a radical, supernatural leadership and church planting school. Duncan is most at home with the poorest, unreached peoples of the world. Wherever they go, the Holy Spirit does extraordinary miracles as the love of the Father and grace of Jesus are poured out to the world.

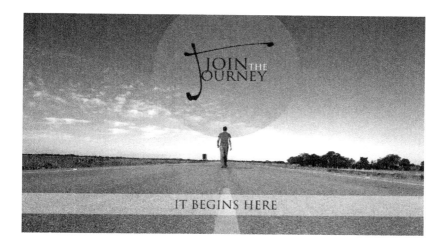

The School of Revival is a 2-year, US-based program designed to raise up leaders and church planters immersed in the Father's love. We are a non-residential school with no age limit.

So if you are 18 years or older and have a passion to be transformed and see whole nations changed by the love and power of God then join us on our 2-year adventure here in Raleigh, North Carolina.

International Students who wish to attend the School of Revival may apply for the M-1 Student Visa with the United States Citizen and Immigration Services (USCIS). The School of Revival is fully authorized by the US Government to accept international students and has been awarded the M-1 Academic Institution Student Visa category.

www.schoolofrevival.com

Printed in Great Britain
by Amazon

81289112R00174